The Return of the Epic Film

The Return of the Epic Film

Genre, Aesthetics and History in the
Twenty-first Century

Edited by Andrew B. R. Elliott

EDINBURGH
University Press

For my parents
who introduced me to epic films on VHS
and forgave me when I recorded over them by accident.

© editorial mater and organisation Andrew B. R. Elliott, 2014
© the chapters their several authors, 2014, 2015
This paperback edition 2015

Edinburgh University Press Ltd
The Tun – Holyrood Road
12 (2f) Jackson's Entry
Edinburgh EH8 8PJ
www.euppublishing.com

First published in hardback by Edinburgh University Press 2014

Typeset in Monotype Ehrhardt by
Servis Filmsetting Ltd, Stockport, Cheshire

A CIP record for this book is available from the British Library

ISBN 978 0 7486 8402 1 (hardback)
ISBN 978 1 4744 0284 2 (paperback)
ISBN 978 1 4744 0285 9 (epub)
ISBN 978 0 7486 8403 8 (webready PDF)

The right of the contributors to be identified as author of this
work has been asserted in accordance with the Copyright,
Designs and Patents Act 1988 and the Copyright and Related
Rights Regulations 2003 (SI No. 2498).

Contents

List of Figures vii
Acknowledgements ix

1 Introduction: The Return of the Epic 1
 Andrew B. R. Elliott

Part I Epics and Ancient History
2 Sir Ridley Scott and the Rebirth of the Historical Epic 19
 Jeffrey Richards
3 The Decline and Fall of the Roman Empire and America since the Second World War: Some Cinematic Parallels 36
 Kevin J. Harty
4 'There's Nothing So Wrong with a Hollywood Script that a Bunch of Giant CGI Scorpions Can't Solve': Politics, Computer Generated Images and Camp in the Critical Reception of the Post-*Gladiator* Historical Epics 57
 Mark Jancovich
5 Popcorn and Circus: An Audience Expects 74
 Robert Stow

Part II Epic Aesthetics and Genre
6 Colour in the Epic Film: *Alexander* and *Hero* 95
 Robert Burgoyne
7 Defining the Epic: Medieval and Fantasy Epics 110
 Paul B. Sturtevant
8 Special Effects, Reality and the New Epic Film 129
 Andrew B. R. Elliott

Part III Epic Films and the Canon

9 Pass the Ammunition: A Short Etymology of 'Blockbuster' 147
   Sheldon Hall
10 Epic Stumbling Blocks 167
   Saër Maty Bâ
11 The Greatest Epic of the Twenty-First Century? 188
   Deborah Bridge
12 The *Ramayana* and Sita in Films and Popular Media: The Repositioning of a Globalised Version 201
   Aarttee Kaul Dhar

Notes on the Contributors 216
Index 219

Figures

3.1	American values triumph over communism in *Sign of the Pagan*	39
3.2	The enemy within and without: Honoria and Attila in *Attila*	41
3.3	*The Fall of the Roman Empire*: 'a great civilisation is not conquered from without until it destroys itself from within'	45
3.4	Commodus as the unheroic counterpart of the hero Maximus in *Gladiator*	46
3.5	*Centurion*: Quintus and his men are a strange coalition of the willing and the unwilling	48
3.6	*The Eagle*: Esca as a wild animal who, to Roman eyes, is not worth training	52
5.1	*Gladiator* contains everything one respondent expected in a movie about Romans	80
5.2	The armour and weapons in *Centurion* are some of the most accurate committed to film	83
5.3	Etain in *Centurion*	86
6.1	The hero's entry into Babylon in *Alexander*: 'at this one glorious moment in time, Alexander was loved by all'	100
6.2	*Hero* uses the traditional forms of Chinese culture, such as martial arts, music, calligraphy and painting, to attract a global audience	104
6.3	In its elaborate use of colour frequencies associated with female knights, *Hero* presents a variation on typical epic themes	107
7.1	*Kingdom of Heaven*'s defence of Jerusalem: when Balian acts with and for larger group causes, the film acquires a mythic dimension and becomes an epic	115
7.2	*King Arthur* defines the British as a liminal people, born of a marriage between idealistic remnants of a crumbling Empire and a proud, native people living in tune with the land	120

viii FIGURES

8.1	The digital creation of 'the largest fleet that ever sailed' in *Troy* (2004)	132
8.2	CGI aerial shots in *Agora* transform the city of Alexandria into a site of spectacle wherein the personal and the political are interwoven	136
9.1	Trade advertisements in the 1930s and 1940s frequently showed long queues of patrons in lines extending around the block	149
9.2	*Bombardier* was advertised as 'the blockbuster of all action-thrill-service shows'	151
9.3	An appeal for industry support for a fund-raising campaign drawing upon readers' presumed awareness of the blockbuster bomb and its connotations of massive impact	152
9.4	Paramount's 'Big Guns'	157
9.5	Weapons of Mass Distribution	159
10.1	*300*'s Queen Gorgo serves two purposes: to fulfil male sexual needs and have babies	172
10.2	*Planet of the Apes*: Opaque entities . . .	174
10.3	. . . and complex reversals	174
10.4	*Amazing Grace*: Equiano shows a scar on his chest, in tears	176
10.5	White opacity rules: 'we were apes; they were humans'	176
10.6	*Zulu Dawn*: mythified and xeno-racist: Lord Chelmsford	179
12.1	In *Sita Sings the Blues* the goddess Laxmi creates a forceful identification between the Earth itself and womanhood, recalling a range of ideas drawn from Indian mythology	207
12.2	The songs of *Sita Sings the Blues* frame the epic around a familiar and relatable problem with global appeal	210

Images in Chapter 3 are drawn from the contributor's own collection.

Images from *Variety* used in Chapter 9 are drawn from the contributor's research.

Images from *Sita Sings the Blues* (Paley 2009) used in Chapter 12 are taken from http://www.sitasingstheblues.com/press.html#stills, and have been reproduced here under the film's CC-SA licence.

All other images are taken from screenshots from DVD copies of the film, generated either by the editor or the individual contributor, and have been acknowledged accordingly. They are reproduced here under the Fair Use Policy for educational materials used to illustrate discussions of specific films. In all instances basic screen capture techniques have been employed using free software, with no modification of the image, and with no commercial intentions.

Acknowledgements

This book is the product of a number of different people, and not only those whose names are listed on the contents page. Many of the ideas put forward here were first raised in a conference held at the University of Lincoln in July 2011. My thanks are owed to those who helped me to organise the conference: Professor Ann Gray, Dr Erin Bell, Dr Sarah Barrow, Carolyn Williams, and Suzanne Etherington, without whom the whole thing would probably have fallen apart. I also heartily thank the presenters, attendees, and those who supported the conference itself, especially Dr Finn Pollard and Nigel Morris.

My genuine gratitude is owed to all at Edinburgh University Press, especially Gillian Leslie, Jenny Peebles, Michelle Houston and Eddie Clark, who put their trust in me to deliver an ambitious project, and were patient, kind and supportive throughout the whole process. Matthew Wilhelm Kapell's sage advice throughout the project was indispensable, as was that of Professor Steve Neale and the anonymous reader, both of whose criticism and ideas were insightful, professional and – perhaps most importantly of all – helpful. They have all contributed to making this a better book as a consequence.

However, none of this would have been remotely possible without the excellent ideas, scholarship and willingness of the contributors themselves, who worked to impossible timescales, accommodated increasingly unreasonable (and sometimes self-contradictory) demands from me, but nevertheless managed to deliver excellent manuscripts on time. Particular thanks go to the editorial board of *rebeca* (*Revista Brasileira de estudos de cinema e audiovisual*) for kindly allowing us permission to reprint Chapter 6 in this volume.

My final thanks go to the people who keep me going once the office door closes: Sara, Antonella, Daniele and Abigail always listen to me; Brian, Pat,

Alastair, Leanne, Louise, Jamie, Lorna and Tom do too, but only because they have to. I can only apologise for the number of times I've made them all talk about, watch, rewatch and critique epic films – they'll probably never realise how much they have helped.

CHAPTER 1

Introduction: The Return of the Epic

Andrew B. R. Elliott

In the spring of 2000, some three decades after the well-publicised flops of *Cleopatra* (Mankiewicz 1963), *The Fall of the Roman Empire* (Mann 1964) and *The Greatest Story Ever Told* (Stevens 1965), unsuspecting cinema audiences were once again presented with the lavish and costly historical epics which had ruled the box office a generation earlier. Ridley Scott's *Gladiator*, in a seemingly sudden departure from many of Scott's previous films, told the epic tale of a Roman general-turned-gladiator 'who defied an emperor' and who (albeit posthumously) founded a new Roman Republic. Though few could have predicted it at the time, the global success of his film 'resurrected long-standing traditions of historical and cinematic spectacles',[1] and Scott would later find himself credited with re-launching a genre which had lain dormant for 35 years, heralding 'a sudden resurrection of toga films after thirty-six years in disgrace and exile', which prompted critics and scholars alike emphatically to declare the return of the epic.[2] Indeed, looking back over the first decade of the twenty-first century, in terms of films and box-office takings the effect of this return is clear: in each year from 2000 to 2010, historical epics have made the top ten highest-grossing films, and attracted numerous awards and nominations.[3] Accordingly, from *Gladiator* to *The Immortals* (Singh 2011), via *Troy* (Petersen 2004), *Kingdom of Heaven* (Scott 2005) and *Alexander* (Stone 2004), the decade came to be characterised by a slew of historically-themed, costly, spectacular, lavish – in a word, 'epic' – films which, though not always as profitable as might have been hoped, performed respectably at the box office.

THE PROBLEM OF A RETURN

Yet, at the same time, the triumphant declaration of the return of the epic is not without its difficulties, which scholarship has been slow to assess. First, claims about the return of the epic immediately confront issues regarding the term 'epic' itself, a word which has 'joined the long list of words which are rapidly losing their original meanings'.[4] One of the crucial prerequisites for discussing the return of the epic is that we know precisely what we mean by the term itself. *Lord of the Rings* (Jackson 2001, 2002, 2003), for example, seemed to fall squarely within the historical epic tradition, even if the 'historical' context of the film was demonstrably untrue; by the same criterion, however, *The Da Vinci Code* (Howard 2006) was excluded, since despite its epic sweep of history, the main focal point for the action was the present. Such criteria are, however, ambiguous when it comes to the *Harry Potter* films (which, in Chapter 11, Deborah Bridge argues ought to be included), which adopt a form of temporal dislocation, but would not disbar *Pirates of the Caribbean* (Verbinski 2003), given that the action is past, and the epic cinematography and stirring score belong to the production stable of Jerry Bruckheimer, a man who is no stranger to the epic. Yet, somehow, to site *Pirates of the Caribbean* alongside 'serious' epic fare like *Gladiator* or *Troy* (Petersen 2004) instinctively feels as though we are comparing two very different kinds of films.

It quickly becomes evident, then, that the definition of 'epic' is a largely personal issue, since (as Paul Sturtevant shows in Chapter 7) one person's fantasy is another's sci-fi, and in films like *Clash of the Titans* (Leterrier 2010) or *300* (Snyder 2006), the line between history and mythology becomes considerably less clear. Indeed, one critic discussing the problems of defining the term 'epic' suggests that rather than confronting such a nebulous term in theory, we should examine each film on a case-by-case basis, so that 'we could then send the term "epic" on vacation until some of the confusion died down and was forgotten'.[5]

Second, even more problematic than the term itself, however, is its uncritical application to a group of films, which often unthinkingly assumes the existence of an identifiable, coherent and self-contained genre, an assumption which, after a generation of scholarly works on genre outlining significant difficulties with the term, is by no means straightforward. As Steve Neale observes, attempts to define genres of films are problematic, are often formed on the basis of assumptions of cultural worthiness, or of iconography, and are at times self-contradictory:

> What emerges [from studying genre] is that genre as a term has been used in different ways in different fields, and that many of its uses have been governed by the history of the term within those fields ... rather than by logic or conceptual consistency.

Neale's proposed responses to this '*require thinking of genres as ubiquitous, multifaceted phenomena rather than as one-dimensional entities* to be found only within the realms of Hollywood cinema or of commercial cinema'.[6]

Such problems in using genre in imprecise ways, therefore, have serious consequences if we try to classify the return of the epic as the return of a once defunct genre, for they require us first to prove that the epic films under discussion can indeed be treated as a single genre. This would require us to produce a list of criteria for inclusion within that genre: a reasonably straightforward process in the case of films like *Gladiator* and *Troy*, but considerably more complex in the case of lower-budget films like *Centurion* (Marshall 2010), or non-Hollywood fare like *Arn: Knight Templar* (Flinth 2007) or *Hero* (Yimou 2002). These latter kinds of films, sitting at the fringes of our loose term 'epic', rather than clarifying the debate, in fact engender *further* questions about which films, settings, themes and national cinemas might qualify as suitably 'epic'. Thus, by treating the issue in simplified terms of genre, rather than solving problems we are in fact creating new ones even more complex than those that existed in the first place.

Third, along the same lines, claims about the return of the epic film make assumptions about the invisibility of the epic during the 1970s, '80s and '90s, assumptions which overlook a number of key examples which offer some kind of continuation from earlier cycles of epics. We might, for instance, point to the epic film's survival in a number of other forms and media: for instance, the survival of ancient worlds on television, from *I, Claudius* (1976–7) and *Moses the Lawgiver* (1974) to *Xena: Warrior Princess* (1995–2001) and *Hercules* (1995–9), which collectively suggest that epic did not die, but merely moved to television.[7] Similarly, the claim ignores the overlap between Hollywood epics and their low-budget spin-offs in the form of the peplum, such as the hugely popular – though critically disparaged – films centring on the mythological figure of Maciste, or Steve Reeves in *Le Fatiche di Ercole/Hercules* (Francisci 1958) and *Ercole e la regina di Lidia/Hercules Unchained* (Francisci 1959). These low-budget, Italian B-movies set in classical antiquity (however loosely interpreted) survived in one form or another through to the 1980s with Arnold Schwarzenegger's debut *Hercules in New York* (Seidelman 1969), and traces can be found in later films like *Conan the Barbarian* (Milius 1982) which drew on similar themes and muscular heroic figures in fantastical, if not outright classical, worlds.[8]

Finally, to claim the death and rebirth of the epic is to adopt a Hollywood-centric vision which disregards numerous offerings in world cinema, from Pasolini's *Trilogia della vita* (1971–4) and his engagement with classical themes in *Il Vangelo secondo Matteo* (1964), *Edipo Re* (1967) and *Medea* (1969), or Michael Cacoyannis' engagement with ancient Greek theatre in *The Trojan Women* (1971) or *Iphigenia* (1977). Alternatively, we might mention a number of films traditionally ascribed to other genres which engage either directly or indirectly with classical themes. Obvious candidates here might include the kinds of sci-fi and fantasy films which Winkler discusses as 'genre cinema', and which at first sight have 'nothing in common with the ancient world [but which] may still adapt plots or patterns familiar from antiquity, particularly those relating to heroic myth'.[9] However, less obvious candidates might include comedies like *Up Pompeii* (Kellett 1971), *A Funny Thing Happened on the Way to the Forum* (Lester 1966), or *Carry On Cleo* (Thomas 1964); horror such as Hammer's *The Gorgon* (Fisher 1964); biblical musicals such as *Jesus Christ Superstar* (Jewison 1973) and *Godspell* (Greene 1973); 'social problem' films like *The Warriors* (Hill 1979), which uses Xenophon's *Anabasis* to create a myth for New York's underworld; or even pornography in the form of *Caligula* (Brass 1979).[10] While, admittedly, most of these might be difficult to classify as 'epics', to discount them we are forced back to the problematic issue of genre outlined above. The proliferation of films with classical themes throughout the 1970s and '80s, then, challenges the return of the epic by fundamentally questioning whether epic films ever really went away in the first place. The major difference between these films and the epics under discussion here is in their aesthetic, which calls for the kind of study of the formal and aesthetic qualities of the new epic film found in Part II of this book.

A GENRE BY ANY OTHER NAME

Adopting such a formal approach, and setting aside the issue of genre, even a cursory glance at films like *Gladiator*, *Alexander*, *Troy*, *Kingdom of Heaven* and *Agora* (Amenábar 2009) reveals a range of comparable qualities which allow us to group these films together as an important body of films which have enjoyed popularity at the box office and generated significant scholarly discussion.[11] Most scholars working in the field – Robert Burgoyne, Mark Jancovich, Constantine Santas, Jeffrey Richards, Jon Solomon, Martin Winkler, Monica Cyrino, Joanna Paul and Maria Wyke, among others – are broadly in agreement that there is a certain group of films with comparable styles, settings and themes which fell out of favour in the mid-1960s, but which have regained popularity over the past decade. Even more compelling is that all point to *Gladiator* as the first instance of this kind of film's revival: Cyrino describes it 'as the first Roman epic made after the end of the Cold War'; Winkler calls the film 'the first ancient epic produced for the silver screen since the mid-1960s'; Aknin terms it 'the first real production of this kind since the 1960s'; Solomon describes it as 'the first heroic tragedy on the cinema screen set in the Graeco-Roman world at the turning point of two millennia'.[12]

Moreover, not only do they point to *Gladiator* as the first of a long line of ancient-world epics, but many also credit the film as the catalyst, if not the cause, for the revival of the epic; Winkler argues that 'its gigantic box-office success has made epic cinema a promising venue for commercial filmmaking', and Cyrino agrees that '*Gladiator* initiated a sudden resurrection of toga films after thirty-six years in disgrace and exile'.[13] James Russell likewise proposes that '*Gladiator*'s success inspired another wave of epics', and Jerome de Groot points to the resurgence of these toga films as 'signals [of] a return to the mainstream historical imagination of epic narratives and of classical heroism'.[14] Even Wolfgang Petersen himself acknowledged that it was 'the gigantic and wholly unsuspected worldwide success of *Gladiator* [which] made *Troy* possible'.[15]

However, despite such unanimity (or, perhaps, precisely because of it), even if we can accept the return of the epic, to date no critical study has examined differences between this recent cycle and earlier waves of epics, or their coherence as a single body of films under the epithet 'epic'. In defining earlier cycles of sword-and-sandal films, for example, critics have variously referred to them as a 'wave' (Russell), a 'genre' (Wyke), a 'cycle' (Richards, Hall and Neale) or else as 'cross-cultural popular forms' (Burgoyne) which are to be understood variously as aesthetic labels, generic distinctions, or industrial niches.[16] Looked at from an industrial perspective, the term 'epic' can be used 'to identify, and to sell two overlapping contemporary trends: films with historical, especially ancient world, settings; and large scale films of all kinds which used new technologies, high production values and special modes of distribution and exhibition'.[17]

Questions raised about recent epics, then, are concerned with much more than genre. As Sheldon Hall's chapter in this volume suggests, when we look in depth at a term like 'blockbuster' we are often dealing more with industrial concerns and critics' nomenclature than with any identifiable properties of the films themselves. Neale and Hall's *Epics, Spectacles and Blockbusters* eloquently argues that the epic is a loose term, 'as indicative of size and expense as it was of particular kinds of historical settings, of protagonists who are caught up in large-scale events as it was of those who sway the course of history of the fate of nations'.[18] As such, it is perhaps more productive simply to describe them in terms of a cycle, or '*filone*' (an Italian term whose rough translation might be 'strand', or 'thread'), as much as a genre.

Understanding the films as a cycle also offers a secondary benefit in that, as well as sidestepping problematic issues of genre, the sense of decline and return implicit in the term usefully allows us to tie these films back to earlier cycles of epics much more clearly. Jeffrey Richards, for instance, makes the important point that the new epic film was as much about earlier epics as it was about history.[19] Consequently, he discusses the return not as a *new* foray into classical myths, but as a revival of the earlier cycle of films, suggesting that 'the astonishing worldwide success of [*Gladiator*] sent film producers scampering back to the stories that had inspired the previous cycle of Ancient World epics in the 1950s and early 1960s, and new versions of the tales of Troy, Thermopylae, Alexander the Great and Julius Caesar duly appeared'.[20]

It is certainly true that *Gladiator* as a film bears a clear resemblance in terms of plot, aesthetics and even characters to *Spartacus* (Kubrick 1960) and *The Fall of the Roman Empire*, to the extent that Claude Aziza rather unkindly terms it a 'capable (but disguised) remake'.[21] Cyrino's analysis, though more charitable, nevertheless insists upon the film's debt to earlier cycles in her observation that 'any interpretation of *Gladiator* must take into account its relationship to the Roman epics made in Hollywood in the 1950s and early 1960s'.[22] Likewise, as Mark Jancovich points out in his chapter, *Village Voice* film critic Michael Atkinson responded to another film in the cycle by referring directly back to earlier cycles: '*Troy* is everything old made new again: matte-image palaces (digitized, of course), hordes of shield-holding extras (also CGI), dialogue that may well have been burped out by a Hercules-movie-digesting mainframe . . . and risible "ancient" loungewear.'[23]

However, rather than dismissing the recent epics as merely derivative recycling of earlier themes, we must also remember that the earlier cycle of 1950s epics were often themselves reworkings of silent-era epics. *Ben-Hur* (Wyler 1959) was a direct remake of Fred Niblo's classic 1925 version, which was in turn an adaptation of Lew Wallace's novel *Ben Hur: A Tale of the Christ*. Mervyn LeRoy's 1951 *Quo Vadis* had already seen two earlier outings in 1925 and 1913, both of which were in turn adaptations of Sienkiewicz's novel. Robert Wise's 1956 *Helen of Troy* was by no means the first to bring the Trojan War to the screen, with a host of earlier versions including one in 1924 (*Helen of Troy*, Noa), a largely lost version in 1927 (*The Private Life of Helen of Troy*, Korda) and the short film *The Fall of Troy* by Borgnetto and Pastrone in 1911. In 1956, Cecil B. De Mille even recycled his own material, making an updated version of his earlier version of *The Ten Commandments* (even if Essoe and Lee argue that the second version 'hardly resembled his 1923 effort').[24] The fact, then, that all four have seen recent remakes in the twenty-first century (a TV version of *Ben Hur* appeared in 2010 and a film version is slated for 2015; *Quo Vadis* was remade by Jerzy Kawalerowicz in 2001; Petersen's *Troy* was followed by a made-for-TV version in 2005; *The Ten Commandments* has seen a number of versions in 2006–7 and even a musical version in 2006) can be seen in some ways as part of a natural pattern in which the new returns to the old as much for inspiration as for legitimacy. Such a common reuse of earlier themes reminds us that 'popular conceptions of particular genres are invariably based on the features of earlier cycles', which suggests that recycling is perhaps a constituent part of epic filmmaking.[25] It is perhaps in this sense that we can see Oliver Stone's three different versions of *Alexander* as a normal part of the continual reinvention and repackaging of the epic film.²⁶ As Michel Lagny claims, the genre is in some ways destined to be remade, since 'a measure of its success is the way films of the same type were made again and again over a period of years: mass production of this kind is justified only when attendances generate healthy profits (and it ceases as soon as profits fall off)'.²⁷

It is, in fact, likely that even the earliest cinematic outings of ancient Greece, Rome and the Bible were in themselves indebted to classical settings in other media, especially theatre, opera and novels, demonstrating a 'continuity between the painting and drama of the nineteenth century both in Britain and the United States and the emergence and development of the Ancient World epic in Hollywood'.²⁸ The emergence of film came at a time when filmmakers, themselves often having been trained in other visual arts, would cast about for suitable topics to film and most likely fall back on the sources most familiar to them. As a consequence, the relationship between cinema and the epic dates back to cinema's very earliest days, in which filmmakers would readily seize on classical plots; from the very moment 'when the cinema emerged . . . it turned naturally to the ancient world and scores of short films were produced with pocket versions of the familiar stories from the Bible, ancient history and classical mythology'.²⁹ Likewise, Santas observes that 'from the outset, epic film has feasted on the collective myths of East and West, dipping into the inexhaustible resources of stories from the Bible; from Greek, Egyptian, Babylonian, Roman and medieval cultures; and from Oriental and Eastern myths'.³⁰ However, Sam Leith, more bluntly, observes that

> the attraction of classical antiquity to filmmakers has never been hard to fathom: it has sex (from Theda Bara's heavy-lidded Cleopatra in 1917, the idea of the ancients being constantly "At It" has persisted), violence (plenty of scope for gladiatorial hurly burly and epic battles) and grand narrative. Graeco-Roman antiquity offers filmmakers a giant out-of-copyright myth kitty.³¹

In this way, then, the return of the epic film becomes more explicable as a body of films loosely based around historical – usually ancient or classical, but also medieval – periods which returned to the big screen and from the very outset began to be aped as part of an industrial strategy to tap into a lucrative market. Such a return seems less surprising, too, when we can understand these films not as genres but as part of a broader pattern of cycles which periodically fall out of favour through cost or surfeit, and which return at other key moments when a combination of technical prowess, audience popularity or industrial strategies create the perfect conditions for germination.

WHY NOW?

Thus, if the epic is a cyclical phenomenon which comes and goes, the final question which the return of the epic poses is not 'Why are they back?' but rather 'Why are they back *now*?'. This final question is no less problematic than any of the others broached above, in part because the response is contingent on the responses to these other questions. However, it is also difficult to answer because the reason for the epic's return by necessity depends on which reasons are offered for its disappearance in the 1960s.

The most often cited reason for the demise in the 1950s and '60s is that the huge costs associated with producing an epic became unsustainable, eventually culminating in the near bankruptcy of several of the major studios.[32] In his classic study of epics, Elley describes the climate of one-upmanship which saw the major studios – particularly MGM and 20th Century Fox – taking on increasing risks as they sought to film ever bigger, more lavish and spectacular epics depicting the classical world.[33] These include *The Fall of the Roman Empire*'s spectacular re-creation of the Roman forum, which remains one of the largest cinema sets ever constructed, and one 'which was populated by most of the residents of Las Matas'.[34] Over the course of the decade, as budgets spiralled out of control, such competition would eventually lead to financial gambles in which excessive spending would place them at the mercy of audiences. With so much having been spent on making the film, the break-even point was dependent on ever greater returns at the box office, at times approaching *Ben-Hur*'s whopping 7.6 per cent of the total box-office takings.[35] The argument runs that the increasing reliance on spectacle – created both through the profligacy of studios and the increasingly sophisticated visual effects designed to achieve greater authenticity – would lead studios to breaking point rather than to break-even point. In the case of *Cleopatra*, *The Fall of the Roman Empire* and *The Greatest Story Ever Told*, for example, the fortunes of major studios such as Paramount were to ride almost entirely on the success or failure of the massive epics.[36]

It is worth noting, however, that even here critical opinion is somewhat divided; while most agree that cost was a major factor which all of the studios suffered equally, many pinpoint individual films which, they argue, acted as cautionary tales sounding the death knell of the cycle, offering stark forecasts of dwindling audience interest. Where Cyrino and Elley date the demise of the epic at 1964, with Mann's *The Fall of the Roman Empire*, Winkler (rightly) disputes Bronston's role as sole architect of the epic's demise, and instead insists that, if we must blame any individual film it should be *Cleopatra* on the grounds of its cost and wastefulness.[37] While it may seem unfair to criticise one film for its cost when many others saw eye-watering budgets far above the norm, *Cleopatra* in particular does stand out as marked by the kind of wasteful expenditure which, no matter how well the film performed, in practical terms stood little chance of ever being recouped. Using different criteria, Hall suggests that the epic came to an end in 1965 with *The Greatest Story Ever Told* (again, rightly, on the basis that this was the last film released which we might describe as part of that epic cycle), while Santas opts for Mankiewicz's *Cleopatra* from two years earlier as the point at which alarm bells began to ring.[38] Searles, however, rejects all of these, protesting the unfairness of the legacy left by these films, on the grounds that it is markedly unfair to blame a handful of films for the demise of an entire style of filmmaking without taking into account external factors such as dwindling audiences in general, changing tastes, younger teen audiences for whom the historical epic held little attraction, and a general satiation with the epic as a whole. So although in Searles' view '*Cleopatra* is generally credited with being a prime contributor to the demise of the expensive historical spectacular', it is clear that both trends (dwindling audiences and rising costs of the epics) were set to continue, which suggests that the demise of the epic was on the cards long before any of these films went into pre-production.[39]

Nevertheless, if the epic cycles of the 1950s and '60s did indeed draw to a close because of industrial factors such as cost, then the preconditions for their return would logically need to be the same, or else the epic would remain unfeasible. Consequently, this would mean either that by 1999 the studios were willing once again to risk such make-or-break sums on their blockbuster films, or else that the costs associated with such films had finally fallen to a manageable level. As we shall see in my discussion of special effects in Chapter 8, both positions are vaguely tenable; CGI and crowd-building software meant that the enormous costs of physical sets and hordes of extras were no longer required, and the escalating budgets of 1990s blockbusters means that 'despite proclamations of doom amongst Hollywood commentators, more money was being invested in epics [at the end of the 1990s] than at any time since the 1960s'.[40] And yet, neither of these propositions can fully explain the return either. CGI and visual effects had been used consistently in other genres throughout the 1970s and '80s when allegedly no epics were being made, so why was *Gladiator* not made earlier? Equally, the runaway budgets of *Titanic* became, according to Paula Parisi, something of a wake-up call for 20th Century Fox's accounts department,[41] which suggests, if anything, that the major studios would have been far *less* likely to invest sizeable sums in a unsafe kind of film which had not been made since the 1960s and which, furthermore, had almost bankrupted the studios at that time.

Nor do such arguments take into account other factors, some of which have nothing to do with film at all. For example, Russell and Aknin both suggest that rather than any industrial concerns, it was merely the intervention of a generation gap which allowed filmmakers to relive their youth by making the epics they saw as children and which, perhaps, inspired them to make films in the first place; 'as the baby boomers reached maturity, broader demographic shifts . . . seem to have contributed to a popular belief that the historical epic was once more a relevant form of cinematic expression'.[42] Aknin seems to concur here, suggesting that 'it was necessary for the last witnesses of the disastrous venture of *Cleopatra* to disappear, and for an entire new generation to take up the baton, before a new classical epic could see the light of day'.[43] In this case, any in-depth study of production ecologies and Hollywood investment strategies is potentially undermined by a combination of luck, nostalgia and Malthusian population theory.

PRESENTISM

One other argument regarding the epic's return concerns the issue of 'presentism' (see Chapters 2 and 3). James Chapman describes it as 'a truth universally acknowledged . . . that a historical feature film will often have as much to say about the present in which it was made as about the past in which it was set'.[44] The intercorrelation between the past and the present – otherwise called a conflation of temporal planes by Sobchack and White – is an idea most prominently proposed by Siegfried Kracauer in his argument that historical films reflect the collective cultural consciousness, and one carried forward by Pierre Sorlin.[45] This is especially true in the depiction of ancient history, as Jeffrey Richards reminds us, since 'the Ancient World epics tell us as much about the preoccupations and values of the period in which they were made as about the period in which they were set'.[46]

According to this way of thinking, a historical film might use the past as a way of talking about, pointing to, parodying or rejecting the present, and indeed from the outset *Gladiator*'s screenwriter Franzoni openly acknowledged that 'the movie is about us. It's not just about ancient Rome, it's about America.'[47] However, one of the risks of this argument is that it can be taken further to suggest that, instead of simply using the past to comment on the present, the ways in which films and television treat the past unwittingly reveal more about our values than they do about anything historical. This position in effect transmutes the conscious use of past-as-commentary to an unconscious, vaguely Freudian, revelation of our deepest fears, in much the same way as dreams are conceived as revelations of our unconscious thoughts. To read historical films in such a way is to oversimplify Peter C. Rollins' assertion that 'without intending to act the role of historian, Hollywood has often been an unwitting recorder of national moods', since this discredits the historical film's ability to say anything important about the past, but rather patronisingly asserts instead that they can only ever slavishly mirror the era in which the film was made.⁴⁸ As a useful way around this, in an excellent study of classical antiquity in modern culture Martin Winkler terms these unconscious uses of history a 'cultural seismograph', a concept which allows for a reading of historical films as in part a reflection of the present, but which does not preclude an earnest attempt to retell historical events, thus reconciling these positions with traditional criticism of historical films.⁴⁹

If the past is thus a safe but effective way of critiquing the present, it makes some logical sense to look at the politico-ideological context of the return; just as the Cold War provoked so many useful metaphors about naming-and-shaming (such as *Spartacus*),⁵⁰ or the threat of pagan, proto-communist enemies at the gates who risk derailing white Christian values and ways, or communist moles operating from within, perhaps what Chomsky terms America's 'hegemony or survival' approach prompted an introspective critique which emerged as a metaphor in *Gladiator*'s neo-imperial designs, as Cyrino persuasively argues.⁵¹ In this way, as the Cold War was replaced by a global 'War on Terror', so too would new versions of past worlds emerge to critique armed incursions in the Middle East (*Kingdom of Heaven*, *Robin Hood* (Scott 2010), *Arn*), or to offer warnings based on past efforts at conquest (*Alexander*) or else actively to endorse them (*300*). In the aftermath of openly falsified justifications for war in Iraq, we find attacks on unjustified warmongering (*Troy*, *Centurion*), or scepticism towards cynical political manoeuvring (*King Arthur* (Fuqua 2004), *The Eagle* (Macdonald 2011), *The Last Legion* (Lefler 2007)); amid contentious debates about religious ideologies we find scathing attacks on fundamentalism of all stripes (*Agora*, *Kingdom of Heaven*, *King Arthur*).

Accordingly, then, we might suggest that the epic came back because, simply, we *needed* it back; we needed it to serve a purpose it had once fulfilled as a convenient series of metaphors to critique the present, and the complex industrial, commercial, creative and demographic conditions for its return just so happened to have fallen into place at the turn of the millennium.

ABOUT THIS BOOK

It is clear, then, that the only way out of such a multifaceted debate is to recognise the return of the epic as a real phenomenon, but one whose motivations probably include a combination of all of these factors in varying degrees. Whatever the reasons for its return, as the following chapters argue, ancient and medieval worlds are back on our screens, and alive and well in the box office at the time of writing.

The undisputed popularity of *Gladiator* and its successors calls for a coherent study moving beyond genre theory to one which examines how we define these epics, and what criteria we are using to do so, whether there are any formal and aesthetic qualities which unite these films, and whether the term 'epic' relates exclusively to a North American, or more specifically Hollywood, canon. Given that, as I have tried to show above, there are potentially as many answers to these issues as there are questions, my intentions in this collection were to gather together the thoughts of some of the best critics writing about these issues, alongside those of emerging new voices in the field who have been trained to cross disciplinary lines in order to understand popular culture's uses of the past. The various chapters in this book thus embrace a range of approaches which take into account the entire production process from the industrial context to marketing and reception, and one which questions the canon of films conventionally accepted as epics, as well as the formal and aesthetic aspects of the epic film.

To the three major questions discussed here – questions about what form this return might take, about our definitions of the epic canon, and about the epic's use of history – the response of this book is appropriately threefold. Part I begins by looking at the question of the relevance of ancient history to today's audiences. In Chapter 2, Jeffrey Richards examines Ridley Scott's unofficial trilogy of *Gladiator*, *Kingdom of Heaven* and *Robin Hood* to suggest that they represent, at base, the same film three times, which each reflect Scott's own ideological concerns. This is followed by Kevin J. Harty's discussion in Chapter 3 of the return of the epic in terms of its relevance to contemporary US politics, offering some cinematic parallels between the fall of Rome and the 'American Empire'. In Chapter 4, Mark Jancovich examines the critical reception of the new epic film, using film critics' responses to the epic to show that – somewhat surprisingly – despite *Gladiator*'s initially frosty reception, as the decade wore on critics gradually warmed to the spectacle and CGI which accompanied these films. Chapter 5 sees Robert Stow using the results of a revealing audience study of *Gladiator* and *Centurion* to show that when it comes to the public appetite for, and understanding of, these films, a marked divergence between scholarly appreciation and public enjoyment reveals that these two audiences come to the epic films with very different expectations.

In Part II, the focus moves to aesthetic and formal appreciation. In Chapter 6, Robert Burgoyne argues for a new mode of analysing the epic, namely a focus on colour which allows us to tie together films like *Alexander* and *Hero*. In Chapter 7, Paul Sturtevant examines the idea of genre in more depth to argue that the relationship between a hero and wider national concerns allows us to understand why some epic films seem more naturally suited to the epithet 'epic' than others. This is followed by my own analysis in Chapter 8 of the CGI and special effects which have become associated with the epic film, in which I argue that they serve a dual purpose in the modern epic: to increase the epic's traditional sense of spectacle but also to enhance verisimilitude and/or narrative plausibility.

Part III turns to examine the epic canon, using a range of films falling outside of traditional definitions of epics to argue against what we might term the 'epic canon'. In Chapter 9 Sheldon Hall looks at the etymology of the term 'blockbuster', situating it in the immediate aftermath of the Second World War, showing that its association with expensive pictures thus places it firmly in a Hollywood industrial context. This is followed in Chapter 10 by Saër Maty Bâ's study of 'planetary humanism', in which he argues that cultural assumptions about the white body prevent us from seeing the black body in cinema in what he calls an 'epic stumbling block'. In the same vein, in Chapter 11 Deborah Bridge offers a persuasive challenge to include Harry Potter in the epic canon; looking at the reasons for dismissing the films, she uses traditional definitions of the epic to make the case for the inclusion of the Potter franchise and thus, by extension, poses wider questions about our assumptions of what is, or is not, epic. Such a challenge is continued in Chapter 12, which sees Aarttee Kaul Dhar examine two remakes of a fundamental Indian epic, the *Ramayana*, to question whether a global myth can become epic and still keep in touch with its national roots.

Overall, each of the chapters included in this volume rethinks the epic in one way or another, by examining the return of the epic and its use of history, as well as questioning what we tend to include in the epic canon and what this reveals about our values and ideas. As editor I am happy to give full credit for all of the great ideas in the chapters which follow to the authors themselves, and to acknowledge responsibility for any factual or typographical errors as wholly my own. If the great William Wyler was unable to spot the wristwatch on one of his extras, if Ridley Scott missed a pair of sunglasses in his Colosseum crowd, and if Wolfgang Petersen managed to miss an aeroplane in the background of the Trojan landscape, should any errors be discovered in this text I should think myself to be in very good company indeed.

NOTES

1. Martin M. Winkler (ed.), *Gladiator: Film and History* (Oxford: Blackwell, 2005), p. 110.
2. Monica S. Cyrino, '*Gladiator* and Contemporary American Society', in Winkler 2005, pp. 124–49 (p. 125).
3. Source: www.the-movie-times.com, last accessed 1 August 2010.
4. Derek Elley, *The Epic Film: Myth and History* (Cinema and Society) (London: Routledge & Kegan Paul, 1984), p. 9.
5. J. B. Bessinger Jr, 'The *Gest of Robin Hood* Revisited', in Stephen Knight (ed.), *Robin Hood: an Anthology of Scholarship and Criticism* (Woodbridge: Brewer, 1999), p. 43.
6. Stephen Neale, *Genre and Hollywood* (London: Routledge. 2000), p. 26 (my emphasis).
7. See, for example, James Russell, *The Historical Epic and Contemporary Hollywood: From Dances with Wolves to Gladiator* (New York: Continuum, 2007), p. 5.
8. For more on the Italian peplum, see Michèle Lagny, 'Popular Taste: The Peplum', in

Richard Dyer and Ginette Vincendeau (eds), *Popular European Cinema* (London: Routledge, 1992), pp. 163–80; Domenico Cammarota, *Il Cinema Peplum* (Rome: Fannuci Editore, 1987); Laurent Aknin, *Le Péplum* (Paris: Armand Colin, 2009); Claude Aziza, *Le Péplum, Un Mauvais Genre* (Paris: Klincksieck, 2009); Gideon Nisbet, *Ancient Greece in Film and Popular Culture* (Exeter: Bristol Phoenix Press, 2006); Elley, *The Epic Film*.

9. Martin M. Winkler (ed.), *Classical Myth and Culture in the Cinema* (Oxford: Oxford University Press, 2001), p. 3. For an in-depth argument about how, for example, *Frankenstein* uses classical myth, see Brett M. Rogers and Benjamin Stevens, 'Classical Receptions in Science Fiction', *Classical Receptions Journal*, 4.1 (2012), pp. 127–47.
10. For a more comprehensive list of these see Jon Solomon's excellent 'In the Wake of Cleopatra: The Ancient World in Cinema Since 1963', *The Classical Journal*, 91 (1995), pp. 113–40. See also Martin M. Winkler, *Classical Myth and Culture in the Cinema*.
11. To mention only a few of these, see Martin M. Winkler, *Troy: From Homer's Iliad to Hollywood Epic*; Martin M. Winkler, *Gladiator: Film and History*; Maria Wyke, 'Are You Not Entertained? Classicists and the Cinema', *International Journal of the Classical Tradition*, 9 (2003), pp. 430–45; Joanna Paul, *A Spectacle of Destruction: Pompeii and Herculaneum in Popular Imagination* (London: I. B. Tauris, 2012); Joanna Paul, 'Cinematic Receptions of Antiquity: The Current State of Play', *Classical Receptions Journal*, 2 (2010), 136–55; Monica Cyrino, *Big Screen Rome* (Oxford: Wiley-Blackwell, 2005); Jon Solomon, *The Ancient World in the Cinema* (New Haven, CT: Yale University Press, 2001); Sandra R. Joshel, Margaret Malamud and Donald T. McGuire Jr (eds), *Imperial Projections: Ancient Rome in Modern Popular Culture* (Baltimore, MD: The Johns Hopkins University Press, 2001); Paul Cartledge and Fiona Rose Greenland (eds), *Responses to Oliver Stone's Alexander: Film, History, and Cultural Studies* (Madison, WI: University of Wisconsin Press, 2010); Richards, *Hollywood's Ancient Worlds*; Robert Burgoyne (ed.), *The Epic Film in World Culture* (London: Routledge, 2010).
12. Cyrino, *Big Screen Rome*, p. 239; Winkler, *Gladiator: Film and History*, p. xi; Aknin, *Le Péplum*, p. 109 (my translation); Jon Solomon, 'Gladiator from Screenplay to Screen', in Winkler (ed.), *Gladiator: Film and History* (Oxford: Wiley-Blackwell, 2005), pp. 1–15 (p. 15).
13. Solomon, 'Gladiator from Screenplay to Screen', p. xi; Cyrino, 'Gladiator and Contemporary American Society', in *Gladiator: Film and History* (Oxford: Blackwell, 2005), pp. 124–49 (p. 125).
14. Russell, *The Historical Epic*, p. 7; Jerome De Groot, *Consuming History: Historians and Heritage in Contemporary Popular Culture* (London: Routledge, 2009), p. 226.
15. Winkler, *Troy: From Homer's Iliad to Hollywood Epic*, p. 3.
16. Russell, *The Historical Epic*; Maria A. Wyke, *Projecting the Past: Ancient Rome, Cinema, and History* (London: Routledge, 1997); Richards, *Hollywood's Ancient Worlds*; Sheldon Hall and Steve Neale, *Epics, Spectacles, and Blockbusters: A Hollywood History* (Detroit, MI: Wayne State University Press, 2010); Burgoyne, *The Epic Film in World Culture*.
17. Neale, *Genre and Hollywood*, p. 85.
18. Hall and Neale, *Epics, Spectacles, and Blockbusters*, p. 5.
19. Richards, *Hollywood's Ancient Worlds*.
20. Ibid., p. 1.
21. Aziza, *Le Péplum*, p. 87.
22. Cyrino, *Big Screen Rome*, p. 125.
23. Michael Atkinson, 'Natural Born Killer: Tousled Bleach Jobs, One-eyed Stiffs, Neo-epic Drops Its Veils but Keeps the Nookie Offscreen', *Village Voice*, 16 Nov. 2004.

24. Gabe Essoe and Raymond Lee, *DeMille: The Man and His Pictures* (New York: A. S. Barnes, 1970), p. 222.
25. James Russell, '"A Most Historic Period of Change": The Western, the Epic and *Dances with Wolves*' in Lincoln Geraghty and Mark Jancovich (eds), *The Shifting Definitions of Genre: Essays on Labeling Films, Television Shows and Media* (Jefferson, NC: McFarland, 2008), pp. 142–58 (p. 143).
26. For a candid discussion of Stone's problems with 'letting the film go from my consciousness', see Stone's Afterword in Cartledge and Greenland, *Responses to Oliver Stone's* Alexander, pp. 337–51, p. 341.
27. Lagny, 'Popular Taste: The Peplum', p. 163.
28. Richards, *Hollywood's Ancient Worlds*, foreword; see also Chapter 1, pp. 1–23 of the same work.
29. Richards, *Hollywood's Ancient Worlds*, p. 25.
30. Constantine Santas, *The Epic in Film: From Myth to Blockbuster* (Lanham: Rowman & Littlefield, 2007), p. 4.
31. Sam Leith, 'The Return of Swords 'n' Sandals Movies', *The Financial Times*, 14 May 2010.
32. Baird Searles, *Epic! History on the Big Screen* (NY: Abrams, 1990), p. 228; Richards, *Hollywood's Ancient Worlds*, p. 55.
33. Elley, *The Epic Film*, p. 21.
34. Carl J. Mora, 'The Image of Ancient Rome in the Cinema', *Film-Historia*, VII (1997), pp. 221–43 (p. 234).
35. Russell, *The Historical Epic and Contemporary Hollywood*, p. 45.
36. This, for instance, is the argument made convincingly by Jeffrey Richards in *Hollywood's Ancient Worlds*. However, in a review of this work Winkler does raise some objections, claiming that 'Bronston's financial problems were considerably more complex', *Film and History*, 41.1 (Spring 2011), pp. 112–15 (here p. 114); see also Martin M. Winkler (ed.), *The Fall of the Roman Empire: Film and History* (Oxford: Wiley-Blackwell, 2009); Bruce Babington and Peter William Evans, *Biblical Epics: Sacred Narrative in the Hollywood Cinema* (Manchester: Manchester University Press, 1993).
37. Cyrino, 'Gladiator and Contemporary American Society', p. 125; Elley, *The Epic Film*, p. 18; Winkler, *The Fall of the Roman Empire: Film and History*, p. 10.
38. Sheldon Hall, 'Selling Religion: How to Market a Biblical Epic', *Film History*, 14 (2002), pp. 170–85 (p. 170); Santas, *The Epic in Film*, p. 116.
39. Searles, *Epic!*, p. 46.
40. Russell, *The Historical Epic and Contemporary Hollywood*, pp. 157–8.
41. Paula Parisi, *Titanic and the Making of James Cameron: The Inside Story of the Three-year Adventure That Rewrote Motion Picture History* (New York: Newmarket Press, 1998); see also Matthew Wilhelm Kapell and Stephen McVeigh (eds), *The Films of James Cameron: Critical Essays* (Jefferson, NC: McFarland, 2011).
42. Russell, *The Historical Epic and Contemporary Hollywood*, p. 107.
43. Aknin, *Le Péplum*, p. 109 (my translation).
44. James Chapman, *Past and Present: National Identity and the British Historical Film* (London: I. B.Tauris, 2005), p. 5.
45. Hayden White, 'The Modernist Event', in Vivien Sobchack (ed.), *The Persistence of History: Cinema, Television, and the Modern Event* (London: Routledge, 1996), pp. 17–38 (p. 17); Siegfried Kracauer, *From Caligari to Hitler: A Psychological History of the German Film* (Princeton, NJ: Princeton University Press, 2004); Pierre Sorlin, *The Film in History: Restaging the Past* (Tutowa, NJ: Barnes and Noble, 1980).

46. Jeffrey Richards, *Hollywood's Ancient Worlds*, foreword.
47. Quoted in Cyrino, 'Gladiator and Contemporary American Society', p. 125.
48. Peter C. Rollins, *Hollywood as Historian: American Film in a Cultural Context* (Lexington, KY: University Press of Kentucky, 1998), p. 1.
49. Winkler, *Classical Myth and Culture in the Cinema*, pp. 3–22, see also his introduction to *Troy: From Homer's Iliad to Hollywood Epic*, p. 4, note 13.
50. For more on this relationship, see Frederick Ahl, '*Spartacus*, Exodus and Dalton Trumbo: Managing Ideologies of War', in Martin M. Winkler (ed.), *Spartacus: Film and History* (Oxford: Wiley-Blackwell, 2007), pp. 65–86; Duncan S. Cooper, 'Dalton Trumbo vs. Stanley Kubrick: The Historical Meaning of Spartacus', in the same volume, pp. 56–64. See also Steve Neale, 'Swashbucklers and Sitcoms, Cowboys and Crime, Nurses, Just Men and Defenders: Blacklisted Writers and TV in the 1950s and 1960s', *Film Studies*, 7 (2005), pp. 83–103.
51. Cyrino, 'Gladiator and Contemporary American Society'.

PART I
Epics and Ancient History

CHAPTER 2

Sir Ridley Scott and the Rebirth of the Historical Epic

Jeffrey Richards

It was Sir Walter Scott who, in the first decades of the nineteenth century, invented the historical novel. It was Sir Ridley Scott (no relation) who, in the first decades of the twenty-first century, reinvented the historical epic. Of Walter Scott's medieval romances, Henry Beers wrote:

> Scott apprehended the Middle Ages in their spectacular and more particularly their military sides. He exhibits their large, showy aspects: battles, processions, hunts, feasts in halls, tourneys, sieges and the like. The motley medieval world swarms in his pages, from the King on his throne down to the jester with his cap and bells . . . it was . . . the noise, bustle, colour, stirring action that delighted him.[1]

It is a vision that is already inherently cinematic, and it was in the 1950s – by which time Scott's novels were largely unread – that Hollywood turned three of his most celebrated medieval romances into big-budget films: *Ivanhoe* (Thorpe 1952), *The Talisman* (filmed as *King Richard and the Crusaders* (Butler 1954)) and *The Adventures of Quentin Durward* (Thorpe 1955). However, Walter Scott had a political agenda. First, he sought to define and elaborate chivalry as the appropriate code of behaviour for gentlemen, and it was to become the dominant code of masculinity in both Britain and America for a century and a half. Second, as a practical upholder of the Hanoverian settlement and the Anglican Church who dreamed romantically of Jacobitism, the sacred lost cause of Scotland, and of an idealised medieval past, he sought in his novels consistently to dramatise the idea of reconciliation: between Cavalier and Roundhead, highlander and lowlander, Norman and Saxon, Jacobite and Hanoverian, in the interests of building a unified nation.

What I want to explore in this chapter is the political agenda lying behind what has been so far a trio of historical epics by Sir Ridley Scott: *Gladiator*

(2001), *Kingdom of Heaven* (2005) and *Robin Hood* (2010). Looking at his films purely cinematically in terms of scale, spectacle and visual style, the filmmaker Ridley Scott most recalls is Cecil B. De Mille. While De Mille never filmed Robin Hood, he did re-create the Middle Ages in his version of Joan of Arc, *Joan the Woman* (1916) and *The Crusades* (1935) as well as evoking the Roman Empire in *The King of Kings* (1927), *The Sign of the Cross* (1932) and *Cleopatra* (1934). Both Scott and De Mille have demonstrated a mastery of the large-scale set-piece, can handle huge crowds with confidence and imagination, and are supreme visual stylists, their imagery – as they both admitted – being fundamentally influenced by famous paintings, particularly Victorian and Renaissance paintings. Where they differ is in the ideology underpinning their films. Fundamental to De Mille's cinematic vision was Christianity. That was not what influenced Ridley Scott.

Now I should make it clear that I belong firmly to the school of historians whom Robert Burgoyne in his thought-provoking book *The Hollywood Historical Film* calls 'presentists', that is to say historians who believe that historical films can tell us far more about the period in which they are made than about the period in which they are set.[2] The objective presentation of historical facts in feature films is practically impossible, given the demands and constraints of the medium. There is the question of running time. There is a limit to the amount of history you can include in a two- or three-hour film, particularly if it claims to be covering twenty or thirty years. There are the demands of the drama. Characters are eliminated or merged, events telescoped and simplified, historically insupportable confrontations invented, chronology altered. And films don't have footnotes.[3]

There is no doubt that enormous research went into the 'look' of historical films: costumes, settings and appearances exhaustively researched, to support the invariable claim to historical authenticity. But even that had its limits. When Josef von Sternberg was making his epic film *I Claudius* (eventually abandoned after Merle Oberon playing the Empress Messalina was involved in a car accident), the designer prepared accurate dress designs for the six Vestal Virgins, who were to be authentically middle-aged and fully clothed. Sternberg vetoed this saying 'I want sixty and I want them naked', and in the surviving footage there are sixty, swathed in skimpy chiffon and of course young and beautiful.[4]

It is even worse in the narratives of historical films where the filmmakers play fast and loose with the facts. In Mel Gibson's *Braveheart* (1995), his epic film about William Wallace, the Scots wear woad a thousand years too late and clan tartans five hundred years too early. The medieval politics is wholly wrong and Wallace impregnates Isabelle of France, Princess of Wales, with the future Edward III whereas she did not arrive in England until two years after his death in 1305. Is this the first known case of artificial insemination? I think we should be told. Take the case of Shekhar Kapur's *Elizabeth* (1998). The producer Alison Owen said of it: 'Although it is a film that is very true to Tudor times, historical veracity has not been the main point of contact. We have not changed facts but manipulated time-periods.'[5] They have certainly manipulated time periods since they cram events from a twenty-year period into the nine years of the film, 1554–63. But they have also invented facts. The director said he had modelled his Elizabeth on Indira Gandhi and the film was constructed as a fast-moving conspiracy thriller in which spymaster Sir Francis Walsingham – who did not actually become a key adviser of Elizabeth until 1573, ten years after the action of the film – uncovers a plot to assassinate her and persuades her that in a lightning coup, all the plotters should be executed or murdered. The plotters are the Spanish ambassador De Quadra, Bishop Stephen Gardiner, the Earls of Sussex and Arundel and the Duke of Norfolk. As a matter of fact, none of them was executed or murdered, all dying of natural causes except for the Duke of Norfolk, and he was not executed until 1572. As historian Christopher Haigh wrote of the film: 'By all means enjoy *Elizabeth* – I did – but don't suppose that it's telling you anything about history.'[6]

These objections are not mere historians' pedantry. There is nothing more tiresome than critics who simply list historical errors without explaining why. I mention them to underline the fact that historical films have political agendas. The filmmakers select events and personalities from the historical record in order to create their dramas. That is as true of Ridley Scott as of any of his cinematic predecessors. The question then is not so much what they include as what they leave out and why they make the selections they do and to what end.

Gladiator (2000) was a remarkable and unexpected worldwide success, single-handedly reviving a genre – the Ancient World epic – which had languished in the cinema since the box-office failure of *The Fall of the Roman Empire* in 1964. Fittingly perhaps, Scott chose to tell the same story as the earlier film, showing how it should have been done to achieve maximum audience satisfaction. Russell Crowe won an Oscar for his performance as Maximus Decimus Meridius, general of the armies of the North, reduced to the status of slave and gladiator, who becomes a hero of the people and succeeds in overthrowing the tyranny of the Emperor Commodus and restoring the Roman Republic.

Gladiator is not really an attempt to tell an accurate story from Roman history. The script is full of provable historical errors. The heroine Lucilla was executed for plotting against her brother Commodus and therefore did not survive him as she does in the film. Her son Lucius Verus, who also plays a significant role in the film, died in infancy. There is no evidence that Marcus Aurelius was murdered. No one seriously contemplated restoring the Republic. Commodus was not killed in single combat but strangled by a wrestler hired by his mistress Marcia while lying drunk in his bed. However, none of this matters remotely so far as the film's entertainment value is concerned.

But how far is the film in any way based on history? The direct inspirations for *Gladiator* were not histories of Imperial Rome. They were Roman epics of the 1950s and 1960s and nineteenth-century paintings of the Roman world. Scott was persuaded to take on the project when producer Douglas Wick showed him a print of Jean-Léon Gérôme's 1872 painting *Pollice Verso* (Thumbs Down), in which a gladiator straddles a fallen opponent in the arena and waits for the crowd's verdict of thumbs up or down. This moment is reproduced in the film, as are scenes from several other Gérôme paintings.

The script of *Gladiator* is a cunning fusion of the plots of *The Fall of the Roman Empire* (Mann 1964), the least successful of the earlier cycle of Roman epics, and *Spartacus* (Kubrick 1960), one of the most successful. The characters of Marcus Aurelius, Lucilla and Commodus in *Gladiator* derive as much from Anthony Mann's *The Fall of the Roman Empire* as they do from Roman history. They are joined by characters inspired by *Spartacus*. The Numidian Juba is the counterpart of the African Draba in *Spartacus*. Proximo, the ruthless businessman who becomes 'a good guy' at the end, recalls Batiatus in *Spartacus*. The republican senator Gracchus in *Gladiator* is lifted directly, even to his name, from *Spartacus*. Maximus is a composite of Livius, the fictional hero of *The Fall of the Roman Empire*, and Spartacus. This habit of borrowing from earlier films rather than from history has now become the norm in Hollywood. This is superbly demonstrated in Colin McArthur's study of *Braveheart*, in which he lists and explains the errors and distortions and details the film's borrowings from *The Vikings* (Fleischer 1958), *Spartacus*, *The Adventures of Robin Hood* (Curtiz 1938), *The Wild Bunch* (Peckinpah 1969) and *Major Dundee* (Peckinpah 1965).[7]

Gladiator omits the disastrous anti-climactic ending of *Fall* in which Livius rejects the throne and walks away, allowing the empire to decline. This is replaced by the much more dramatically satisfying but completely unhistorical ending of *Gladiator*, in which the dying Maximus implements the last wish of Marcus Aurelius – the restoration of the Republic. Both films omit the short reign of Pertinax. But *Gladiator* ought to have ended with the auction of the imperial title which featured in *Fall* and resulted in Didius Julianus gaining the throne. This was followed by the arrival of the African-born general Septimius Severus and the Pannonian legions to behead Julianus and inaugurate the Severan dynasty which restored order and stability to the Empire. But of course that would not have suited the politics of either film version. For the politics of *Gladiator* were not Roman at all but those of contemporary America. Scriptwriter David Franzoni said 'the movie is about us. It is not about Ancient Rome; it's about America', and producer Douglas Wick thought the Roman obsession with the games had a direct parallel with present-day America: 'The whole population is distracted by entertainment from the serious issues like today.'⁸ In the light of such comments, *Gladiator* can fairly be seen as a critique of Clintonian America. It is now America and not Britain or Russia that is 'the evil Empire'. The film was made at a time when the American government was mired in financial and sexual scandals and embroiled in overseas adventures (the Balkans, Somalia) – the Somalia intervention actually features in Ridley Scott's 2001 film *Black Hawk Down*; meanwhile the public was immersed in a culture of sports, entertainment and celebrity. *Gladiator* opens with Rome engaged in a costly high-tech war, defeating the last enemy to become the sole global superpower. Marcus Aurelius wants peace, denounces the corruption that has crept into public life, urges the restoration of power to the people and the re-energising of the supine Senate. The republic that Marcus Aurelius wants restored is not so much the Roman Republic as the Republic of Jeffersonian America, the eighteenth-century construct led by honest men and devoted to democratic ideals. However, when Commodus seizes the throne, he institutes what is in effect a fascist regime. This is indicated visually by Scott when he stages Commodus' triumphal entry into Rome exactly like Hitler's arrival in Nuremberg in Leni Riefenstahl's *Triumph of the Will* (1935). Commodus then distracts the people with games, blinding them to their loss of freedom. When Commodus and Maximus finally face each other, they embody rival visions of Rome, Commodus' of a totalitarian Empire and Maximus' of a democratic Republic. It is Maximus' vision, symbolised by family and farm like that of a good eighteenth-century American yeoman, which triumphs.

A different political ideal was adumbrated in *The Fall of the Roman Empire*, produced by Samuel Bronston and directed by Anthony Mann, which was once again constructed to reflect contemporary preoccupations. Anthony Mann explained, in an article published at the time, what had drawn him to the subject:

> The reason for making *The Fall of the Roman Empire* is that it is as modern today as it was in the history that Gibbon wrote. The past is like a mirror; it reflects what actually happened, and in the reflection of the fall of Rome are the same elements in what is happening today, the very things that are making our empires fall.⁹

In *Fall*, the Emperor Marcus Aurelius, depicted as an idealised statesman-ruler (his persecution of the Christians conveniently forgotten), seeks after seventeen years of continual border warfare to transform the Empire from a state of being permanently at war to one of being permanently at peace. He calls all the kings and governors of the Empire to an assembly where he proposes to grant Roman citizenship to all, creating a 'family of equal nations', all dedicated to the preservation of the *pax romana*. It is in essence a blueprint for the United Nations. The United Nations ethic lay practically and ideologically behind all of Samuel Bronston's epics, notably *King of Kings* (Ray 1961), *El Cid* (Mann 1961), and *55 Days at Peking* (Ray 1963). However, when in *Fall* it is learned that Marcus Aurelius plans to disinherit his degenerate and unstable son Commodus in favour of general Livius, who shares Marcus' ideals and also loves his daughter Lucilla, Commodus' cronies poison Marcus Aurelius before he can do so and Commodus duly succeeds to the throne.

In the Senate, the philosopher Timonides, the Greek ex-slave acting as Livius' spokesman, advocates a policy for the empire which is based on freedom, equality, peace, common citizenship, the end of slavery and an open door for immigrants. In other words, he proposes to turn the Roman Empire into an idealised form of the USA, complete with Civil Rights. Commodus prefers to turn the Empire into a totalitarian tyranny. The film ends with Livius killing Commodus in a duel. But when he is hailed by the legions as the new Emperor, Livius walks away with Lucilla, leaving rival claimants to bid for the throne and the support of the all-powerful legions. It is the beginning of the fall of the Empire.

But no hero worth his salt, having disposed of an evil tyrant and being offered the chance to implement Marcus Aurelius' vision, would simply walk away. However, the scriptwriters faced the problem that there never was an Emperor Livius and the whole point of the film was to explain the fall of the Empire. Although the final complete rejection of empire may have chimed with the view of the three scriptwriters (Philip Yordan, Ben Barzman and Basilio Franchina), who were either liberal or leftist, Anthony Mann subsequently described the ending as 'defeatist' and at least one critic noted of Livius' abdication of responsibility that the film implied that 'this pusillanimous prig was indirectly responsible for the fall, and not Commodus'.[10] No epic in this cycle garnered such excellent reviews or crashed so spectacularly at the box office. The times were evidently unreceptive both for the epic form and the film's message. The assassination of President Kennedy in November 1963 had traumatised not only the USA but the whole Western world as it signalled the end of the optimistic, idealistic age of Camelot, and the dramatic escalation of American involvement in Vietnam under Kennedy's successor, Lyndon Johnson, presaged a major era of war and not of the *Pax Americana*. At the same time, the old studio system was breaking up and the audience changing from a presumed family audience aged from six to sixty to a largely youthful audience under thirty with different values and attitudes from their elders. The cinema box office tells that story. The top six films at the US box office in 1963 were *Cleopatra* (Mankiewicz 1963), *The Longest Day* (Marton et al. 1962), *Irma La Douce* (Wilder 1963), *Lawrence of Arabia* (Lean 1962), *How the West Was Won* (Ford et al. 1962) and *Mutiny on the Bounty* (Milestone 1962), all of them except for *Irma La Douce* epics. The top six films at the US box office in 1965 were *Mary Poppins* (Stevenson 1964), *The Sound of Music* (Wise 1965), *Goldfinger* (Hamilton, 1964), *My Fair Lady* (Cukor, 1964), *What's New Pussycat?* (Donner 1965) and *Shenandoah* (McLaglen 1965), none of them an epic, only the last historical, all of them feelgood or escapist films. *The Fall of the Roman Empire* fell into the enormous chasm between the two eras.

Scott's second historical epic, *Kingdom of Heaven* (2005), was conceived in the aftermath of the attack on the Twin Towers on 11 September 2001 and released after the invasion of Iraq in 2003. It proposed to examine the relations between Christianity and Islam, in such a way as to point to a moral – and it was an impeccably liberal one. Scriptwriter William Monahan said: 'The film proposes that it's better to live together than to be at war. That reason is better than fanaticism. That kindness is better than hate. That it's better to discard the world – money, position, power, whatever your times are telling you to do – than to endanger your integrity.'[11] But the subject of the Crusades was an immensely problematic one. When, in 2001, President George W. Bush described the War on Terror as a 'crusade' he set off a political storm since the Crusades were anathema to the Muslims and had long had the reputation of being the product of greed, land hunger and racial and religious prejudice.

William Monahan did his research and then played fast and loose with history. He declared: 'For a creative writer doing history, the technique is to read everything and then use what you need – which is often very little . . . No-one should expect stageplays and screenplays to be history. And historiography is never "Historically accurate" . . . In our case we have tried to do something very balanced and ethical.'[12] The film takes place in the 1180s and covers the final years of the Crusading kingdom of Jerusalem, culminating in the surrender of Jerusalem in 1187 to Sultan Saladin after the defeat of the Crusader army at the Battle of Hattin. All the leading characters in the film are genuinely historical figures apart from Godfrey of Ibelin and the Hospitaller, who were invented and were there for a particular purpose. Godfrey, who dies of his wounds early on, is there to teach his illegitimate son, Balian, the meaning of chivalry. He sets out the precepts of chivalry as being to tell the truth, do no wrong, protect the helpless and defend the King and the people, and he defines the objective of the Crusade as being to establish the Kingdom of Heaven on earth – a kingdom of conscience which involves peace and living in harmony with the Muslims, and which is a place where a man can be whatever he wants to be; in other words, it is an idealised version of the USA. The Hospitaller, who is killed at the Battle of Hattin, is there to show – as Monahan put it – 'Christianity done right' – and to balance the more hot-headed fanatical Christians in the story. His big speech sums up his position: 'I put no stock in religion. By the word religion I have seen the lunacy of fanatics of every denomination be called the will of God. Holiness is right action and courage on behalf of those who cannot defend themselves.' So in the film there are fanatical fundamentalists on both sides. There is the Saracen Nasir, who wants a holy war against the Christians and to exterminate them all, and among the Christians there are the greedy ruthless Crusaders Reynald of Chatillon and Guy of Lusignan, who deliberately start a war to exterminate the Muslims. Set against the fundamentalists are the noble and enlightened Sultan Saladin and King Baldwin IV of Jerusalem, the leper king in his silver mask, supported by the character the film calls Tiberias, who is in fact Count Raymond of Tripoli, who want peace and coexistence with the Muslims. Baldwin wants Jerusalem to be a place of pilgrimage for all faiths and executes Templars for killing innocent Muslims. However, it is noticeable that apart from the fictional Hospitaller, the representatives of organised religion all come off very badly. The French village priest beheads Balian's wife after her suicide, and steals her crucifix; the Templars slaughter innocent Muslims, and the Patriarch Heraclius of Jerusalem is a cynical politico, who advises Balian when negotiating the surrender of Jerusalem 'Convert to Islam – repent later'.

The changes that Monahan and Scott made are what interest me here. After Monahan produced his first draft script, Scott worked closely with him to revise it, and in so doing brought it into line with *Gladiator*. The basic line-up of characters follows the classic interpretation given by Sir Steven Runciman, in his history of the Crusades published in the 1950s. He saw the Kingdom of Jerusalem divided between two parties. One party, 'the good guys', seek an understanding with the Muslims and consist of the native barons led by Count Raymond of Tripoli and the Ibelin brothers, Baldwin and Balian, and the Hospitallers. The other party, 'the bad guys', comprises the Templars and newcomers from the West. This party, 'aggressive and militantly Christian', seeking war with the Muslims, was led by Reynald of Chatillon, Guy of Lusignan, the Grand Master of the Templars Gerard of Ridefort and the Patriarch Heraclius.[13] But Runciman's interpretation has latterly been challenged by revisionist historians, who are more critical of Saladin than earlier writers who accepted the idealised picture painted by Arab historians and sanctified by Walter Scott in *The Talisman*, and less critical of Chatillon, Lusignan and Heraclius than their predecessors. However, the Runciman line-up was too satisfying in dramatic terms to abandon.

Christopher Tyerman, in his recent book *The Debate on the Crusades*, wrote the following about Runciman's three-volume history of the Crusades, published between 1951 and 1954:

> Even when published, dated in technique, style and content; derivative, misleading and tendentious, a polemic masquerading as an epic; Runciman's three volumes represent the most astonishing literary phenomenon since Michaud [a French historian who published a multi-volume history of the Crusades between 1811 and 1822]. Almost sixty

years after the publication of his first volume, in educated circles in Britain, if anyone talks about the crusades, 'Runciman' is almost certain to be invoked. Across the Anglophone world he continues as a base reference for popular attitudes, evident in print, film, television, and on the internet.[14]

Describing Ridley Scott's film as 'lamentable', Tyerman warned that it was 'imperative to insist that the medieval wars of the cross were of a different nature, in a different time and between different peoples and have nothing directly to say to modern problems'.[15]

The key to Ridley Scott's agenda lies in the changes made to Balian of Ibelin and Princess Sibylla. The real Balian of Ibelin was the greatest feudatory in the Kingdom of Jerusalem after Raymond of Tripoli. He was middle-aged, had spent his entire life in the Levant, dying there in 1193, and was married to Maria Comnena, widow of King Amalric of Jerusalem and stepmother of King Baldwin IV. In fact he would have been effectively played by Liam Neeson, who in the film plays the fictional Godfrey of Ibelin. Ridley Scott's Balian, as played by Orlando Bloom, is youthful, is a French blacksmith, and is the humble-born illegitimate son of the Crusader Lord Godfrey of Ibelin. He inherits the fief of Ibelin and there runs it as an ideal multicultural society in which Christians, Muslims and Jews peacefully coexist. He is part of the significant democratisation of the story. For although he imbibes and seeks to live by the precepts of chivalry, at one key moment during the siege of Jerusalem he knights all the servants and men-at-arms in the city, showing they are just as good as the gentry, whereas what the real Balian did was knight every boy of noble birth.[16]

Ridley Scott's Balian is given an entirely fictional romance with Princess Sibylla, sister of King Baldwin IV. In a plot line that actually recalls *The Fall of the Roman Empire* and the actions of Livius, King Baldwin urges Balian to marry Sibylla and take the throne. But since this would have involved executing Guy of Lusignan, who is her intended husband, Balian refuses on grounds of conscience. If he had done so, he could have carried out King Baldwin's plan for peace with the Muslims and conceivably have avoided the fall of Jerusalem. In the event, after the surrender of Jerusalem, Sibylla renounces her royal status and follows Balian back to France as an ordinary citizen. In reality what happened was that Baldwin IV died aged twenty-four in 1185 and was briefly succeeded by Baldwin V, the seven-year-old son of Sibylla by her deceased first husband, William of Montferrat. Baldwin V does not appear in the cinematic release print. However, the director's cut, released on DVD, which is forty minutes longer, and is a richer, more complex and altogether superior version, does include Baldwin V, who is crowned and then poisoned by his mother when he shows the early signs of leprosy. Historically, the cause of Baldwin V's death is unknown. Rumours of poison circulated, though not aimed at his mother. But then rumours of poison always circulated at times of sudden and inconvenient deaths.

Baldwin V dies in 1186 and Sibylla is crowned Queen; she immediately crowns her second husband, Guy of Lusignan, King, and he heads the Crusading army to disaster at Hattin. History tells us that Sibylla was a devoted and far from reluctant wife to Guy, made him King willingly, and never left him, dying in 1190 still happily married. The democratising agenda of the film, however, requires her to renounce both her status and her unworthy husband. The idea of the romance with Balian was probably inspired by the fact that Balian's elder brother Baldwin had in fact unsuccessfully sought Sibylla's hand in marriage.

It was Walter Scott who cemented into the popular consciousness the chivalric relationship of mutual admiration between Sultan Saladin and King Richard the Lionheart of England in his novel *The Talisman*. This reached the screen in colour and cinemascope in 1954 as *King Richard and the Crusaders*. Directed by David Butler, best known as the director of *Calamity Jane* (1953) and *Road to Morocco* (1942), it emerged as a sort of cross between a large-scale western and a way-out musical comedy.

The strangeness of the enterprise is compounded by the casting. The Scottish hero, Sir Kenneth of Huntingdon, the Knight of the Leopard, is played in his Hollywood debut by Lithuanian-born Laurence Harvey, who made an improbably willowy but suitably earnest hero, though his Scottish accent came and went scene by scene. In the book Sir Kenneth is revealed at the end to be Prince David of Scotland. The film abandoned this revelation, making Sir Kenneth the younger son of the Earl of Huntingdon, but never explaining why in that case he should be Scottish. Glamorous Warner Bros contract star Virginia Mayo played a very 1950s, American and fictitious Lady Edith Plantagenet, cousin of the Lionheart and the love interest of Sir Kenneth. Even the director David Butler, who thought *King Richard* 'a very good film', was retrospectively critical of Virginia Mayo's 1950s 'look'.[17] George Sanders was very curious casting as Richard the Lionheart. Sanders' suave insolence and dry wit made him a natural for the role of King Charles II, which he played twice in his career (*Forever Amber*, *The King's Thief*). But this hardly fitted him for the role of the twelfth-century warrior king. He resolved the problem triumphantly by playing Richard I as Charles II, enjoying himself hugely and revelling in the colourful invective he was given to speak by scriptwriter John Twist. The strangest casting of all was that of Rex Harrison as Saladin. He steals the picture as Saladin, elegant, courteous and raffishly charming, whether spouting pseudo-Arab proverbs, singing love songs or wielding bow and lance in combat. The curious casting is probably to be explained by his previous experience as an exotic potentate when he played the

King of Siam in *Anna and the King of Siam* (Cromwell 1946). For Hollywood in its heyday, one foreign potentate was much like another.

True to Scott's intention, the film's motivating ethic is chivalry. The film, set during a truce in the Third Crusade in 1191, embellishes the narrative with opening and closing fights, an assassination attempt on Richard (who in the book merely has a fever) and a joust between Richard and Kenneth, and takes a distinctly jaundiced view of the Western allies, notably France and Austria, whose rulers plot and squabble among themselves, seeking to undermine the leadership of Richard. He is threatened more by his internal enemies than his external ones – the Saracens.

The most villainous are Sir Giles Amaury, Grand Master of the Knights of the Castle Refuge, and the scheming Venetian Count Conrad of Montferrat (a Marquis in the book). They plan to assassinate Richard and use the army to carve out a kingdom for themselves in the East. Richard is wounded by an archer in Giles' pay but healed when the Saracen Sultan Saladin sends his physician Ilderim of Kurdistan (actually Saladin in disguise) to treat him. Sir Kenneth, the epitome of chivalry, admires and serves Richard (even though Richard distrusts the Scots). He also admires Saladin, the most civilised and attractive of the film's characters, and he declares: 'the warriors of Saladin and the knights of Richard have a guiding creed in common – chivalry.' Sir Kenneth denounces Amaury and his knights for preying on defenceless Muslims and holding innocent pilgrims to ransom. When the King's banner is torn down, while Kenneth is on guard, he is disgraced, stripped of his knighthood and banished. He takes refuge with Saladin. Saladin seeks to marry Lady Edith and cement peace between Christians and Islam. But when Saladin's peace envoys are murdered and Lady Edith is carried off by Amaury and his men, Crusaders and Saracens join forces to rescue her. Kenneth fights and kills Amaury, is restored to knighthood and will marry Edith. True chivalry triumphs over racial and religious differences between Westerners and Saracens, and over the greed and ambition of false Christians. The film cost 3 million dollars to make and thirty years later had still not recouped its costs.

There are still echoes of Walter Scott in Ridley Scott – the desert encounter between Western hero and Saracen, who develop mutual respect, the unequal romance between Princess and ex-blacksmith echoing that of Lady Edith, fictional cousin of King Richard, and a lowly Scottish knight (dismissed by Richard as 'a Scottish swineherd'). But there are notable differences. Ridley Scott insisted that the Muslims be played by Arab actors, notably the Syrian actor Ghassan Massoud, a memorably dignified Saladin.[18] Queen Sibylla renounces her regal status to go with Balian, whereas King Richard is reconciled to the marriage of his cousin to the Scottish knight. Most interestingly, where the forces of organised religion are the villains of *Kingdom of Heaven*, Hollywood demanded changes in 1954 to *The Talisman*. In the book the villains are the Knights Templar and their Grand Master, Brother Giles Amaury, who is a monk. In the film, they are replaced by the invented Knights of the Castle Refuge, the Castellans, and Amaury is made Sir Giles and his monastic status removed. This was in line with Hollywood's deep fear of offending religious sensibilities, a fear which led the villain in *The Hunchback of Notre Dame* (Dieterle 1939), Archdeacon Frollo, to be secularised as Count Frollo, and in *The Three Musketeers* (Sidney 1948), caused Cardinal Richelieu, to lose his cardinal's hat and become merely prime minister of France. The Templars, being a historical monastic order, are spared villain status in *King Richard and the Crusaders*.

Although it was the First Crusade which was in European terms the successful one, it was the unsuccessful Third Crusade that entered popular mythology, and that was largely due to Walter Scott's celebration of the relationship of chivalric respect between Richard I and Saladin, in *The Talisman*. Cecil B. De Mille's *The Crusades* (1935) is one of his least-known and most impressive epics. Although not an adaptation of Scott, it bears Scott's imprint in its characterisations of Richard as proud, stubborn and violent, of Saladin as wise, dignified and chivalric, and of Philip of France and Conrad of Montferrat as treacherous and self-interested. *Time* magazine (2 September, 1935) called the film 'historically worthless, didactically treacherous, artistically absurd', but added, 'None of these defects impair its entertainment value'. On the other hand, *The Motion Picture Herald* (10 August 1935) called it 'an inspiring martial story, powerful, but humanly understandable, that transcends all racial and religious prejudice', and *The New York Times* (22 August 1935) said: 'Mr De Mille has no peer in the world when it comes to bringing the panoplied splendor of the past into torrential life upon the screen ... At its best *The Crusades* possesses the true quality of a screen epic.'

Despite extensive historical research, the film is full of errors and inaccuracies, not least the idea of Peter the Hermit preaching the Third Crusade when in fact he had preached the First a century earlier. But De Mille argued that the film was more a distillation of the spirit of the Crusades than an accurate historical re-creation, writing in his autobiography:

> The history conveyed to the audience in *The Crusades* was simply that there was a time when Christian men, kings, knights and commoners, with motives ranging from purest faith to the blackest treachery and greed, left their homes by the thousands and sought to wrest the Holy Land from its Moslem possessors who were not, as the propaganda of the time would have it, infidel dogs, but highly civilized and chivalrous foemen. I submit that if anyone in the audience took that conception home with him, he had a very good idea of what the crusades were all about.[19]

In a film of trumpet calls, banners, shields and war songs, De Mille certainly conveys in broad strokes the ferocity of battle and all the treachery and rivalry of the Crusading princes. But he also is keen to stress the genuine religious inspiration, strikingly conveyed by the scene in which wounded, dying and exhausted Crusaders drag themselves up a long staircase, bathed in light, for a glimpse of the True Cross, and in the martyrdom of the Hermit, transfixed like Saint Sebastian by Muslim arrows as he urges the Crusaders on to attack. The contrast here is with *Kingdom of Heaven*, decried by Professor Jonathan Riley-Smith for ignoring the genuine religious inspiration and idealism of Crusaders, now strongly stressed by revisionist historians.[20] For all its factual alterations, De Mille's epic is more in line with one of the now-dominant interpretations of the Crusades than *Kingdom of Heaven* is.

But like Walter Scott and Ridley Scott, De Mille preaches reconciliation between Crusaders and Muslims. In this version, Richard only goes on Crusade to escape marriage to Alice of France, and he marries Berengaria of Navarre purely to obtain vital supplies for his Crusaders from her father. But he spends the rest of the film falling in love with her. In the end, he is humbled, repents and asks God for forgiveness. Berengaria moves from hostility to Richard to a willingness to sacrifice herself to Saladin to save Richard from assassination. In the end Saladin releases her and it is Berengaria who pleads with the two of them for peace, saying that much blood has already been shed, Christ was the Prince of Peace, and they all worship God by different names. A truce is agreed, with access to Jerusalem for pilgrims of all faiths. Ian Keith gives the best performance of his career as Saladin, creating a convincing portrait of a man of wisdom, dignity and genuine chivalry. He warns Richard about his potential assassination, liquidates the treacherous Conrad of Montferrat, restores Berengaria to her husband and, having crushed the Crusading army, agrees to peace and the admission of pilgrims of all faiths to Jerusalem.

Like *King Richard and the Crusaders*, *The Crusades* was a box-office failure. This may be in part due to the fact that neither Henry Wilcoxon, who played Richard, nor Loretta Young, who played Queen Berengaria, were major stars, and the film's failure certainly ended Wilcoxon's career as a potential major star. Shooting had overrun by eighteen days and the film came in $336,000 over its one million dollar budget. But it lost $795,000 on its initial release, and even after a 1951 reissue was still showing a loss of $444,000. *Kingdom of Heaven*, budgeted at 130 million dollars, had by the end of 2005 grossed only 211 million worldwide. This is in marked contrast to *Gladiator*, which cost 103 million and made 456 million worldwide. The temper of the times was not perhaps conducive to films preaching reconciliation between Christians and Muslims at the height of the War on Terror. But then Crusading epics had in the past also been box-office failures.

Kingdom of Heaven ended with Richard I setting out on the Third Crusade and Balian of Ibelin declining to join him. Ridley Scott's latest epic, *Robin Hood* (2010), opens with Richard I 'bankrupt of wealth and glory', returning from the Crusade and 'plundering his way back to England'. Richard is killed at the siege of Chalus, his feckless brother John becomes King and the villainous Sir Godfrey sets out to create division within England as a prelude to the invasion and conquest of England by King Philip of France. Into this scenario rides Robin Longstride, who by the end of the film has become the outlaw Robin Hood.

This Robin completes the process of proletarianisation that has been going on in the Robin Hood myth since the 1970s. Whatever his actual historical origins, Robin had been securely gentrified by the sixteenth century, becoming the alter ego of the Earl of Huntingdon. Thereafter, in accordance with the dominance of the chivalric myth, Robin, as played by Douglas Fairbanks, Errol Flynn, Richard Todd and Richard Greene, remained securely a gentleman if not an aristocrat. It was in 1976 in *Robin and Marian* (Lester), following the social and cultural revolution of the 1960s, that Robin – played by Sean Connery – became for the first time unequivocally a peasant. The rejection of chivalry as the dominant code of masculinity and the rise of the working-class individualist – rebellious, nonconformist and devoted to immediate gratification – provided the context in which Robin's devotion to a tyrannical Richard I is seen as irrational. Post-Vietnam disillusionment with war leads Robin to dismiss the Crusade as a parade of massacre, torture and looting, all blessed by the Church. The whole film is an elegy for old-time heroism and a valedictory for Merrie England, with Robin dying at the end.

Robin in *Robin of Sherwood*, the 1980s television series, is also a Saxon peasant, Robin of Loxley, son of a villager killed in a rising of Saxons against the Norman oppression. Ideologically he is now what he had never been before – an English socialist and proletarian rebel, a man of the people, who opposes excessive taxation, the absence of representative government and England's involvement in expensive foreign wars.

Robin of Sherwood heavily influenced the next Robin Hood film, *Robin Hood – Prince of Thieves* (Reynolds 1991). Starring Kevin Costner, whose Robin is the son of Lord Locksley and newly returned from the Crusades with a wise and enlightened Muslim sidekick Azeem, this emerged as a precise analogue of Costner's own *Dances with Wolves* (1990), a paean of praise to the life of the American Indians, harmony with nature and man as eco-warrior. Costner's Robin is a democrat ('Don't call me sire', he tells the outlaws) and a 'New Man' (cheerfully attending a natural childbirth in the forest), and he prefigures Russell Crowe's sentiments in Scott's film when he declares 'Nobility is not a birthright. It is defined by a man's actions'. With the Crusade standing in for the American Civil War, the Sherwood outlaws for the Sioux Indians, the murderous Celts for the savage Pawnees, and the Sherriff's guards for the US cavalry, Costner reruns *Dances with Wolves*. Its central theme becomes mutual respect between two men of different races, with the Moor Azeem replacing the Sioux medicine man Kicking Bird, and with the telescope and nude bathing scenes from *Dances with Wolves* reproduced exactly in case anyone missed the point.[21]

Ridley Scott's Robin Hood is Russell Crowe, who plays him as a surlier and even more taciturn version of his Maximus from *Gladiator*, and with an accent that wanders about from shire to shire. Robin Longstride is a Saxon archer, son of a stonemason, who lectures Richard I on his unjustified slaughter of innocent Muslims, ending up in the stocks for his pains. Echoing Balian's knighting of the men at arms in *Kingdom of Heaven*, Longstride agrees to impersonate the dead Crusader Sir Robert of Loxley, declaring 'There is no difference between a knight and any other man aside from what he wears'. He does so to prevent the Loxley lands being seized by the crown and ends up falling in love with Sir Robert's widow, Marian – though there is absolutely no chemistry between Crowe and Cate Blanchett's Marian. Longstride organises the forest outlaws to resist the depredations of Sir Godfrey and his French soldiers. He discovers that he is the son of a visionary democrat Thomas Longstride, who drafted the original version of Magna Carta, prescribing liberty for all under the law, fair trials, and equality of opportunity for each individual, what might be summed up as 'life, liberty and the pursuit of happiness'. He seeks to impose it on King John, who agrees to accept it until after Robin and his band help repel the French invasion. John then reneges, burns the charter and outlaws Robin, who takes to the greenwood as Robin Hood, proclaiming a philosophy of 'fair shares for all at Nature's table' and determined to secure the implementation of Magna Carta.

The film also contains a notable example of cinematic borrowing, with the French invasion of England sequence strongly influenced by the Normandy landings in Steven Spielberg's *Saving Private Ryan* (1993). Interestingly, this is not the first time Robin Hood has sought to impose Magna Carta on King John. In *Rogues of Sherwood Forest* (Douglas 1950), Robin, son of Robin Hood, and since the death of his father Earl of Huntingdon, returns from Crusade, reunites his father's old band and resists the tyranny of King John, who announces his intention to reverse the 'democratic tendencies' of his brother Richard's reign. This had involved low taxation and consultation of the barons. Eventually Robin Junior successfully forces King John to sign Magna Carta at Runnymede, where Archbishop Stephen Langton reminds him that he rules now only by the consent of his subjects. So in 1950 we get a satisfying closure and the victory of law and justice. But in 2010 we get no closure: only the beginning of a struggle to change society.

So what can we conclude about the politics of Ridley Scott's trilogy of historical epics? I suggest that they are essentially the same film made three times. Structurally they each contain the 'unleash hell' sequences: the attack on the Germanic barbarians at the start of *Gladiator*, the siege of Chalus at the start of *Robin Hood* and the siege of Jerusalem at the end of *Kingdom of Heaven*. But more significantly, the politics are identical. All three films have a working-class hero: gladiator, blacksmith, archer. The heroes all have arrogant upper-class opponents: Emperor Commodus, Guy of Lusignan, King John of England. Each hero has a wise, experienced and enlightened aristocratic adviser to counsel him: Senator Gracchus, Count Tiberias and Chancellor William Marshal. All three heroes become military leaders, physically courageous but also morally and intellectually committed. Morally and intellectually committed to what? – to something that did not exist when the films are set: freedom and democracy. But it is democracy American-style, with Maximus wishing to turn Rome into the eighteenth-century Jeffersonian Republic, Balian being instructed to create the Kingdom of Heaven on earth, which is an idealised form of the USA, and with Robin Hood seeking to introduce a combination of Declaration of Independence and Bill of Rights into medieval England. It is this consistent political agenda which, I suggest, makes it imperative to examine the process of selection in the historical narrative. To be aware of historical errors, omissions and inventions is not the pedantry of blinkered historians looking down on the cinematic medium. It is an integral part of the critical evaluation of all historical films and their ideological projects.

NOTES

1. Henry Beers, quoted in Jeffrey Richards, *Swordsmen of the Screen* (London: Routledge, 1977), p. 10.
2. Robert Burgoyne, *The Hollywood Historical Film* (Oxford: Blackwell, 2008), p. 10.
3. This applies only to the talkies. I am indebted to Sheldon Hall for pointing out that some silent films, notably D. W. Griffith's historical films, did have footnotes, conveyed by the intertitles.
4. John Armstrong, interviewed in the BBC documentary *The Epic That Never Was* (1965).
5. Susan Doran and Thomas S. Freeman (eds), *Tudors and Stuarts on Film* (Basingstoke: Palgrave Macmillan, 2009), p. 124.
6. Doran and Freeman, *Tudors and Stuarts on Film*, p. 134.
7. Colin McArthur, *Brigadoon, Braveheart and the Scots* (London: I. B. Tauris, 2003), pp. 123–90.
8. Franzoni is quoted in Martin M. Winkler (ed.), *Gladiator: Film and History* (Oxford: Blackwell, 2004), p. 125; Wick is featured in the documentary 'Strength and Honour' on the DVD Special Edition of *Gladiator*. The contemporary relevance of *Gladiator* is discussed at length in Monica Cyrino, '*Gladiator* and Contemporary American Society' in Winkler (ed.), *Gladiator*, pp. 124–49.
9. *Films and Filming*, 10 (March 1964), pp. 7–8.

10. *Monthly Film Bulletin*, 31 (May 1964), p. 69.
11. Diana Landau (ed.), *Kingdom of Heaven: The Ridley Scott Film and the History Behind the Story* (London: Pocket Books, 2005), p. 59.
12. Landau, *Kingdom of Heaven*, p. 50.
13. Bernard Hamilton, *The Leper King and His Heirs* (Cambridge: Cambridge University Press, 2000), p. 1.
14. Christopher Tyerman, *The Debate on the Crusades* (Manchester: Manchester University Press, 2011), p. 192.
15. Tyerman, *The Debate on the Crusades*, p. 236.
16. Landau, *Kingdom of Heaven*, p. 45. On Scott's use of landscape and camera movement to convey ideals and motivations see John M. Ganim, 'Framing the West, Staging the East: Set Design, Location and Landscape in Movie Medievalism', in Nickolas Haydock and E. L. Risden (eds), *Hollywood in the Holy Land* (Jefferson, NC and London: McFarland, 2009), pp. 40–3.
17. Irene Kahn Atkins, *David Butler Interviewed* (Metuchen, NJ: Scarecrow Press), p. 256.
18. Landau, *Kingdom of Heaven*, pp. 61–5.
19. Cecil B. De Mille, *Autobiography* (London: W. H. Allen). p. 315.
20. Nicholas Haydock (ed.), *Movie Medievalism* (Jefferson, NC: McFarland, 2008), p. 137.
21. Jeffrey Richards, 'Robin Hood on Film and Television since 1945', *Visual Culture in Britain*, 2 (2001), pp. 65–80.

CHAPTER 3

The Decline and Fall of the Roman Empire and America since the Second World War: Some Cinematic Parallels

Kevin J. Harty

> I am going to tell you what you need to hear if we want to be the world's leaders, not the new Romans. – Thomas L. Friedman[1]

The Founding Fathers clearly looked to ancient Rome as a model for their new American republic. A 2009 exhibition at the National Constitution Center in Philadelphia traced the classical Roman influence that shaped the American nation from its founding through its growth and expansion to the present day, noting that the lessons which the rise and fall of Rome offered fuelled both 'the hopes for national greatness and fears for the fate of the American republic'.[2] Those same Founding Fathers consciously rejected Greek models in favour of Roman ones, and the lasting influence of Rome continues to be felt in both political and everyday life in the United States. Let some random examples suggest how.[3]

For lessons in oratory, the Founding Fathers looked to Cicero's *De oratore*. America borrowed the idea of the decadal census from the Romans, enshrining the requirement for the census in the Constitution in Article 1, section 1, clause 3, and using that requirement as the basis for determining the system of representational apportionment in the House of Representatives. The style consistently used for the neo-classical architecture of the seats of power and of the national monuments in Washington, DC, is Roman not Grecian. And Washington continues to be the site of monument wars about what is and is not an appropriate edifice to be built almost anywhere in the District of Columbia. Most (in)famously, the first Washington monument, a 1841 statue by Horatio Greenough featuring a nearly-naked, toga-clad Washington in the pose of a Roman god or emperor, was the cause not only of debate but of scandal. America has a 'senate', not a 'parliament'. American coins featured recognisably Roman designs thanks to the Coinage Act of 1792. No president's head appeared on an American coin until 1907, the centennial of Abraham Lincoln's birth.[4]

But is America the new Rome? Recently, any number of political commentators seem to think so, as they bewail America's loss both of prestige abroad and morality at home and see these losses in terms of the causes of the decline and fall of the Roman Empire.[5] The particulars of the current comparative concerns are not the subject of this chapter – but they have only been exacerbated for those in the Tea Party and others on the right by the re-election of Barack Obama. Rather, those concerns, cinema might suggest, are not anything new. Indeed, they were noted in 1959 by Harvard historian Samuel P. Huntington in an essay in *Foreign Affairs*.[6] And, evidently, these concerns had currency, as the films discussed below show, even earlier, since at least the Second World War. These films, all historical epics of one stripe or another, provide more than simply spectacle on the silver screen. They also comment on issues which were at the centre of American politics at the times when they were released.

ATTILA AND THE RED SCARE

At least since Gibbon, the official fall of Rome has been linked to the name of Odoacer and dated 476 CE, when Odoacer became the first barbarian King of Italy.[7] But in the popular imagination, it is the Hun Attila, not Odoacer, who is most associated with Rome's (almost) demise thanks to his march on the eternal city in 452 CE, from which he was turned back under mysterious (some would say miraculous) circumstances after a supposed conference with Pope Leo the Great, about the specifics of which history remains silent. Attila's siege of Rome and subsequent retreat, perhaps in light of a conversation with the Pope, had been the subject of art – most notably Raphael's 1514 fresco in the Stanza di Eliodoro of the Vatican's Apostolic Palace now identified as *Meeting between Leo the Great (painted as a portrait of Leo X) and Attila* – and opera – Verdi's opera premiered in Venice in 1846.[8] Film only took up Attila's story in 1954, at the height of McCarthy's Red Scare in the United States, in two films with overlapping plots, Douglas Sirk's *Sign of the Pagan* (1954) with Jack Palance in the title role, and Pietro Francisci's *Attila* (1954), with Anthony Quinn as the so-called 'scourge of God'.[9]

Attila and his Huns are nearly perfect stand-ins for the villains in an American geopolitical scenario that sees Communists everywhere intent upon undermining freedom and democracy. They threaten from the East, relying upon moles among those whom they aim to conquer (the enemy within) to further their cause. They are godless – at least in a Christian sense. They are ruthless, unethical, conniving, and deceitful. They are intent upon world domination at all costs. They break treaties – the list goes on.

The Sirk film underscores the opposition between those in the West and those in the East in its very title. That title plays upon the motto which Constantine first adopted after winning a battle (when a cross supposedly appeared in the sky) and then continued to use upon his subsequent and consequent conversion, along with that of the Roman empire, to Christianity: *in hoc signo vinces* (in this sign you shall conquer). An internal memorandum detailing the publicity campaign for the film makes clear the producers' intent in linking events in the film to contemporary American political and religious concerns as 'a good emotional hook' for marketing the film and increasing its media buzz and box-office receipts.[10]

Sirk and company could rely upon a general familiarity on the part of the American public with Attila and with the reasons he was known as the 'scourge of God', and they sought to capitalise on that familiarity in promoting the film. Attila was 'history's greatest villain', in whose footsteps Hitler and Stalin followed.[11] Sirk and company also sought to tap into any connections American audiences, Catholic or not, might make with papal anti-Communism: 'nowadays . . . the present Popes are waging such a militant war against Communism'[12] and are following in the footsteps of Leo, 'who wasn't afraid to lock horns with an Eastern barbarian'.[13] It seems that 'Attila the Hun . . . was one of the most superstitious people who ever lived. And one of his superstitions involved a great fear of men whose names stood for animals.'[14]

Both the Sirk and the Francisci films surround Attila with soothsayers to help him interpret various signs and portents. In the Sirk film, Attila is overly respectful of Christian churches and religious practices. At one point in the film, while is he invading Roman territory, Attila rescues two Scottish pilgrims on their way to the Holy Land from his own hordes, and shortly thereafter the so-called scourge of God flees a church filled with pilgrims pleading to be saved from his hordes by divine intervention (and anachronistically singing Gregorian chant) when he is confronted with an upraised processional cross. In the Francisci film, Attila is specifically warned to fear men who bear the names of animals – *leo* is, of course, the Latin word for 'lion'. For Sirk and company, especially, 'associating Pope Leo's confrontation with Attila and the Catholic church's current anticommunism was considered "a good gimmick" in the promotion' of the film.[15]

Sign of the Pagan opens with scenes of marauding hordes with red capes and red horse blankets rampaging in every direction as they wreak havoc on the borderlands of the Roman Empire, now split into two halves, with two rival emperors. The Huns' battle standard parodies the central Christian symbol; it is cross-shaped, but skull-studded. Attila has been victorious and has captured the envoy from Rome, Marcian, who bears a message from Emperor Valentinian in the West to Emperor Theodosius in the East. Theodosius is the film's enemy within, as he has secretly made treaties with the barbarians

Figure 3.1 American values triumph over communism: Jack Palance and Jeff Chandler in *Sign of the Pagan* (Douglas Sirk 1954).

against his Roman counterpart. He will soon make a similar treaty with Attila. The film never misses an opportunity to assert its message that Christianity makes Rome invincible, a message that would not fall on deaf ears for an audience used to praying for the conversion of Russia.[16]

Attila's superstitions get the better of him throughout the film. He is haunted by a vision his wet nurse had of him lying upon the ground under the shadow of a cross, and a more recent portent from his Persian soothsayer of 'a cloud of misty white and in that cloud a man in white followed by a host in white'. Imperial politics in the film are as complicated as history attests them to have been. Theodosius is eventually deposed by his sister Pulcheria who will finally ascend the throne of a reunited Roman Empire with Marcian at her side, Valentinian having fled in terror in advance of Attila and his hordes. Leo confronts Attila outside Rome's walls. In a wonderfully over-the-top entrance, he seems literally to float on a cloud to the accompaniment of angelic voices. Leo introduces himself as 'the servant of the servants of God', and warns Attila that 'he who lives by the sword shall perish by the sword'. In light of his encounter with the Pope, Attila turns back, but continues his marauding ways with Marcian and the Roman troops in hot pursuit.

The real Attila died of an unknown illness a year after he left the Italian peninsula. In the film, he is killed by a Roman woman, Ildico, whom he has held as a captive bride since the beginning of the film ('Let her join my wives!'). Indeed, Sirk and company had intended her treatment in the film to be further evidence of what they hoped would be the establishment of Attila's (and Palance's consequent) status as 'one of the greatest screen villains'.[17] The instrument of Attila's death is a dagger with an oversized cross-shaped hilt. The death scene directly fulfils the prophecy of his wet nurse. The dagger hilt casts a shadow as the dead Attila lies under the shadow of the sign of the cross – the sign of the pagan is vanquished by the sign of the cross. The threat of Communism will, the film less than subtly asserts, be held at bay by a god-fearing America keenly alert to the threat and continuing menace from the godless Communists in Russia and China.

Pietro Francisci's *Attila* tells a similar story with some interesting variations upon the plot of the Sirk film. Again, the film opens with repeated shots of marauding hordes on horseback burning and pillaging towns and cities and murdering their inhabitants. The Huns have already made a peace treaty with Rome, and the emperor's legate, Ezio, has arrived to renew the terms of the treaty. The Huns have two rulers, a more pacifist Bleda, and his brother, Attila, who thinks of peace as weakness. Indeed, Attila, who kills his brother, has dreams of world domination in terms that, as Jeffrey Richards notes, echo a familiar enough Nazi mantra: 'One race, one blood, one destiny. Today the Romans – tomorrow the world.'[18] At the same time, Attila refers to recent events in the Huns' past when they were surrounded and lay 'frozen in the north', a comment that links them to the Russians under siege by Nazi forces at Leningrad during the height of the Second World War. And Attila's goal of world domination was certainly matched by leaders of the Communist world throughout the Cold War.[19]

In *Attila*, the enemy within is the Emperor Valentinian's own sister, Honoria, who first seeks a secret alliance with the Hun, and then offers to marry him promising him half of the Western Empire as a dowry. In a later crucial battle, she is rewarded for her perfidy when she is killed by a Roman soldier. Valentinian is a snivelling coward and momma's boy. What little power that seems to remain in the Western Empire, with its capital now at Ravenna, lies in the hand of the Emperor's mother Galla Placidia, but her initial distrust of Ezio and his motives leads to the eventual defeat of the ill-prepared and vastly outnumbered Roman army by the Huns. Ezio himself is killed in battle, so the only power left in the Western Empire to confront Attila is papal. Attila's captains, however, dismiss any threat from Leo out of hand: 'How many men and swords can the Pope arrange!' Their rhetorical question echoes, of course, Stalin's famous 1935 quip to the French Prime Minister, Pierre Laval, in response to being asked whether Stalin could do anything on

Figure 3.2 The enemy within and without: Honoria (Sophia Loren) and Attila (Anthony Quinn) in *Attila* (1954).

behalf of the Catholics in Russia so as to help Laval win favour with the Pope to get him to help counter the increasing Nazi threat: 'The Pope! How many divisions has he got!'[20]

Attila has been warned several times earlier in the film 'to beware the man in white who will face you without any weapons'. His failure to heed that warning becomes apparent when he meets Pope Leo coming out of the city of Rome. The Pope on horseback seems here to walk on water. Once again, he identifies himself ('I am Pope Leo, the servant of the servants of God'), before warning Attila that 'innocent blood will not be washed away', a warning earlier delivered to Attila by his soothsayer in this film, the Hun woman Grune. A voiceover solemnly announces that 'what the Pope said to Attila no one knows', but that the language of the Gospels was clearly 'comprehensible to all'. Attila turns, remains silent, and rides off as a huge cross appears in the sky.

That the two first film treatments of Attila and his unsuccessful siege of Rome, which in turn is somehow the result of his conversation with the Pope, should appear in the same year is coincidental. That both films should reflect the global geopolitics of their time is not. The so-called Red Scare, thanks in no small part to the unscrupulous efforts of the junior senator from Wisconsin Joseph McCarthy, played out in America from 1947 to 1957, and had international repercussions throughout the Cold War. Both the Sirk and Francisci films directly and indirectly acknowledge the threat that Communism posed to the West in the early 1950s. Just as Attila was poised some 1,500 years earlier to destroy the centre of the civilised world and thereafter achieve global dominance, so too Communism was prepared to do the same in the 1950s, extending its reach from behind the Iron Curtain globally to undermine American institutions with an aim towards world dominance.

DECADENCE ROMAN AND AMERICAN STYLE

The 1960s were surely among the most turbulent of decades in American history. They were a time of tremendous change and upheaval, of a changing of the guard, perhaps first and best symbolised by the election of the 43-year-old John F. Kennedy to succeed the 71-year-old Dwight D. Eisenhower as president. The 1960s also saw the assassinations of President Kennedy, his brother, and Dr King. The 1960s saw the increase in America's involvement in Vietnam and a corresponding increase in opposition to that war at home. The 1960s saw the rise of the Great Society, the Civil Rights movement, Woodstock, the Stonewall riots, the hippy movement, an incumbent president, Lyndon Johnson, driven from office by the anti-war movement, and the election of Richard Nixon and Spiro Agnew (both of whom would eventually leave office in disgrace) in a clear rejection of that same anti-war sentiment.

Anthony Mann's *The Fall of the Roman Empire* is perhaps the perfect film to hold a mirror up to the turbulence that was America in the 1960s and to link Rome and America as two world powers on the brink of being undone by forces internal and external, both beyond their control. Jeffrey Richards quotes the film's director, Anthony Mann, on the appeal of making a film about the fall of Rome in the 1960s:

> The reason for making *The Fall of the Roman Empire* is that it is as modern today as it was in the history that Gibbon wrote: if you read Gibbon, like reading Churchill, it is like seeing the future as well as the past. The future is the thing that interested me in the subject. The past is like a mirror; it reflects what actually happened, and in the reflection of the fall of Rome are the same elements in what is happening today, the very things that are making empires fall.[21]

Richards further notes that Mann saw the film's ending as 'defeatist', suggesting that Mann's film marks the end of an era in filmmaking because that Cold War had ended.[22] I would disagree that the Cold War had ended by the time the film was released – it ended when the Berlin Wall fell in 1989 – and I would suggest that the muddle that is Mann's film reflects the muddle that was

American politics in the 1960s. Communism was still a threat; after all, those who opposed the war in Vietnam were 'hippie pinko commies' – or, if not all, at least some of the above. But Communism was not the only threat. The threat to America in the 1960s was threefold. In addition to the still very real threat of Communism, there was unprecedented organised political dissent at home, and the prospect that America would end up losing rather than winning a war, a first in American history.

The Fall of the Roman Empire neatly falls into two halves. In the first, set on the borders of the empire, Marcus Aurelius, philosopher, general and emperor, holds out the increasingly vain hope of establishing a true *pax romana*. In the second, set almost entirely in Rome, Commodus, his unintended heir, presides over an increasingly dissolute city and an empire threatened from within and from without. While Marcus Aurelius' age, experience and wisdom may suggest a parallel with the same characteristics in President Eisenhower, Commodus is clearly no JFK; the film does not intend that sort of one-on-one symmetry with contemporary events. Rather, more simply, there has been a changing of the guard, and, despite the highest of expectations, not necessarily one for the better.

In Mann's film, Rome is at war, initially in the North, later in the East. Marcus Aurelius has been trying unsuccessfully to conquer the tribes in the North, and faces his death no closer to achieving his goal than he was almost two decades earlier. His choice for heir is his chief general, Livius (played by a very blonde Stephen Boyd), rather than his son, Commodus (played, for obvious contrast, by a very dark-haired Christopher Plummer). Complicating matters is Livius' love for Lucilla, the emperor's daughter, who for political reasons is to be married off to Sohamus, the King of Armenia – the East is where the danger lies. While the emperor may have been unsuccessful in establishing the *pax romana*, life on the frontier has a certain order to it, until Commodus arrives and engineers his father's death by poisoning.

Rome, in contrast, the site of the second half of the film, is in chaos. A new generation, with decidedly different ideas, is in control. Commodus' Rome is the ancient equivalent of a 'be-in' – it is a city, we are told, of light, gaiety and beauty. The camera at several points pans across scenes that suggest contemporary Mardi Gras or Carnevale parades and celebrations. And Commodus' pleasures are to be financed by a doubling of taxes on the East – his father's warning that the East is where the danger lies is unheeded by Commodus, who increasingly seeks to quash all opposition, while also destroying his father's legacy. Commodus does not quite have carte blanche, however; there is still some opposition in the Senate.

When Livius suggests that the barbarians of the North be granted Roman citizenship, he runs the risk of undermining the Senate's opposition to Commodus since both the emperor and a majority of the Senate are opposed to the idea. It falls to the estimable Julianus (played by the equally estimable Finlay Currie) to become the voice of reason in the debate in a brief speech that would surely have contemporary echoes in the 1960s: 'How does an empire die? When its people no longer believe in it. We have changed the world but cannot change ourselves.' The barbarians do eventually achieve citizenship and are given land to farm, coming at one crucial point to Rome's aid by feeding its starving populace, though the previously fierce barbarians seem at that point of the film to be living in nothing more than a hippie commune. Commodus' reading of the famine was that it was simply part of a divine plan to relieve overcrowding in the city – a similar skewed logic might, one could argue, underlie some American foreign policies in the decade.

Marcus Aurelius' warnings about danger from the East go unheeded, as Rome eventually faces invasion from Persia. The film's own politics at this point are completely muddled as Livius has come to the East to put down rebellious Roman provinces, only to find himself facing the combined forces of the Persians and Armenians while the rebellious Roman provinces stand on the sidelines – just who is whose client state is not clear. Commodus' response is a scorched earth policy, with crucifixions and burning by the thousands of those who oppose Rome. Livius defeats Rome's enemies in the East, but his victory is short-lived as he finds himself chained in the Forum under sentence of death by burning – joining him are Lucilla, the former barbarian leader Ballomar, and assorted senators and other barbarians. Commodus' entrance into the forum is pure theatrics. He emerges from the inside of a great upraised hand-shaped monument. In a fight to the death, he is killed by Livius, who is immediately offered bribe after bribe by senators who wish to succeed to the throne. He walks away from them and their offers in disgust – the critic for *Monthly Film Bulletin* lays the blame for Rome's fall in the film at Livius' feet, seeing what others might see as virtue as priggishness.[23]

The film's conclusion, like much of *The Fall of the Roman Empire*, is unsatisfying. A final voiceover solemnly intones 'This was the beginning of the fall of the Roman Empire. A great civilization is not conquered from without until it has destroyed itself from within.' The muddled plot reflects a muddled political agenda, albeit a conservative one that sees the America of the 1960s not as some shining city on the hill but rather as a latter-day Rome in danger of collapse because of destruction from within. The idea that America was a shining city on the hill had first been advanced by the Puritans who settled Massachusetts in the seventeenth century, on the basis of the text of the Sermon on the Mount (Matthew 5:14); it had been cited by John F. Kennedy in 1961 right before his inauguration, and would be invoked multiple times by Ronald Reagan long after the film was released.[24] The defeatism that Mann himself noted at the end of his film may well reflect his reading of a similar defeatism on the national American political landscape.

Figure 3.3 Christopher Plummer and Stephen Boyd in *The Fall of the Roman Empire* (1964): 'a great civilisation is not conquered from without until it destroys itself from within'.

The connection, albeit muddled, of Mann's film to the equally muddled politics of 1960s America becomes even more apparent when the film is compared to its 2000 remake, Ridley Scott's *Gladiator*, which seems to go out of its way to eschew any political message. Both films advance essentially the same plot, but with decidedly different results. Scott's film, despite its use of 'shock and awe' in its opening scene as a weapon against the barbarians in Germania, is simply a story of fraternal rivalry, which just happens to be set in ancient Rome. Maximus and Commodus, who have a pre-history never fully teased out in the film (Maximus has a similar never clearly explained pre-history with Lucilla, Commodus' sister), stand as rival heirs to Marcus Aurelius. They are, of course, as different as night and day.

Maximus is a victorious general – a man associated with the natural world. He is a farmer by trade; he wins his battle in the forests; he literally picks up and touches the earth, whether it be the wheat shafts on his farm in a number of dream sequences or the grit and dirt on the floor of the Arena. Commodus is unnatural in several senses of the word. Mann's Commodus turns out not really to be the son of Marcus Aurelius (his real father, he belatedly discovers, is a gladiator), but Scott's Commodus is biologically the emperor's son. But

Figure 3.4 Commodus (Joaquin Phoenix) as the unheroic counterpart of the hero Maximus in *Gladiator* (2000).

he has an unnatural attachment to his sister (Mann's Commodus' attachment is to his former friend and now rival, Livius – and the level of the homoerotic increases throughout the film). Commodus smothers his father in what is surely an unnatural take on the father–son bond.

Most importantly, if Maximus is at home in nature, Commodus is not. He arrives at his father's camp by what would pass for a luxury coach, cosseted and shielded from the elements, and his Rome, thanks to the set's CGI enhancements, is literally unnatural – it does not actually exist, it is simply a made-up image. He is a megalomaniac like his counterpart in Mann's film, but he seems more plagued by migraines than delusions of grandeur. Unlike his earlier counterpart, Scott's Commodus does not have himself declared divine or lauded with the most elaborate string of honorifics. He is the self-centred, snivelling counterpart to the magnanimous, genuinely heroic Maximus.

Scott's Rome is also unnatural since it is ruled by the chaos that is politics. On the battlefield, there is hierarchy and order. In Rome, there is intrigue and plotting. Indeed, the battlefield is wide open; one can literally see the forest for the trees. Scott's Rome is all corridors and passageways, enclosed rooms – even the massive Colosseum is enclosed, and its lower regions are like a rabbit warren. Politics comes into play in Scott's film – Marcus Aurelius has a dream to return power to the people by returning power to the Senate, but there is no nod to the American political scene per se in the film – *Gladiator* is almost a decade too early to suggest the need for an agenda based on hope and change. The battle for control of Rome between Emperor and Senate is simply a given historical and literary narreme.

THE LOST NINTH LEGION AND TWENTY-FIRST CENTURY AMERICAN POLITICS

The mysterious loss of the Ninth Legion when it marched north in 117 CE to put down the always rebellious Britons marked the beginning of the end for Rome in the British Isles, an occupation that had at best been successful in fits.[25] The Britons had rebuffed Julius Caesar twice, in 55 and 54 BCE, and were more or less subdued by Claudius beginning in 43 CE. But the failure of the Roman Empire to extend to the British Isles completely was signalled by the loss of the Ninth and the subsequent construction of what became known as Hadrian's Wall beginning in 122 CE. Neil Marshall's 2010 film *Centurion* is about the loss of the Ninth Legion, and, more importantly, the consequences of foreign adventuring and attempted nation building so far from home by an imperial world power – read here the USA—Iraq—Afghanistan. The film opens somewhere in the north, far from where the Ninth is quartered in York. In command of a lonely, isolated Roman outpost 'at the asshole of the world' is Centurion Quintus Dias (Michael Fassbinder), the thoughtful son of a former gladiator who sees Roman efforts as producing 'a new kind of war', 'a war without honor and without end'. Quintus is fond of quoting his father's advice throughout the film, and that advice sustains him. He has gotten to know his enemy; he speaks their language; and he understands how they fight, and why. When the Britons rally behind the Pictish leader Gorlacon, the Ninth under the command of General Titus Flavius Virilus is ordered to the field to defeat them by the Roman Governor Agricola who, safely ensconced in heavily fortified Carlisle, represents the Senate and the Roman Empire in Britain. Agricola sends along with the Ninth his tracker, Etain, a Pictish woman who turns out to be loyal still to the Picts and eventually betrays the IX.

Quintus' outpost is overrun by Picts, and he is taken captive, only to escape and literally run right into the Ninth as it marches north. He joins their ranks,

Figure 3.5 *Centurion* (2010): Quintus (Michael Fassbender) and his men are a strange coalition of the willing and the unwilling.

seemingly from the start wary of Etain, who true to form leads the Ninth into an ambush that seals its annihilation about a third of the way through the film. The Picts succeed in taking Virilus captive, and only seven other Romans survive the massacre of the legion. They are, however, far from a magnificent seven as they join forces under Quintus' command to rescue Virilus; one of their number, the cowardly Thax, manages to kill Gorlacon's son in the course of the botched rescue attempt. Gorlacon vows death to the surviving Romans in revenge for his son's death as Etain kills Virilus in hand-to-hand combat. The balance of the film sends the ever-diminishing troop of seven across the northern British wilderness in an attempt to escape Etain and her trackers. In the course of their flight, they encounter and are aided by another Pictish woman, Arianne, who has been banished, and is feared, for being a witch. Eventually Quintus alone makes it back alive to Agricola, only to find that the tale he has to tell is not one Rome wants told. The Romans almost succeed in silencing Quintus, but he manages to escape back into the wilderness where he rejoins Arianne, presumably to live happily ever after, as both reject the futile and pointless wars their nations have engaged in.

Had it been made in the 1960s or 1970s, *Centurion* might easily be seen as a protest against American involvement in Southeast Asia. In 2010, it seems rather easy to read the film in part as a response to Desert Storm and the wars in Iraq and Afghanistan. In preparation for the part of Quintus, Fassbinder admitted to reading the historical novels of Steven Pressfield, including his

2007 *The Afghan Campaign* about Alexander the Great's failed attempt to conquer the region.[26] Literally, Rome's incursion into the British Isles was, of course, nothing short of empire building. Its response to the native inhabitants who opposed Roman forces was nothing short of brutal. Etain has seen the Romans blind and kill her father, and repeatedly rape and eventually kill her mother. She herself as a child is repeatedly raped and has her tongue cut out by the Romans. The cowardly Roman Thax, whose loyalty is only to himself, kills Gorlacon's young son – an innocent civilian and collateral damage in the conflict. There is no attempt on Rome's part to win the minds and hearts of the people of Britain, and their failure even to attempt to do so is their undoing.

Quintus' band of seven are a strange coalition of the willing and the unwilling, including in their number an Indian from the Hindu Kush, a Greek, a Sicilian, someone reared in and by the Roman army, and an African who self-identifies as a Namibian – though Nubian might be more historically possible or accurate. Not the least of the enemies they face is the terrain of northern Britain itself – much as the deserts of Iraq and the mountains of Afghanistan proved more than inhospitable to American and coalition forces. Indeed, the film's director of photography, Sam McCurdy, consciously chose to include extensive aerial shots throughout the chase sequences in *Centurion*: 'The Scottish landscape was always going to be a character in the film; as our heroes try to make their way south to safety, they are at odds with the land as much as they are with the Picts.'[27]

Arianne is outlawed and branded by Gorlacon as a witch and feared by Pict and Roman alike as a necromancer. She joins forces with Quintus against Etain and the Picts, proving that the enemy of my enemy is my friend. Virilus recognises that Rome's campaign in Britain is a lost cause, but he is goaded into pursuing the Picts by Agricola's appeal to his sense of duty and patriotism, an appeal that is hardly one to which Agricola himself would respond. Indeed, the characters' very names in the film speak volumes about their characters and attitudes towards duty. Virilus is a virile man among his men – his bond with his men, it is pointed out, is atypical. Agricola – his name is the Latin word for 'farmer' – is no Cincinnatus content to leave his fields temporarily to defend Rome and then to return to them once the threat to the Republic has been eliminated. He is a politician, an armchair warrior, seeking his own advantage at all costs – even Quintus' life, we learn, at the film's end. Among Quintus' last true companions is Bothos – he, Quintus, and Thax alone make it back to the Roman border, now a construction site for the building of Hadrian's Wall. Thax seeks to betray them both, and is killed by Quintus, while Bothos (Pat Tillman-like?) is killed by friendly fire when he rides towards the Roman lines.[28]

The Eagle (dir. Kevin Macdonald, 2011) is an unintended sequel to *Centurion*, picking up the plot of the earlier film by having Marcus Acquila, the son of Titus Flavius Virilus (called Flavius Aquila in the second film and its source), first posted to Britain in hopes of redeeming his father's good name and his family's honour, and then managing to retrieve the fallen standard of the Ninth Legion from the hands of the Britons north of Hadrian's Wall. The hunt for the missing legionary standard occupies much more of the plot of the film than it does that of the book. The film is a combination buddy/road film in which Marcus and his slave Esca set out north of Hadrian's Wall as a sort of Special Ops or Seal Team – no pun intended since they encounter the Seal People, a surprisingly unredeemed barbarian people, given the mania for political correctness in historical and quasi-historical films in the last quarter century. In a series of (sometimes mis)adventures, all of which stay just shy of the homoerotic, they encounter the remnant of the lost legion, switch roles as master and servant among the Seal People, retrieve the Eagle, and return home.

Missing from the film are sub-plots from its source, Rosemary Sutcliff's 1954 novel *The Eagle of the Ninth* which are in keeping with its genre, young adult fiction. The novel, which is the first in a trilogy of Roman works by the prolific Sutcliff, is more of a coming-of-age story for Marcus than the film – the road trip occupies only about a third of the book.[29] Not only does Marcus have a rite of passage in retrieving the Eagle and in confronting his father's life, death and legacy, but he also finds love and friendship, from a slave, a young woman, and even a wolf cub. In short, in the novel, Marcus matures on a number of levels. The wolf, called Cub, is, like the slave Esca, a wild creature in Roman eyes whose taming is not necessarily deemed wise or possible. In addition, the buddy aspects of the film – and any hint of the homoerotic – are undercut in the novel where Marcus awkwardly discovers love with his uncle's snooty Roman neighbour's daughter, Cottia. The book details a more definite future for Marcus; he will marry Cottia, settle down to a life of farming in Britain as his uncle's heir, and have a lifelong friend in the now-freed Esca, who seems to have no problems assimilating himself to Roman life.

The film plots a different story and comes to a decidedly different end. Missing are the sub-plots with Cub and Cottia – the film's Marcus is older, and more mature than the book's. The journey north of the Wall consumes most of the film's plot, and Marcus and Esca, while returning with the Eagle, and bringing it to the Senate, have clearly seen the symbolism behind the golden standard to be at best empty. In the book, Marcus and Esca return the Eagle to Roman hands, but they decide, almost anti-climactically, with the approval of Uncle Aquila and Legate Claudius, to bury it at a crossroads across which Roman legions would regularly tread:

> 'Here lies the Eagle of the Ninth Legion, the Hispana,' the Legate was saying. 'Many times it found honour in the wars, against foes abroad and

rebellion at home. Shame came to it; but at the end it was honourably held until the least of those who held it died beneath its wings. It has led brave men. Let it lie forgotten.' . . . [Marcus] had failed to redeem his father's Legion, since it was past redeeming, but the lost Eagle was home again, and would never now be used as a weapon against its own people.[30]

In the film, the Eagle meets a different fate.[31] The legionary standard is brought back to Roman hands, but Marcus is stripped of any illusions about Rome and those who run the empire. Marcus has come to see the Eagle as a dangerous symbol in the hands of Roman politicians who have fetishised it for their own purposes, blatantly ignoring both the sacrifices that his father and his legion made and the enduring importance that the Eagle has had as a symbol for the men who fought under it. Throughout the film, Roman authority again seems to rest in the hands of armchair warriors, senators who speak in empty catch-phrases of an idea of Rome that they have appropriated and misconstrued, and of those whom Marcus calls the sons of 'silk-assed politicians'.

The grounds for Marcus' eventual disaffection with Rome – matched by an increased affection for Esca – are laid in a scene in the film before the two set out north of Hadrian's Wall. Marcus and Esca have been out hunting wild boar, and despite Marcus' earlier protestations that he neither wants nor needs a slave, he and Esca have clearly fallen into the prescribed roles of master and servant; Esca, appearing here clearly the more honourable, indicates that he owes Marcus a 'debt of honour' for earlier saving his life in the arena. Their return from the hunt leads to an encounter with the Legate of the Sixth Legion, Claudius Marcellus, Marcus' uncle's old comrade in arms, and Claudius' companion, Servius Placidus, the politically well-connected Tribune to Claudius. Servius has the lean and hungry look of a politician; his protestations that he wishes to spend a life in the legions, but is only disbarred by his father's plan to send him into politics, are totally unbelievable. Even Marcus' uncle recognises that Claudius and Servius have virtually nothing in common with himself and his nephew. It is to Claudius and Servius that Marcus and Esca deliver the Eagle in the film's last scene. And the exchange among the four of them seals Marcus' decision to turn his back on Rome.

While Claudius had earlier expressed the sentiment that Rome had lost honour with the Eagle and that in losing honour Rome had lost all, he is quick to change course once he has the Eagle in his hand. He suggests that the Senate will want to reform the Ninth – earlier, Claudius and the Senate had wanted to wipe out any trace of the legion – and that Marcus might well head that reformed legion. Servius wonders aloud how Marcus has managed to retrieve the Eagle with nothing more than the help of a slave, and Marcus explodes at him. 'He's not a slave. He knows more about honour and freedom that you ever will.'

Figure 3.6 *The Eagle* (2011): Esca (Jamie Bell) as a wild animal who, to Roman eyes, is not worth training.

A coincidental parallel here to the plot of the film in American politics is the rise of the so-called Tea Party, right-wing ideologues who rally around and even fetishise national symbols, blatantly ignoring what the true meaning and importance of those symbols might be. The Senate and Rome have fetishised the Eagle – Marcus' journey to retrieve it has made him the dupe of those unworthy of the sacrifices he and his father and the Ninth have made. Not surprisingly then, he literally turns his back on the Senate (and Rome) and walks out of the Senate chambers with Esca as his equal, suggesting, even more strikingly, that Esca, not Rome, will determine their future.

The mid-term elections of 2010 allowed the Tea Party to establish more than a foothold in both state legislatures across America and, on the national level, in both houses of Congress. In January 2011 as the new Congress was sworn in, members took to the floor of the House of Representatives to read the Constitution aloud to remind their fellow legislators, it would seem, that it would no longer be business as usual in the House. Instead, thanks to their presence, a Congress with newly-elected Tea Party representatives would, for a change, govern strictly according to the tenets of the Constitution. Unfortunately, as the press, both on the right and on the left, at times gleefully pointed out, members skipped over key passages in the Constitution, either out of carelessness or disregard for them, or omitted parts that they felt were irrelevant because they had been repealed or amended.[32]

It would seem that, for Tea Party members, the Constitution was a sacred symbol as long as it was their version of the Constitution that was read, just as in *The Eagle*, the eponymous figurine eventually came to symbolise what the Senate wanted it to symbolise. Rome has fetishised the Eagle; the Tea Party, the Constitution. Kevin Macdonald's *The Eagle* may, therefore, be one of the first 'Tea Party' films thanks to the significant changes that screenwriter Jeremy Block has made to Rosemary Sutcliff's 1954 novel. Rome will not fall for several more centuries, but the seeds of that fall have clearly already been sown in *The Eagle*. The Tea Party, so intent on preserving its version of America, has set into motion legislative gridlock and unswerving bipartisanship across America that do not bode well for its future.

CONCLUSIONS

That Rome was not built in a day has been proverbial since at least the twelfth century CE.[33] Thanks to Gibbon and others, we know that Rome also did not fall in a day. The roots of decline were centuries in the making. For contemporary alarmists on the political right prone to see that decline as a model for America in the twentieth and twenty-first centuries, this fact is less than reassuring. There have been any number of recent cinematic studies that have linked historical films to the politics of their time. Most notably, Alan Lupack has found reactions to America's Red Scare in Arthurian and Viking films;[34] Susan Aronstein has discussed the larger corpus of cinema Arthuriana in terms of what she calls 'the politics of nostalgia';[35] and Nickolas Haydock and E. L. Risden have assembled a collection of essays by diverse hands on the politics that underlie Hollywood's frequent forays into the Holy Land.[36] This chapter has attempted to follow in their footsteps, and those of others, in seeing historical films as at times more than simple spectacle and entertainment. Historical films set in the time of the Roman Empire may also hold a mirror up to the times in which they were made, allowing us today better to understand the ever-changing course of political anxiety in post-Second World War America.

NOTES

1. Quoted by David A. Bell, 'Political Columnists Think America Is in Decline. Big Surprise', *The New Republic*, 7 October 2010. Available at http://www.tnr.com/blog/foreign-policy/7816/america-in-decline-thomas-friedman
2. *Ancient Rome & America, The Classical Influence That Shaped Our Nation* (Philadelphia, PA: National Constitution Center, 2009), p. 3.
3. See Carl J. Richard, *Greeks and Romans Bearing Gifts: How the Ancients Inspired the Founding Fathers* (Lanham, MD: Rowan & Littlefield, 2008).
4. See variously *Ancient Rome & America*, passim; Kirk Savage, *Monument Wars: Washington, DC, The National Mall, and the Transformation of the Memorial Landscape* (Berkeley, CA: University of California Press, 2009); and Arlyn G. Sieber, *Warman's US Coin & Currency, A Field Guide* (Iola, WI: Krause, 2009), 3rd edn.
5. Bell, 'Political Columnists'.
6. Ibid.
7. Edward Gibbon's monumental work, *The History of the Decline and Fall of the Roman Empire*, ran to six volumes and was published from 1776 to 1779.
8. The fresco dates from 1514 and depicts Leo with his hand raised in benediction while St Peter and St Paul, brandishing fiery swords in their hands, appear over him. Attila, who has arrived accompanied by storm clouds and fire, pales opposite the Pope. See Adolph Paul Oppé, *Raphael* (1909; rpt New York: Praeger, 1970) for a reproduction in colour of the fresco.
9. The Francisci film is variously entitled *Attila, flagello di dio* and *Attila the Hun*. Earlier, in 1924, Fritz Lang did follow his medieval German source, *The Nibelungenlied*, in basing the character of Etzel in his film on the historical Attila. But there is no mention of Attila's march on Rome in either the source or the film. Both the Sirk and Francisci films, not unexpectedly, take liberties with historical fact. On the historical Attila and his siege of Rome, see Christopher Kelly, *The End of Empire: Attila the Hun and the Fall of Rome* (New York: W. W. Norton, 2010). On Leo the Great, see Bronwen Neil, *Leo the Great* (London: Routledge, 2009).
10. '"A good emotional hook": Selling *Sign of the Pagan* to the American Media', *Film History*, 3.2 (1989), pp. 115–31.
11. Ibid., pp. 116, 122.
12. Ibid., pp. 116, 122.
13. Ibid., p. 120.
14. Ibid., p. 120.
15. Ibid., p. 130.
16. The original prayers for the conversion of Russia were instituted by a later Pope Leo, Leo XIII, and first offered for the conversion of enemies of the Vatican in general. The fall of Russia to so-called godless Communism accounted for a change in their focus. The prayers were discontinued after changes were made in the rubrics for the Roman Catholic mass following the Second Vatican Council. See Sacred Congregation of Rites, 'Iam inde ab anno', *Acta sanctae sedis*, 16 (1884), pp. 249–50.
17. '"A good emotional hook"', p. 127.
18. Jeffrey Richards, *Hollywood's Ancient Worlds* (London: Continuum, 2008), p. 78.
19. Because he repeated the phrase so often in the 1950s and 1960s, Soviet premier Nikita Khrushchev almost made a catchphrase out of his threat, 'Мы вас похороним!' ('We will bury you!').
20. For details of the several-day-long meeting between Stalin and Laval, which took place in

Moscow, see Winston Churchill, *The Second World War* (1948; rpt New York: Mariner Books, 1986), vol. 1, p. 105.
21. Richards, p. 89.
22. Richards, p. 92, p. 94.
23. John Peter Dyer, 'Review of *The Fall of the Roman Empire*', *Monthly Film Bulletin*, 31 (May 1964), p. 69.
24. The idea that the New World in general and America in particular were to be a 'shining city on the hill' first appears in Puritan colonist and governor John Winthrop's sermon 'A Model for Christian Charity', which he composed and delivered on board the ship *Arabella* in 1630. More than three centuries later, the idea was subsequently invoked by President-elect Kennedy in an address to the General Court of Massachusetts in 1961, and twice by Ronald Regan, first when he accepted the Republican nomination in 1984, and again when he later bid the nation farewell in 1989. See http://religiousfreedom.lib.virginia.edu/sacred/charity.html for the text of Winthrop's sermon. For the text of Kennedy's address, see http://www.jfklibrary.org/Historical+Resources/Archives/Reference+Desk/Speeches/JFK For Reagan's remarks, see http://www.reagan.utexas.edu/archives/speeches/1984/82384f.htm and http://www.ronaldreagan.com/sp_21.html, last accessed 10 April 2013.
25. On the disappearance and loss of the Ninth Legion and the significance of that loss to the Roman Empire, see Sheppard Sunderland Frere, *Britannia: A History of Roman Britain* (New York: Routledge & Kegan Paul, 1987), pp. 122–4; and Duncan B. Campbell, 'The Fate of the Ninth', *Ancient Warfare*, 4.5 (2010), pp. 48–53.
26. Nev Pierce, 'Death and Glory', *Empire*, 245 (November 2009), p. 142.
27. Stanley Manders, 'Romans on the Run', *American Cinematographer*, 91 (September 2010), pp. 76.
28. Specialist Patrick Daniel 'Pat' Tillman gained fame and national acclaim when he quit his promising career as an American football player to enlist in the US Army after the events of 9/11. He served several tours of combat duty as an Army Ranger, for which he was highly decorated, before he was killed in action in the mountains of Afghanistan on 22 April 2004. Subsequent investigations, following a Defense Department cover-up, eventually revealed that his death was the result of friendly fire. See Jon Krakauer, *Where Men Win Glory: The Odyssey of Pat Tillman* (New York: Doubleday, 2009), as well as the 2010 documentary *The Tillman Story*, directed by Amir Bar-Lev.
29. The Sutcliff Roman trilogy consists of *The Eagle of the Ninth* (1954), *The Silver Branch* (1957) and *The Lantern Bearers* (1959).
30. Rosemary Sutcliff, *The Eagle of the Ninth, Now A Major Motion Picture Filmed as The Eagle* (1954; rpt New York: Oxford University Press, 2011), p. 200.
31. There is a curious ancient artefact housed in the Museum of the City of Reading in England known as the Silcester Eagle, dated to the second century CE, that is sometimes associated with the Eagle in the Sutcliff novel. See J. M. C. Toynbee, *Art in Roman Britain* (London: Phaidon Press, 1962), p. 50 and figure 60.
32. See, for instance, Stephen Dinan, 'Constitution Read on House Floor, and Debated Too', *Washington Times*, 7 January 2011: A1; Philip Rucker and David A. Fahrenthold, '"To Form a More Perfect Union", but Reading Sparks Some Division', *Washington Post*, 7 January 2011: A1; Jennifer Steinhauer, 'Constitution Has Its Day (More or Less) in House', *New York Times*, 7 January 2011: A15. See also the special 10th Annual History Issue of the weekly American news magazine *Time* published on 4 July 2011, in which Richard Stengel asked whether what the Founding Fathers intended still mattered in the twenty-first century.

33. The so-called *Li proverbe au Vilain* allows 'Rome ne fu pas faite/toute en un jour'. The unknown author was a poet in the court of Philippe of Flanders during the second half of the twelfth century. See John Bednar (ed.), *Li Proverbe au Vilain, A Critical Edition* (New Orleans, LA: University of the South, 2000), p. 45 (Proverb 98).
34. Alan Lupack, 'An Enemy in Our Midst: *The Black Knight* and the American Dream', in Kevin J. Harty (ed.), *Cinema Arthuriana, Twenty Essays* (2002; rpt Jefferson, NC: McFarland, 2010), pp. 64–70. Alan Lupack, 'Valiant and Villainous Vikings', in Kevin J. Harty (ed.), *The Vikings on Film* (Jefferson, NC: McFarland, 2011), pp. 46–55.
35. Susan Aronstein, *Hollywood Knights, Arthurian Cinema and the Politics of Nostalgia* (New York: Palgrave Macmillan, 2005).
36. Nickolas Haydock and E. L. Risden (eds), *Hollywood in the Holy Land* (Jefferson, NC: McFarland, 2005).

CHAPTER 4

'There's Nothing So Wrong with a Hollywood Script That a Bunch of Giant CGI Scorpions Can't Solve': Politics, Computer Generated Images and Camp in the Critical Reception of the Post-*Gladiator* Historical Epics

Mark Jancovich

In 2001, Ridley Scott's *Gladiator* won the Academy Awards for Best Actor and Best Picture. However, on its original release, it was not the critical success that one might assume in retrospect. On the contrary, many of the most respected mainstream publications gave the film lukewarm, and in some cases overtly hostile, reviews, a situation that demonstrates the ways in which critical judgements can change over time. The following chapter is a study of the reception of the cycle of films that followed *Gladiator*, films that were understood as resurrecting the epics of the post-war cinema which included *The Ten Commandments* (De Mille 1956), *Ben-Hur* (Wyler 1959) and *Spartacus* (Kubrick 1960). The aim here is not to portray this reception as an example of 'failed criticism',[1] nor as possessing an authentic moment that represents the 'truth' of these films; rather, it is to explore the meanings of films in specific periods, meanings which may be different from those of the present but which are just as 'real'; and require one to recognise that the current meanings of films are as historically contingent as those of other periods.

Indeed, when I embarked on this study, I expected to find a process in which the evaluation of the cycle changed from a celebration of *Gladiator* to a condemnation of *Clash of the Titans* (Leterrier 2010), an expectation that was quickly confounded. If reviews of *Gladiator* were more critical than I had remembered, reviews of *Clash of the Titans* were far more positive. Instead the change of attitudes proceeded from a general dismissal of *Gladiator*, through a frustration with the various examples of the cycle that immediately followed it – *Troy* (Petersen 2004), *King Arthur* (Fuqua 2004), *Alexander* (Stone 2004) and *Kingdom of Heaven* (Scott 2005) – to wholesale derision at *300* (Snyder 2006), a film that was separated from these others by its association with Frank Miller's graphic novel and thereby the 2005 Robert Rodriguez/Frank Miller film, *Sin City* (which was also based on Miller's graphic novels), rather than with the historical films of the 1950s and 1960s. However, if *300* marked the lowest point in the critical evaluation of these films, *Clash of the Titans*, maybe surprisingly, marks a kind of high point. Freed from the cultural pretentions that marked other films in the cycle, and that provoked many of the critical attacks, *Clash of the Titans* was often indulged by critics as ludicrous fun. As Xan Brooks of the *Guardian* put it: 'I think it was Robert Bresson who put it best: there's nothing so wrong with a Hollywood script that a bunch of giant CGI scorpions can't solve.'[2]

However, Brooks' comment also reveals another aspect of this reception. If these films were understood as a coherent cycle, despite their considerable differences from one another, owing to the ways in which they were presumed to reference the previous cycle of historical epics, they were also seen as very different from those of the earlier period. Some reviewers noted the difference in pace, so that, for example, Anthony Mann's *The Fall of the Roman Empire* (1964) was described as 'stately and formal' while *Gladiator*, which borrowed heavily from it, was described as 'vital, visceral and pulse-quickening'.[3] Many reviewers also made reference to the political context of the later films, given that as Richards (Chapter 2) and Harty (Chapter 3) suggest, they often dealt with military struggles involving the Middle East, at a time when the USA was entering into conflicts in Afghanistan and Iraq.

However, despite their rhetoric, reviewers were usually most critical of other features of the films. Many reviews complained that contemporary stars were simply not fit for the roles. If some complained that these films lacked 'actors with built-in emotional clout [such as] Richard Burton, Fredric March, Claire Bloom' (who had all starred in Robert Rossen's 1956 version of *Alexander the Great*), others complained that contemporary stars not only lacked the 'presence of a Richard Burton'[4] but were also inappropriate in other ways:

> Pitt is a good actor and a handsome man, and he worked out for six months to get buff for the role, but Achilles is not a character he inhabits comfortably. Say what you will about Charlton Heston and Victor Mature, but one good way to carry off a sword-and-sandal epic is to be filmed by a camera down around your knees, while you intone quasi-formal prose in a heroic baritone. Pitt is modern, nuanced, introspective; he brings complexity to a role where it is not required.[5]

It is also fascinating how often critics latched onto, and celebrated, the presence of older stars, such as Richard Harris, Oliver Reed, Peter O'Toole and, to a much lesser extent, Julie Christie, as figures that referred back to an earlier era and possessed the sense of *gravitas* supposedly lacking in the younger stars.

Similarly, these films were seen as defeating their directors. Although often directed by major figures (Ridley Scott, Wolfgang Petersen and Oliver Stone), epics of this period were seen as strangely anonymous works: 'Visually, Wolfgang Petersen's new committee work could have been birthed out of a pod.'[6] If this suggests that the problem lies with the vast commercial investment that these films required, investment that made their directors no more than one element in a larger corporate machine, this comment goes on to hint at something else, too: 'it trudges along in a de-individualized daze with repetitive helicopter shots of milling byte-crowds.'

Here, the reference to 'byte-crowds' reiterates one of the main complaints about these films – their association with computer generated imagery (CGI) as discussed in Chapter 8 of this book. Rather than simply *using* CGI, these films would not have been made without it. CGI did more than simply make the films financially viable, but the films themselves were designed to demonstrate the spectacle of CGI. If Brooks jokingly sees the 'giant CGI scorpions' as compensating for *Clash of the Titans*' other failings, it should be borne in mind that this is not only an ironic comment, but also that CGI was well established by 2010. Critics were not only long past complaining about CGI, they also had more immediate complaint. Critics were indulgent about the use of CGI in *Clash of the Titans*, and in some cases even celebrated it, but they were brutal about its use of 3D, a new technological spectacle that, after *Avatar*, had become a more insistent object of critical condemnation.

'THUNDEROUS HOKUM': ACTION, SPECTACLE AND SPECIAL EFFECTS IN THE RECEPTION OF *GLADIATOR*

Although *Variety* claimed *Gladiator* was both 'thrilling' and 'compelling', many other mainstream reviewers were less positive.[7] J. Hoberman in *Village Voice* declared it to be 'thunderous hokum', an evaluation that was shared by Elvis Mitchell in *The New York Times*, who condemned it as 'grandiose and silly'.[8] However, while 'silly' can sometimes imply a positive sense of innocent joy, this was not the case here and Robert Ebert contrasted *Gladiator* with *Raiders of the Lost Ark* (Spielberg 1981), a film that he claimed was 'just as dim-witted but 12 times more fun'.[9] For these critics, then, *Gladiator*'s main crime was its pretension – it just took itself too seriously. As Ebert goes on to say, it not only 'lacks joy' but 'employs depression as a substitute for personality'.

Certainly, there was some praise for specific members of the cast, particularly

Oliver Reed and Russell Crowe, who 'confirms his position as one of the best star character actors around' and provides 'the most virile presence in a film of this kind since Richard Burton ... in *The Robe*'.[10] Nonetheless, the film was generally seen as an anonymous Hollywood disaster that was closer to the embarrassments in Scott's career than to its highlights: 'in the Scott oeuvre, the movie is far closer to *1492* or *Legend* than *Blade Runner*.'[11]

The film was even unfavourably compared to earlier examples of the 'tarnished and often derided genre' that it supposedly resurrected and, as we have seen, references to the earlier pictures were often used to emphasise the difference between *Gladiator* and its forebears: '*Gladiator* borrows from *Spartacus* as well, although the conflict here is less a matter of collective injustice than individual payback.'[12]

As I have demonstrated elsewhere, one of the most 'derided' features of the historical epic of the post-war period was its use of the male body as spectacle, a feature that it had in common with later action movies, particularly those associated with stars such as Schwarzenegger and Stallone.[13] It is therefore interesting that many critics maintained a sense of distinction between *Gladiator* and earlier epics by displacing this issue onto these later stars. Mitchell made a point of claiming that the last 'revisionist take on the gnashing-teeth, sweaty-torso, clanging-steel epic' took place back when 'Arnold Schwarzenegger crushed all the consonants under his sandaled feet in *Conan the Barbarian* almost 20 years ago'.[14] However inaccurate this claim may have been, it was hardly unique, and Ebert described the film as '*Rocky* on downers', while Mitchell again went one better and suggested that the film did not even have the integrity of *Rocky* but was more a 'brazen mix of blood sport and soap opera: *Rocky* by Ross Hunter'.[15]

If the film was seen as a compromised mixture of masculine and feminine genres, at other points it was not even really a drama but rather associated with extra-cinematic entertainments. For example, Mitchell's 2000 review claimed that *Gladiator* lacks 'the exultant lift of Hong Kong period-action pictures like the "Once Upon a Time in China" series, where the fights have the eye-popping panache of dance sequences in a musical', but instead felt much more 'like "W.W.F.: The Motion Picture," complete with chest puffing and the hero challenging his boss to a duel'. Even then the film was supposed to be too feminine to work as masculine sports entertainment: '*Gladiator* suggests what would happen if someone made a movie of the imminent extreme-football league and shot it as if it were a Chanel commercial.'[16]

If references to 'Hong Kong period-action pictures' were used to suggest stylistic borrowings that marked *Gladiator* as inferior, other references were used to express political revulsion. For Mitchell, combatants in the film 'move in formation out of Leni Riefenstahl's *Triumph of the Will*', the famous exercise in Nazi propaganda, and while the film may have explicitly condemned the violence of the arena, it has 'each scene composed for an audience's delectation of the constant slaughter', so that 'you can't take your eyes off it even though you are repelled by its purpose'. 'The power to amuse the mob' is ultimately 'the only kind of power *Gladiator* desires'.[17] Even supportive critics such as Philip French in the *Observer* and Richard Corliss in *Time* largely praised the film as an action entertainment, with French identifying Scott as 'a most impressive exponent of screen violence' and Corliss referring to *Gladiator* as 'quite a good movie – a big, fat, rousing, intelligent, daring, retro, many-adjective requiring entertainment'.[18] However, both demonstrated ambivalence about this action. If French simply claimed that it 'appeals to much that is primitive and atavistic in us', Corliss shared with other critics the sense that the film was essentially hypocritical: 'Violence is an issue directors love to deplore and exploit.'

Furthermore, concerns with the spectacle of violence also bring us back to CGI. Scott's style was described as 'inhuman, glossy' and unconcerned with reality; and his action was supposed to take place in 'Mount Olympus . . . or some other mythical area, since the Roman Collosseum [*sic*] is roughly the size of the Death Star from *Star Wars*, thanks to the magic of computer graphics'.[19] Similarly, Ebert complained about the film's 'shabby special effects' and that its 'colosseum in Rome looks like a model from a computer game'.[20] Indeed, these elements were brought together explicitly by Hoberman, who complained: 'Some might reasonably consider *Gladiator* an inferior *Star Wars* without the cute critters. The digital animation is far more evident here than in *The Phantom Menace*.'[21] As a result, Hoberman claimed that the film is 'self-reflexive' but only insofar as 'Proximo might be speaking for James Cameron when he explains to Max that "the power to amuse a mob" *is* power'. The invocation of Cameron was no idle comment here; Hoberman even started his review with the observation that *Gladiator* 'has been as rapturously received by some reviewers as *Titanic* was three years ago . . . and the projects are not dissimilar. Like *Titanic*, *Gladiator* is a fearfully expensive, relentlessly high-tech revival of deeply retro material.' Complaints about CGI then were simply the latest versions of a long-standing assumption that 'high-tech' is somehow 'inhuman' and dominates the spectator through spectacle. Awe at special effects, it is presumed, can only result in uncritical submission and deference.[22]

'HONORABLE FAILURE': CGI, SERIOUSNESS AND CAMP IN THE CRITICAL RECEPTION OF *TROY*, *KING ARTHUR*, *ALEXANDER* AND *KINGDOM OF HEAVEN*

By the time of *Troy*, the second film in the cycle, Ebert was already 'getting tired of computer generated armies' and the sight of 'two masses of 50,000 men marching toward each other across a sea of special effects'.[23]

However, there were other complaints. *Variety* observed that 'the women come off a distant second best' and that the film was largely preoccupied with 'dashing men'.[24] As we have seen, Pitt was also seen as being uncomfortable in the role of Achilles, and the film was supposed to feature one scene in which he 'strolls out of his love tent, like a petulant movie star summoned from his trailer'.[25] In other words, he was seen as 'too contemporary' and as displaying the 'narcissism . . . of a modern celebrity: he fights because it will bring him fame, not to serve the gods or the glory of the Greek nation or, least of all, his corrupt king. His loyalty is to individuals . . . rather than to causes.'[26]

For many critics, however, Pitt's presence raised other anxieties, and they seemed more than a little perturbed by his 'modeling [of] the latest in Hellenic leisure wear',[27] an issue that became most explicit in McCarthy's discussion of the film:

> What's really going on, however, is the cinematic fetishizing of an actor on a virtually unequalled level. Appearing almost impossibly buffed, brazened and chiseled, Pitt is lavished with elaborate photographic attention by Petersen and lenser Roger Pratt, in the way Greta Garbo and Marlene Dietrich – but very few men – have been. By way of immortalizing the actor's physical beauty, pic endeavors to turn his character into an icon with godlike status which surely won't hurt in attracting audiences of women and gay men.[28]

In other words, while the problem was partly claimed to be that 'Pitt's charisma doesn't withstand the scrutiny', it was also the case that many critics were clearly uncomfortable or embarrassed by this 'fetishizing' of a male actor, being far more used to films that directed such attention at women instead.

If most critics had something positive to say about Peter O'Toole's performance in the film, which was supposed to highlight the problems with the rest of the cast, the main positive feature was supposed to be its handling of politics. For several, the film's distinction was 'its refusal to take sides', while the *New York Times* noted that it was written by David Benioff, who had written the 'screenplay for Spike Lee's *25th Hour* (based on his own novel)' and decided to read the film through that lens.[29] Seen from this perspective the film was 'fundamentally a story about treachery and brotherhood – about the fallibility and fragile nobility of men'. It was a story of corrupt kings with 'imperial ambitions', a reading that hinted at contemporary relevance related to Bush's military campaigns in the Middle East.

However, such potentially positive readings were overshadowed by complaints about the film's spectacle. The *New York Times*, for example, deplored the scale of the production, 'which cost something approaching the gross national product of modern Greece', while *Village Voice*, as we have already seen, objected violently to the film's use of CGI:

> *Troy* is everything old made new again: matte-image palaces (digitized, of course), hordes of shield-holding extras (also CGI), dialogue that may well have been burped out by a Hercules-movie-digesting mainframe ... and risible 'ancient' loungewear.³⁰

Consequently, although the film was commended for making 'an effort to tell the unsimple tale instead of settling for gotcha effects alone', the final judgement was that it failed. Even one of its most indulgent critics, Philip French, couldn't say much more about the film than '*Troy* isn't terrible' but that 'it isn't good either'.³¹

Failure was also the verdict on *King Arthur*, which 'claims to be "the untold story that inspired the legend"' and shifted the action back to roman times.³² If *Time Out* complained that the film had 'ditched much of the familiar legend' in the process, and *Time* felt that there was 'too much realism' and 'not enough magic', *Variety* argued that, while it would 'disappoint viewers expecting a *Camelot*-like love triangle', the film's 'telling is as credible as any other'.³³ Furthermore, although *Time* missed the 'magic', other reviewers praised the film for the ways in which it 'curtails the use of computer effects', a curtailment that was associated with a 'surprising seriousness of purpose' and made it 'unexpectedly gritty'.³⁴ Again, the film was also said to feature 'a story with uncanny parallels to current events in Iraq', and it was also said to be 'impressively well made and acted' so that its cast 'don't seem out of time and place like the cast of *Troy*'.³⁵

However, for all these positive features, the film was largely seen as a failure, and even its defenders damned it with faint praise. For example, Ebert's judgement was that it 'is not a bad movie, although it could have been better' and that its main virtue was simply that 'it isn't flat-out silly like *Troy*'. For others, however, its lack of silliness was part of the film's failing. *Time* condemned the film as 'joyless', and while the *New York Times* argued that the film was 'not a complete drag', this was due to 'an element of brawny camp' that other critics found to be insufficient.³⁶ *Time* declared that the film was badly in need of 'flash, sass and genial trash', while the *Guardian* claimed to 'miss the days when Hollywood epics would give us Gina Lollobrigida doing a very 1950s frug in *Solomon and Sheba*, or John Wayne speaking reams of ludicrous dialogue while wearing a spiked hubcap in *The Conqueror*'.³⁷

Oliver Stone's *Alexander* received a similar reception. Although the material was seen as well suited to Stone's interests, and despite the film being described as 'intelligent and ambitious' by some and as 'ambitious and sincere' by others, the film was ultimately deemed to be 'an honorable failure', even by its most sympathetic critics.³⁸ For the *Guardian*, the 'soldier's masculine brotherhood and its closed world of secret fears and private affections has long been a favorite theme for Oliver Stone', while *Time* claimed that Stone's films are usually 'celebrations and autopsies of overweening machismo'.³⁹ It also noted that 'for this agit-historian' the figure of Alexander 'is a clear model for George W. Bush, pursuing destiny or delusion from the civilized West into Babylon-Baghdad, completing the quest George H. W. Bush left unfinished'.⁴⁰ But despite its potential, the film was claimed to have 'brought out the worst' in Stone and to have defeated his attempts to give any sense of shape to the narrative.⁴¹ Consequently, while *Alexander* 'far outreaches *Troy* in ambition', the latter film at least 'tells a story that has some structure and clarity, and those are precisely the qualities that *Alexander* lacks'.⁴² The absence of 'structure and clarity' is therefore claimed to make the film 'wildly boring'; and *USA Today* summed matters up succinctly: 'Short life, long movie. After *Alexander* ... don't look for Oliver Stone to be on anybody's A-list to direct or co-write a screen treatise on the life and times of Methuselah.'⁴³

In this case, the critics rounded on the silliness, but not as a celebration of the film. *Village Voice* noted several moments of 'unintentional hilarity' while the *Guardian* claimed that the scenes between Alexander and his mother 'ignite a flame of silliness and absurdity in the film which never goes out'.⁴⁴ It was also claimed that the film exploded in 'a festival of risible wiggery' that most critics couldn't help ridiculing; *Village Voice*, for example, noted that throughout his campaigns Colin Farrell's Alexander sports 'a tousled bleach job, his gypsy-moth eyebrows and dark brooding roots suggesting less the eponymous myth figure in his battlefield prime than a *Vanity Fair* hairdresser ablaze with purpose during a high-pressure Kirsten Dunst cover shoot'.⁴⁵ *Time Out* also claimed that, for much of the film, Farrell 'battles uphill against his blonde wig', which was variously described as 'Anistonian hair' or as 'conquering Clairol blonde'.⁴⁶

However, even the high camp of Angelina Jolie's Olympias was not seen as enough to overcome the tedium, although it provided the critics with considerable ammunition against the film: 'Rarely since Joan Crawford rampaged through the B-movie sunset of her career has a female performer achieved such camp distinction'.⁴⁷ This 'mother of all monstrous mothers' was seen as 'part Yiddishe Mama, part Natasha of *Rocky and Bullwinkle* fame', and as 'like Antony Perkins mom in *Psycho*' or 'Dracula's daughter'.⁴⁸

As a result, the critics had a lot more to work with than the problems of CGI, which was still seen as fakery: 'The climactic battle with Indian elephants has a certain bizarre friction until you realize to what outlandish degree that Stone is digitally shake-and-baking the images'.⁴⁹ Furthermore, many critics were coming to accept CGI, and some even praised the 'careful CGI work' that enabled 'visions of antiquity, the likes of which have never before been put on screen'.[50]

This growing acceptance of CGI was most pronounced in the reception of *Kingdom of Heaven*, another film that was generally seen as sincere and intelligent but ultimately a dull failure. For example, *Variety* noted: 'With CGI improving all the time, the mix of live and computerized elements creates numerous extraordinary canvases of virtually seamless quality.'[51] Similarly, the *Guardian* praised the film's 'beautifully realized ancient world'.[52] However, most critics found Orlando Bloom's hero 'bland', largely because he 'lacks the authority that Crowe brought to his role' in *Gladiator*.[53] As *Variety* observed, given that his character is 'a cipher needing to be filled, a bigger personality than Bloom's would have helped'.[54]

Nonetheless, despite the film's failings most critics demonstrated an appreciation of the film. *Variety* praised it for being 'historically quite respectable' and for 'never betraying the subject matter'; while the *Guardian* noted that it 'enables you to relate it to modern life without making it too obvious', the relation again being to issues surrounding the Iraq War.[55] For example, most critics praised Scott for 'carefully' handling the conflicts between Christians and Muslims on which its story centres,[56] and Corliss describes the film as 'fascinating', while Ebert calls it 'brave', given its political context, seeing it as a plea for 'Christians and Muslims . . . to co-exist peacefully' and as a condemnation of 'extremists on both sides' who seek to benefit from creating conflict.[57] If this interpretation resulted in praise for Scott, who was now re-evaluated as doing the epic 'better than anybody', others still objected that it was *too* liberal, that its hero was an anachronistic 'representation of early 21st-century liberal thinking',[58] while the Muslims were too idealised:

> The movie brings to mind those liberal westerns of the Cold War era in which the Indians are presented as cultured and peaceful, the European settlers seen as ameliorative and considerate, and all would be well were it not for a few headstrong braves going on the warpath, and the whisky-selling, gun-running renegades bent on corrupting native Americans.[59]

However, if these objections were presented as minor quibbles, *Village Voice* was a rare dissenting voice that continued to complain about 'computer generated masses' and declared the film's politics to be not only hypocritical but to be offering 'a fascist or at least newly Riefenstahlian perspective'.[60] Indeed, for *Village Voice*, the film's historical trappings are nothing more than a disguise for a plot right out of *Star Wars*, with Bloom's Balian being 'Luke Skywalker', and Liam Neeson being 'Obi-Wan'. As a result, the film is condemned for its 'simplistic narrative cosmology [that] drags on the eyelids like a covert *Star Wars* sequel'.[61]

'ALL BUT UNWATCHABLE': *300*, *CLASH OF THE TITANS* AND THE EXTREMES OF HISTORICAL FANTASY

As the critics were fond of noting, many of these films did not make their money back, and it was therefore something of a lurch when, the year following *Kingdom of Heaven*, the cycle scored a massive hit with *300*, a film that attracted unparalleled venom from the critics. If *King Arthur*, *Alexander* and *Kingdom of Heaven* were seen as being intelligent but dull, *300* was seen 'fantastically silly' by some and 'stupid' by others.[62] It was claimed to provide a 'blustering' and 'bombastic spectacle' that was condemned not just for a lack of intelligence but as being symptomatic 'of a culture slowly and painfully going mad'.[63]

Furthermore, the issues that were supposedly driving that culture mad were usually taken to be the ongoing 'War on Terror', but, while Denby was generous enough to see *300* as a symptom, other critics attacked it as an active instigator. For many critics of the film, the story of 'macho white guys vs. effeminate Orientals' was clearly a metaphor for the war in Iraq.[64] Indeed, numerous critics noted that Persian arch-villain Xerxes is 'an 8-foot-tall godking who looks like RuPaul beyond the Thunderdome', or 'a queenly strop-fest pitched somewhere between RuPaul and Ming the Merciless'.[65] Similarly, Ebert comments:

> I am just about prepared to believe that the ancient Persians went in for the piercing of ears, cheeks, eyebrows, noses, lips and chins. But [Xerxes'] eyebrows have been plucked and re-drawn into black arches that would make Joan Crawford envious.[66]

Consequently, many saw the villains as being portrayed as camp and the heroes as 'militaristic psychopaths', so that the film felt like 'an Army recruiting film'.[67]

If some dissented from this view, it was largely on the grounds that they found it difficult 'to credit the picture with that much relevance, though it'll doubtless be huge in US Army camps'.[68] Furthermore, critics seemed far more horrified by the sexualised opposition between the Greeks and the Persians. If some treated this with potential humour and declared the film 'an absolute riot of ambiguous sexual signage', others were clearly horrified by 'its outrageous sexual confusion'.[69]

Much was therefore made of the male bodies on display, from the 'speedo wearing' hero who spends the film 'modeling an unattractive pair of trunks' to the suggestion that the Spartans' real advantage over their enemy is not discipline or democracy but access to 'superior health clubs and electrolysis facilities'.[70] Again the film was seen as hardly even being a film and its protagonists as lacking any sense of character and being more like sporting figures: 'professional wrestlers' and 'linebackers'.[71]

Unfortunately, the nature of the criticism remained largely incoherent. Certainly, the reviews mobilised all the evidence that they needed to point out that, rather than being motivated by homosexual pleasures, the film is profoundly homosocial – that is, it places men on display but rigorously deflects any association with homosexuality onto the Persian enemy. In other words, the film could be attacked as profoundly homophobic. But most critics seemed content to simply snigger at the film's fascination with heroic male bodies, and to adopt their own homophobia. It is therefore declared that 'the movie is totally gay',[72] while there was also the implication that only sexually confused young boys would exhibit such fascination with male bodies. In other words, it was assumed that, once young boys grow up, they have either have *straightened out* or *come out*. Consequently, the *Guardian* claimed that the film features 'the kind of tremulous fervour that only prepubescent boys can work up', while *Village Voice* claimed that the film marshals 'the full capacities of hardcore fanboy nerditude'.[73]

As *Variety* put it, 'nowhere outside of gay porn have so many broad shouldered, bulging biceps and ripped torsos been seen on screen', while Bradshaw called it a 'homoerotic battle fantasy'.[74] For *Time Out*, the film was 'positively tumescent with macho posturing', and Scott declared it a must for devotees 'of the pectoral, deltoid and other fine muscle groups'.[75]

In fact, one of the implicit criticisms of the film was that, unlike other films in the cycle, it was not concerned with its cinematic heritage as a historical epic but drew its influences from the 'muscle magazine' or was stuck in 'slavish, frame-by-frame devotion to Miller's source material'.[76] In other words, its original was 'Frank Miller's comic-book version of Greek history rather than the 1962 vintage swords-and-sandals epic, *The 300 Spartans*', and while it was claimed that the historical confrontation could have made 'a great tale of derring-do, [*300*] in no ways does justice to it'.[77]

Furthermore, the obsession with the male bodies was also related to another issue. If CGI was becoming more respectable by *Kingdom of Heaven*, *300* used developments in CGI that had been pioneered in *Sin City*, and Roger Ebert paid penance for giving the previous film 'a four star rating' and saw *300* as the punishment that 'I deserve'.[78] If discussion of the film's male bodies sought to identify them as 'pumped up', unnatural products of artifice – 'health clubs', 'steroids' and 'protein shakes' – many noted that they were also the product of CGI.[79]

As Ebert put it, the filmmakers relied 'so heavily on CGI that many shots are entirely computer generated', and although the actor's 'faces are convincing, I believe their bodies are almost entirely digital creations'. This not only revolted Ebert's tastes but was also supposed to create some kind of epistemological crisis. If these bodies were 'artistic renderings, not human beings', he was also forced to acknowledge that, when Xerxes confronts the Spartan commander Leonidas, the Persian despot 'towers over' the Spartan to such an extent that it can only be the result of CGI and that therefore 'we know his body isn't really there'.[80]

Complaints about CGI once again erupted in these reviews, and there were accusations that the film was 'computer tooled blood-letting' that employed 'the latest technical know-how', but ended up having 'something secondhand and suffocating about it'.[81] Similarly, the *New York Times* claimed that despite the film's new technology, its visuals looked very old-fashioned: the film was supposed to be 'rendered in images that might have been airbrushed onto a customized van sometime in the late 1970s'.[82] Moreover, the problem was not just that the film was 'synthetic' but that cinema was not its major reference point: 'I would happily pay a nickel less, in quarters and arcade tokens, for a vigorous 10-minute session with the video game that *300* clearly aspires to become.'[83]

Ultimately, then, Scott dismisses the film 'more tiresome than entertaining' and being 'camp' but in the wrong way. As Johnston complains, 'it might have been one of the great all-time mad, bad movies but for one thing – it's just sooo boring'.[84]

The contrast with *Clash of the Titans* could not have been more pronounced, and while the latter film was seen as 'cinematic camp' or 'an amiable upgrade of the camp 80s epic', it was deemed by many critics to be 'a very entertaining ride' and 'highly enjoyable'.[85] Rather than being uncomfortable with the film, critics seemed to have positively relished its lack of pretention and its willingness to be nothing more than 'old-school', 'popcorn' entertainment.[86] Rather than condemn its follies, critics seemed to extract fun from them: Mount Olympus 'looks more like something one might encounter in Las Vegas, with its fake Greek pillars and campy atmosphere. Indeed, Neeson's Zeus is outfitted in gleaming armour that shines worse than one of Liberace's jackets.'[87] Ebert confessed:

> I like this kind of stuff. I don't say it's good cinema, although I recognize the craftsmanship that went into it. I don't say it's good acting, when the men have so much facial hair they all look like Liam Neeson. I like the energy, the imagination, the silliness. So do I recommend this movie? Yes, if you intuit that this review is affectionate and have the same tolerance for goofy Greek gods as I do.[88]

Indeed, for all its CGI, a lot of critics positively relished the film's old-fashioned qualities, particularly its unembarrassed 'silliness'. Corliss, for example, particularly liked its lack of irony, in which 'the movie proceeds without winks or nudges; it doesn't cue its viewers to easy laughs. As Worthington told an interviewer, "We take it serious so the audience doesn't have to take it too serious."[89]

Consequently, although Corliss complained that 'the critical cry has arisen against *Clash of the Titans*', the film received some of the most indulgent reviews of the entire cycle. Certainly, many critics felt the need to pay homage to the original film, so that the *New York Times* observed: 'Harryhausen isn't listed in the credits for the *Clash of the Titans* makeover. He should be.'[90] *Variety* was more pointed, but even here its review could hardly be described as a 'critical cry':

> Once state-of-the art, Harryhausen's work is surely dated from a technical standpoint compared to the magic CGI can conjure; still, this *Titans* reboot merely demonstrates that building a more elaborate mousetrap doesn't necessarily produce a more entertaining one.[91]

On the contrary, although most critics agreed that CGI images were not necessarily better than Harryhausen's creations, which were supposedly distinguished by their creativity, rather than their realism, the CGI did not provoke the same horrified responses as in previous films. Part of the reason may, ironically, have been that many critics felt that the CGI was 'still rather fake looking', and that, rather than seeing this as a problem, they claimed that the effects 'are fitting rather than astounding'.[92] In other words, there was an implication that the effects were integrated with narrative and character and performed a job, rather than becoming an end in their own right. There was also a sense that, as in Harryhausen's films, the 'wobblesome special effects' were part of the pleasure and Ebert therefore affectionately referred to the film's 'terrifying battles between mortals and special effects'.[93]

Another reason was that, as a post-*Avatar* release, the critics had their sights set on another technological feature and presented the real problem with *Clash of the Titans* as being its 'conversion to 3D'.[94] For some, the 3D was simply 'superfluous' and provided 'no discernible improvement', but for others it was 'rather painful' and even 'all but unwatchable, blurring the image to a headache inducing degree'.[95]

CONCLUSION

The films of this cycle might be seen as a fairly eclectic group, some claiming historical sources (*Gladiator, Alexander, Kingdom of Heaven, 300*); others claiming mythic sources (*Troy, Clash of the Titans*); and one even claiming to represent the authentic historical events that gave rise to a myth (*King Arthur*).

However, despite their diversity, these films were identified with one another on the grounds that they supposedly shared a common reference back to the post-war historical epic, although they were largely judged to be inferior to this earlier cycle of films. Although most critics engaged in political readings of these films in an attempt to add weight and significance to the practice of film reviewing, these readings were not very developed; and it is clear that these critics were more concerned with the use of spectacle in these films, particularly the use of CGI. In the process, these critics repeated familiar (yet unsubstantiated) claims that spectacle makes audiences passive, uncritical and open to totalitarian politics, claims that were insistent in relation to both *Gladiator* and *300*. Certainly, some films were seen as more culturally ambitious, but this did not necessarily endear them to reviewers, who saw *Alexander*, *King Arthur* and *Kingdom of Heaven* as pretentious and even boring exercises. It is therefore only *Clash of the Titans* that was largely indulged by critics, and this was due precisely to its *lack* of cultural pretentions on the one hand, and a change in the target of critical attack from CGI to 3D on the other.

NOTES

1. Barbara Klinger, *Melodrama and Meaning: Culture, History and the Films of Douglas Sirk* (Bloomington, IN: Indiana University Press, 1994).
2. Xan Brooks, 'Review of *Clash of the Titans*', *The Guardian*, 1 April 2010.
3. Todd McCarthy, 'Review of *Gladiator*', *Variety*, 23 April 2000.
4. Mike Clark, '*Alexander* the Great: Barely Even Mediocre', *USA Today*, 23 November 2004; John Hiscock, 'Sex and Sandals', *Daily Telegraph*, 2 May 2004.
5. Roger Ebert, 'Review of *Alexander*', *Chicago Sun Times*, 24 November 2004.
6. Michael Atkinson, 'They Build Horses, Don't They? Could Be Verse: Brad Pitt's Beefcake Achilles Is a Heel in a Streamlined, Digitized *Iliad*', *Village Voice*, 4 May 2004.
7. McCarthy, 'Review of *Gladiator*'.
8. J. Hoberman, 'Natural Selection', *Village Voice*, 2 May 2000; Elvis Mitchell, 'Film Review; That Cruel Collosseum', *New York Times*, 5 May 2000.
9. Roger Ebert, 'Review of *Gladiator*', *Chicago Sun Times*, 5 May 2000.
10. Philip French, 'Rome with a View: Ridley Scott's Exhilarating and Ferocious Gladiator Brings the Epic Back to Life', *Observer*, 14 May 2000.
11. Hoberman, 'Natural Selection'.
12. McCarthy, 'Review of *Gladiator*'; Hoberman, 'Natural Selection'.
13. Mark Jancovich, '"Charlton Heston is an Axiom": Spectacle and Performance in the Development of the Blockbuster', in Andrew Willis (ed.), *Film Stars: Hollywood and Beyond* (Manchester: Manchester University Press, 2004), pp. 51–70.
14. Mitchell, 'That Cruel Collosseum'.
15. Ebert, 'Review of *Gladiator*'; Mitchell, 'That Cruel Collosseum'. Ross Hunter was the producer of numerous glossy woman's pictures of the 1950s and 1960s, including Douglas Sirk's *Magnificent Obsession* (1954), *All that Heaven Allows* (1955) and *Imitation of Life* (1959).
16. Mitchell, 'That Cruel Collosseum'.

17. Ibid.
18. French, 'Rome with a View'; Richard Corliss, 'Cinema: The Empire Strikes Back', *Time*, 8 May 2000.
19. Mitchell, 'That Cruel Collosseum'.
20. Ebert, 'Review of *Gladiator*'.
21. Hoberman, 'Natural Selection'.
22. For an account and a critique of these assumptions, see Joanne Hollows, 'Mass Culture and Political Economy', in Joanne Hollows and Mark Jancovich (eds), *Approaches to Popular Film* (Manchester: Manchester University Press, 1995), pp. 18–23.
23. Roger Ebert, 'Review of *Troy*', *Chicago Sun Times*, 14 May 2004.
24. Todd McCarthy, 'Review of *Troy*', *Variety*, 4 May 2004.
25. A. O. Scott, 'Film Review; Greeks Bearing Immortality', *New York Times*, 14 May 2004.
26. McCarthy, 'Review of *Troy*'; Scott, 'Greeks Bearing Immortality'.
27. Scott, 'Greeks Bearing Immortality'; see also Michael Atkinson, 'Natural Born Killer: Tousled Bleach Jobs, One-eyed Stiffs, Neo-epic Drops Its Veils but Keeps the Nookie Offscreen', *Village Voice*, 16 November 2004.
28. McCarthy, 'Review of *Troy*'.
29. Richard Corliss, 'That's What You Call a Homer', *Time*, 2 May 2004; Scott, 'Greeks Bearing Immortality'.
30. Scott, 'Greeks Bearing Immortality'; Atkinson, 'Natural Born Killer'.
31. Philip French, 'Troy', *Observer*, 16 May 2004.
32. A. O. Scott, 'Film Review: The Once and Future Fury: These Knights Go for the Jugular', *New York Times*, 7 July 2004.
33. DC, 'Review of *King Arthur*', *Time Out London*, 28 July–4 August 2004; Richard Schickel, 'Movies: Dark Knights', *Time*, 19 July 2004; Todd McCarthy, 'Review of *King Arthur*', *Variety*, 5 July 2004.
34. Roger Ebert, 'Review of *King Arthur*', *Chicago Sun Times*, 7 July 2004; McCarthy, 'Review of *King Arthur*'.
35. Ebert, 'Review of *King Arthur*'; McCarthy, 'Review of *King Arthur*'; Ebert, 'Review of *King Arthur*'.
36. Schickel, 'Dark Knights'; Scott, 'The Once and Future Fury'.
37. Schickel, 'Dark Knights'; Rob Mackie, 'Review of *King Arthur*', *The Guardian*, 3 December 2004.
38. Todd McCarthy, 'Review of *Alexander*', *Variety*, 20 November 2004; Roger Ebert, 'Review of *Alexander*', *Chicago Sun Times*, 24 November 2004; McCarthy, 'Review of *Alexander*'.
39. Peter Bradshaw, 'Review of *Alexander*', *The Guardian*, 31 December 2004; Richard Corliss, 'It's His Same Old Story', *Time*, 21 November 2004.
40. Manohla Dargis, 'With No More Parents to Conquer, He Wept', *New York Times*, 24 November 2004.
41. Ibid.
42. Ebert, 'Review of *Alexander*', *Chicago Sun Times*, 24 November 2004.
43. NB, 'Review of *Alexander*', *Time Out*, 5–12 January 2005; Mike Clark, '*Alexander* the Great: Barely Even Mediocre', *USA Today*, 23 November 2004.
44. Atkinson, 'Natural Born Killer'; Bradshaw, 'Review of *Alexander*'.
45. Atkinson, 'Natural Born Killer'.
46. NB, 'Review of *Alexander*'; Atkinson, 'Natural Born Killer'; Clark, 'Barely Even Mediocre'.
47. Dargis, 'With No More Parents'.

48. Ibid.; Bradshaw, 'Review of *Alexander*'; Corliss, 'It's His Same Old Story'.
49. Atkinson, 'Natural Born Killer'.
50. McCarthy, 'Review of *Alexander*'.
51. Todd McCarthy, 'Review of *Kingdom of Heaven*', *Variety*, 1 May 2005.
52. Rob Mackie, 'Review of *Kingdom of Heaven*', *The Guardian*, 7 October 2005.
53. McCarthy, 'Review of *Kingdom of Heaven*'.
54. Ibid.
55. Ibid.; Mackie, 'Review of *Kingdom of Heaven*'.
56. Manohla Dargis, 'An Epic Bloodletting Empowered by Faith', *New York Times*, 6 May 2005; Richard Corliss, 'Movies: To War or Not to War', *Time*, 1 May 2005.
57. Corliss, 'To War or Not to War'; Roger Ebert, 'Review of *Kingdom of Heaven*', *Chicago Sun Times*, 5 May 2005.
58. Ebert, 'Review of *Kingdom of Heaven*'; Corliss, 'To War or Not to War'.
59. Philip French, 'Saladin Days: Great Spectacle, Sweeping Narrative, Heroic Deeds and Lots of Gore. Ridley Scott Delivers All the Goods for a Mighty Epic', *Observer*, 8 May 2005.
60. Michael Atkinson, 'Holy Crap: The Empire Strikes Back: Uneasy Nods to Contemporary Politics Is All This *Heaven* Knows', *Village Voice*, 26 April 2005.
61. Ibid.
62. Peter Bradshaw, 'Review of *300*', *The Guardian*, 23 March 2007; A. O. Scott, 'Battle of the Manly Men: Blood Bath with a Message', *New York Times*, 9 March 2007.
63. Todd McCarthy, 'Review of *300*', *Variety*, 9 March 2007; Scott, 'Battle of the Manly Men'; David Denby, 'Men Gone Wild', *New Yorker*, 2 April 2007.
64. Nathan Lee, 'Man on Man Action: It's Spartan Hotties versus Persian Trannies in Zack Snyder's Far-too-faithful Frank Miller Adaptation', *Village Voice*, 27 February 2007. For a particularly virulent and incoherent articulation of this position, see Rick Moody, 'Frank Miller and the Rise of Cryptofascist Hollywood', *The Guardian*, 24 November 2011.
65. Lee, 'Man on Man Action'; Trevor Johnston, 'Review of *300*', *Time Out*, 21–7 March 2007.
66. Roger Ebert, 'Review of *300*', *Chicago Sun Times*, 9 December 2006.
67. Denby, 'Men Gone Wild'.
68. Johnston, 'Review of *300*'.
69. Ibid.; Lee, 'Man on Man Action'.
70. Lee, 'Man on Man Action'; Bradshaw, 'Review of *300*'; Scott, 'Battle of the Manly Men'.
71. Ebert, 'Review of *300*'; Denby, 'Men Gone Wild'.
72. Richard Corliss, '7 Reasons Why *300* Is a Huge Hit', *Time*, 14 March 2007.
73. Bradshaw, 'Review of *300*'; Lee, 'Man on Man Action'.
74. McCarthy, 'Review of *300*'; Bradshaw, 'Review of *300*'.
75. Johnston, 'Review of *300*'; Scott, 'Battle of the Manly Men'.
76. Lee, 'Man on Man Action'.
77. Johnston, 'Review of *300*'.
78. Ebert, 'Review of *300*'.
79. McCarthy, 'Review of *300*'; Scott, 'Battle of the Manly Men'; McCarthy, 'Review of *300*'; Ebert, 'Review of *300*'.
80. Ebert, 'Review of *300*'.
81. Johnston, 'Review of *300*'; McCarthy, 'Review of *300*'; McCarthy, 'Review of *300*'.
82. Scott, 'Battle of the Manly Men'.
83. Lee, 'Man on Man Action'; Scott, 'Battle of the Manly Men'.
84. Johnston, 'Review of *300*'.

85. Manohla Dargis, 'Beware of Greeks Bearing Buzz Cuts', *New York Times*, 1 April 2010; Xan Brooks, 'Review of *Clash of the Titans*', *The Guardian*, 1 April 2010; Tom Huddleston, 'Review of *Clash of the Titans*', *Time Out*, 1–7 April 2010.
86. Huddleston, 'Review of *Clash of the Titans*'; Kirk Honeycutt, '*Clash of the Titans* – Film Review', *Hollywood Reporter*, 14 October 2010.
87. Honeycutt, '*Clash of the Titans*'.
88. Roger Ebert, 'Review of *Clash of the Titans*', *Chicago Sun Times*, 31 March 2010.
89. Richard Corliss, '*Clash of the Titans*: A Hit from a Myth', *Time*, 2 April 2010.
90. Dargis, 'Beware of Greeks Bearing Buzz Cuts'.
91. Brian Lowry, 'Review of *Clash of the Titans*', *Variety*, 28 March 2010.
92. Huddleston, 'Review of *Clash of the Titans*'; Corliss, 'A Hit from a Myth'.
93. Mark Jancovich and Derek Johnston, 'Genre, Special Effects and Authorship in the Critical Reception of Science Fiction Film and Television during the 1950s', in Elizabeth McCarthy and Bernice M. Murphy (eds), *It Came from the 1950s: Popular Culture, Popular Anxieties* (London: Palgrave Macmillan, 2011), pp. 90–107; Ebert, 'Review of *Clash of the Titans*'.
94. Huddleston, 'Review of *Clash of the Titans*'.
95. Dargis, 'Beware of Greeks Bearing Buzz Cuts'; Anthony Lane, 'Out of Reach', *New Yorker*, 12 April 2010; Huddleston, 'Review of *Clash of the Titans*'.

CHAPTER 5

Popcorn and Circus: An Audience Expects

Robert Stow

In early 2010, I watched *Gladiator* (Scott 2000) with a friend. While discussing it afterwards they asked me how accurate it was and why I thought they had changed things. The discussion got me thinking; I was aware that the re-creation of the ancient world in film was a popular area of research among classicists but was often discussed in relation to arguments and debates about the potential of cinema and film as an educational tool.[1] Martin Winkler's *Gladiator: Film and History* is a prime example of the academic's analysis of historical film; a series of works by professors at the top of their fields either analysing inaccuracy in the films or explaining the historical facts behind what we see in an attempt to inform and convey a proper understanding of the real events. Winkler discusses the problems in faithfully re-creating authenticity and questions how important accuracy and detail really are; his argument is based upon an idea that the production of accurately detailed sets and props does not affect the audience's enjoyment of the film. This raised an unexplored area of research, the lack of academic literature exploring the reception of the historical world from the audience's point of view. Whilst it is understandable that those wanting to teach about the past will want to utilise cinema to their advantage, a different question arises when we begin to ask what the public think. After all, it is *their* tastes that a studio or director will often target to try to produce as commercially successful a film as possible; do they want, or even expect, their films to be historically accurate? Take the following statement by Pierre Sorlin:

> Historians who try to list the historical inaccuracies in [a film] would be ignoring the fact that their job should not involve bestowing marks for accuracy, but describing how men living at a certain time understand their own history. A historical film can be puzzling for a scholar: everything that he considers history is ignored. But at the same time it is

important to examine the difference between history as it is written by the specialist and history as it is received by the non-specialist.[2]

Sorlin makes a clear distinction here between the specialist and non-specialist; it is this idea of the non-specialist and how they receive historical film which I focused on. In this chapter I discuss the difference between what audiences expect and what they want from the genre, and whether there is a common ground between audiences' expectations and the desires of the academics that historical films educate. To this end, I propose not to look at the historical inaccuracy of *Gladiator* in any depth,[3] but instead to use the film as a starting point to analyse the ways in which my focus group members engaged with the classical past on offer.

By way of offering comparative reactions to the classical epic, I also used *Centurion* (Marshall 2010) as a second case study, on the grounds that it offers a different perspective on the historical epic. The first of these differences was that, when carrying out my research, the film had only just been released. Therefore, there was no academic literature to compare and contrast with my participants' views, only public opinion and amateur reviews. Because the film was far less familiar, and had not yet had the opportunity to circulate widely in the public domain, there was less chance that this specific depiction of classical antiquity would have been discussed, disseminated and diluted in the popular imagination in the same way as *Gladiator*. Second, the true version of events behind the film was still widely debated, which precluded any approach which simply listed inaccuracies or divergence from received historical opinion. Modern historians are divided about the legion's fate; a popular theory remains that the main force of the Ninth Legion was wiped out on the northern frontier in modern-day Scotland. This theory does have some merit, as ancient historians and public officials were not averse to covering up large defeats by the Roman field army and Tacitus, the main historian of the period, was the son-in-law of Gnaeus Julius Agricola, the Roman general in charge for much of the conquest of Britain. It is this theory which Marshall used as the inspiration behind his film, and *Centurion*, set in 117 CE, therefore offers a different proposition from *Gladiator*, which replaced known historical events with a fictional plot.

Using these two films as my focus I carried out my research through online questionnaires. These were split into two sections, firstly using a Likert scale on a series of statements with response options of Strongly Disagree, Disagree, Neither Agree nor Disagree, Agree and Strongly Agree. The second section offered a series of qualitative questions to gather responses, which will be analysed throughout this chapter. Altogether seventy-eight people took part in the survey, offering a solid range of data. Where further explanations were required, the study used a comparative approach making use of comments and discussions taking place on websites such as IMDB message boards to further explore the public debate. As discussed in the introduction to this book, the 'sword and sandal' epics have enjoyed a resurgence in popularity of late, started by *Gladiator*, following their disappearance from our screens for thirty-six years after *The Fall of the Roman Empire* (Mann 1964).[4] Analysing what audiences believe the historical epic *should* be also offers an insight into how the recent revival of the genre can maintain its current level of popularity.

Before we can explore any reactions to the films, however, it is first important to establish what is meant by historical accuracy in the first place, and realistic expectations must be set around this. As much of the discussion surrounding historical films makes clear, it is impossible for a film to be a completely faithful re-creation since there are simply too many variants.[5] As one participant put it: 'prove to me what is beyond doubt as being historically accurate'. For one thing, the ancient historians we rely on offer only a brief analysis of the events covered in the films. Winkler highlighted how these historians re-created the past by 'shaping it artistically through their own inventions and interpretations'.[6] Thucydides, for example, emphasised the truthful recording of events whilst admitting to applying an artistic licence in his description, which he claimed was acceptable if you adhere to 'the spirit of the time or circumstance being described'.[7]

If the sources are not fully factual – that is, if there is no universally agreed upon factual basis for the film – then a fictional element is inevitably required, as Kathleen Coleman, the historical consultant for *Gladiator*, discovered when she frequently found her advice ignored in favour of artistic innovation.[8] In a discussion of her experiences on set, Coleman argued that 'the historical consultant should be a person who is intimately involved with the entire process of making the film' and should not simply point out everything that was wrong but suggest how to correct it.[9] It is thus unsurprising that, in ignoring the latter part of her role, *Gladiator* falls outside the academic boundaries of historical acceptability. Reflecting on her experiences, Coleman concluded:

> If the standard for authenticity is determined by what has already been monumentalised on screen, the consultant really has no part to play at all. Maybe there is a residual notion in the film industry that the hiring of a consultant is itself enough to give a film a veneer of responsibility. If that attitude exists, it is, to say the least, unethical, and it is predicated upon the assumption, undoubtedly correct, that the vast majority of cinemagoers have no way of judging the authenticity of a historical film and do not care at all whether it is authentic or not.[10]

The assumption is that non-specialist audiences have no way of judging how historically accurate a film is and therefore that the vast majority of cinemagoers do not care if a film is authentic. This has two implications; either audiences just want to be entertained, or they already trust that a faithful account will be produced, twin assumptions which prompted the basis of my questionnaire. In response to the statement 'It is a given that in films depicting the ancient world the director will alter the portrayal of historical events to suit their plot' the results were overwhelmingly one-sided: thirty-four people strongly agreed with the statement with a further thirty-one agreeing. Only three people disagreed, with nine having no opinion, which can be taken as a clear suggestion that the majority of the participants do not take what they see on screen as fact in either one way or another. Two further statements that elicited similar responses were 'films depicting historical events should aim to be as faithful as possible', and 'film has a responsibility to educate as well as to entertain'. Thirty-eight people agreed with the latter, with twenty-three disagreeing. The basic results suggest a tendency towards wanting a film which is as accurate as possible; however, closer scrutiny of the results of the surveys revealed that even this observation is too simplistic, as the following comments attest:

A: I would much rather the film I see be entertaining, as opposed to being historically accurate. It would be good for a film to be historically accurate, but an entertaining plot for me is much more important than anything else. So if that means a film is historically questionable, so be it.

B: Cinema is for entertainment and making money. Documentary film is for education – many funded by cinema profits.

C: Film's responsibility to educate is a difficult question. Most films like this are only based loosely on historical facts. I believe they should try to stick as close to them as possible, but I go see [sic] a film for entertainment, and in that respect I would rate it as being more important to entertain then [sic] to educate. If it does both, then great, but the entertainment is more important.

D: For me asking if historical film has a need to be accurate is like arguing over whether art has to mimic real life. I believe we have many interesting abstract pieces of work, so the answer for me is a resounding no.

This sample of comments shows a clear recognition and acknowledgement of different forms of cinema, and an assertion that documentaries are made to educate while movies should provide entertainment. An accurate historical drama could still be entertaining, and some participants felt that although entertainment was the priority, historical films had a duty to stick to the facts where possible. The comment identifying cinema as an art form, drawing on the question of whether art should 'mimic real life', brings a view that filmmakers should be able to exert their creative freedom. This supports Coleman's claim that audiences are not concerned whether a film is authentic or not, and Winkler makes a similar argument:

> Who among audiences of Mervyn LeRoy's *Quo Vadis* (1951) paid attention to, or remembered afterwards, that most of the decor of these films was highly authentic and had been re-created lovingly and at great expense? Were not the climatic arena sequences much more fascinating through their visceral appeal?[11]

The unspoken argument is that audiences would have the same experiences even if the sets were not authentic, or indeed that they would not be equipped with sufficient knowledge to judge their accuracy. My research, however, suggests that something else is happening in addition to accuracy: whilst thirty-eight people believed that film had a responsibility to educate as well as to entertain, only twenty-nine said they were concerned when the true nature of events was changed, suggesting that over half of the focus group consciously rated accuracy as a relatively low priority. Consequently, there must be different interpretations of the ways in which cinema can educate. Take the following two comments on *Gladiator*:

> A: I liked the recreation of Rome as a city. More the level of the detail given to the setting rather than the plot.
>
> B: I don't know how accurate it is, but it is a very enjoyable movie and I view it as a picture of what the Roman World would have looked like.

This suggests that authenticity extends beyond the plot and includes the screenplay, the set designs, the characters, and the way it is all brought together on screen. One participant felt 'it is up to the viewer to educate themselves as to the historicity of the film'. In the survey, forty-eight people said that upon seeing either *Gladiator* or *Centurion* they were inspired to carry out their own research into the real events. In a similar vein, Robert Stam's theory on film adaptations suggests that those who read a novel before seeing the film will compare the director's take to their own visualisation, a theory which can be applied to historical film through the reverse sequence; the spectator sees the film before reading the 'novel', or in most cases, before researching the history of the film.[12] Those who were inspired to carry out some research will overlay the visuals from the screen onto any relevant text. Cinema offers a visual scope unavailable to literature, and this side of cinema could be beneficial to those who want to see cinema educate more. One respondent represented this benefit as follows:

Whilst *Gladiator* may not be one hundred percent historically accurate, I feel that it still captured the essence of history. As long as movies like *Gladiator* are entertaining and have the *essence* of history down, I'm good. [italics in original]

The 'essence of history' is an intriguing notion, and fits in with Thucydides' statement about adhering to 'the spirit of the time or circumstance being described'. One participant said:

Gladiator contained everything I'd expected in a movie about Romans; warfare, slaves, gladiators, chariots, villainous Emperors, backstabbing senators and a whole lot of political squabbling!

This evokes the problematic nature of the 'essence of history': that it depends on a prior conception of what it should be. The Roman Republic and (Western) Empire lasted from 509 BCE to 476 CE. If this period is covered by the generic term 'Romans', the reality of trying to capture the real essence of the period is revealed to be impossible. The opening scene of *Quo Vadis* shows Marcus Vinicius enter Rome by chariot, though the Roman army did not use chariots in the first century CE. Although inaccurate, this fits with this participant's belief of what Rome was like, which suggests that, in contrast to Coleman's observations, references to other Roman films at the expense of advice from a historical consultant are not necessarily a cynical manoeuvre on the part of the director, but perhaps something hard-wired into the relationship between spectator and filmmaker.

Allen Ward asked if it is too pedantic to point out that the Roman cavalry in *Gladiator*'s opening battle use stirrups, which were not introduced until the sixth or seventh century CE.[13] Alternatively, should one expect the use of Latin to be accurate? For instance, 'Proximo' must be either dative or ablative and makes no sense as a name, yet participants wholeheartedly rejected such criticisms as having little to do with the feeling of history:

It's being far too picky: name me a single film that doesn't have errors in it. I've seen films set in the modern day with more continuity errors and goofs then [sic] having something misspelt in a language which the majority of people are not going to understand. I mean how many people will have even spotted it? I heard there is a scene where you can see someone in the background wearing jeans. Is the film trying to say Romans invented the jeans? No, it's just an error!

Such insights offer a clearer idea of what the boundaries for accuracy are, and positions those who wanted as much as possible – such as one person who

Figure 5.1 *Gladiator* (2000) contains everything one respondent expected in a movie about Romans.

requested to see a film shot entirely in Latin or Greek – as the minority. The appearance of Latin, regardless of mistakes, appears to be sufficient to create the 'spirit of the time' mentioned above. Yet our perception of history in film is also influenced by the way the characters are brought to life. In the historical sources personalities are constructed over pages; however, when an actor first appears on screen numerous assumptions and opinions are made about their character through their body language, posture, facial expressions, mannerisms, and even accents.[14]

There is also another entity to consider: the performer. While historians are expected accurately to record a character's actions, the actor is given freedom to channel the character through their performance, which is refined by their interpretation of the screenplay and their role, as well as their talent as an actor. Further to this, our impressions are shaped by what we already know about the actor's previous performances and personal life.[15] Discussing Joaquin Phoenix's portrayal of Commodus, Ward observes that 'except for the love of the games, there is not much that is historical about the Commodus we see in *Gladiator*'.[16] Joaquin Phoenix may be physically different from Commodus, but that has no effect on how his performance is received, as demonstrated by the following comment on the IMDB message board for *Gladiator*:

> A: I've read a brief history of Commodus the Emperor, and Joaquin Phoenix was able to project the fact that his character was a misunderstood and misguided soul. He made a villain sympathetic, a difficult thing to pull off, especially when the villain had a few [*sic*] redeemable features. Most actors would opt to portray a villain one dimensionally, but Joaquin was able to give the character depth and 'layers', and each

time you watch the movie there's something new you don't know about Commodus.[17]

For these viewers, the fact that there is no physical resemblance to the real Commodus is irrelevant: the performance is nevertheless believable for a range of other reasons. Another comment suggested:

> Joaquin Phoenix delivered one of the most perfect depictions of a mad Emperor. He fits the role perfectly IMO, in such a way that it seems to be natural. I'm pretty sure that there is some kind of connection between Joaquin's view of life and Commodus'.[18]

This second suggestion also reinforces the link between the actor's personal life and the reception of his performance, yet this was not the only contemporary influence my survey picked up on. Cyrino describes ancient Rome as a city which is symbolic of 'power, intrigue, beauty, brutality and lust'[19] and which therefore provides the ideal screen on which to project our concerns about contemporary international relations, domestic politics and cultural and social tensions.[20] One participant reacted to this by saying:

> I guess it makes sense that there would be modern influences on the film. As long as they make it entertaining and enjoyable it doesn't bother me, if anything it would probably make me appreciate the film more. I would probably find it more accessible than if I was watching a thousand-year-old political debate that was irrelevant to me.

Another respondent felt that it was 'fine if they find some point in the past which is relevant and applicable so they don't have to make too many changes'. Cyrino argues that films about antiquity can play an important role in bridging the gap between past and present because they offer an interpretation of history, literature and mythology that are fully relevant to a contemporary audience.[21] Yet the contemporary version of history is not always so well received:

> Films are primarily for entertainment. I do not believe they have any responsibility to teach. However, I do think that it is entirely inappropriate to knowingly mislead the audience, particularly on important and sensitive subjects. I particularly hate the Americanisation of history by Hollywood. This only furthers America's arrogance and ignorance and almost every other country in the world instantly hates the film because of it (i.e. *U571*).[22]

Rome may have similarities to America, but it also has its own fascinating history, and while these views suggest that audiences are not averse to a film using contemporary resonances to make it accessible and entertaining, they are less willing to accept America imprinting its own history onto film if it fails to capture the 'essence of history'. Given the fictional element of *Gladiator*, it is ironic that Ridley Scott says 'with history your challenge, really, is to see how accurate you can be'. However, here he is not talking about facts: 'the priority was to stay true to the spirit of the period, but not necessarily to adhere to facts. We were, after all, creating fiction, not practicing archaeology.'[23] This sits with the views of *The Fall of the Roman Empire*'s director, Anthony Mann, who claimed that 'the most important thing is that you get the feeling of history', which provides common ground between the director and the audiences.[24] A prime example of this was the expectation that *Gladiator* be violent:

> *Gladiator* is a very violent film; I think it captures the bloody nature of the gladiatorial games very well.

One participant thought *Gladiator*'s battles provided an insight into Roman military tactics, yet the use of the catapults and *ballistae* hurling fire was not a tactic utilised in open warfare. The gladiator bouts are another example; the gladiators should have been divided into categories, each with their own specific armour, weapons and style of fighting, yet there is no sense of this division.[25] In fact, mêlées between large numbers of contestants were more suited to staged battles or criminal executions than gladiatorial combat.[26] The responses to this followed a consistent trend:

> A: The gladiators and games existed as a form of entertainment. It does not bother me if they've changed the styles, I'm still entertained.

> B: I have no idea how accurate the portrayal of the games was and it does not really bother me, what is important is that they caught the sense of excitement. Styles and tastes change; just because a style was popular back then certainly doesn't mean that it would be now.

The implication is that inaccuracies do not necessarily detract from the fights, provided that they fulfil the need to entertain. They also play an important part in the flow of the film; one participant commented on the role the fights played in forming the bond between Maximus and Juba, noting that their relationship would have been far less convincing had they not both faced death in the arena.

Gladiator effectively re-created the violent nature of antiquity; however, the battle sequences in *Centurion* eclipse *Gladiator* in both realism and gore.

Figure 5.2 The armour and weapons in *Centurion* (2010) are some of the most accurate committed to film.

The film provides a glimpse into life on the Empire's northern frontier, and Marshall wanted to portray this as realistically as possible. The Roman legionaries' armour and weapons are some of the most accurate committed to film. The director's desire to get this detail right reinforces an important point; the director's point of view must be considered.

One inaccuracy with *Centurion*'s props is the use of the *lancea*, the long spear, a weapon that did not become standard fare for the Roman army until the third century CE. Marshall wanted to use the thinner *pilum*, but encountered problems getting these to register on screen properly. Despite the director's best intentions, a faithful re-creation is sometimes not possible. This attention to detail may not be recognised by the wider audience, but there is nevertheless a general perception regarding what looks believable in a film representing this time period.

> I was really enjoying Centurion, until they met Arianne . . . not only did it completely throw the pace of the film off, [but] it really shattered the illusion they'd created. It's like they'd just wandered into modern Scotland. She was wearing lipstick for starters! She's meant to be an outcast witch living in the Scottish wilderness. She just wouldn't look like that.

While make-up did exist in antiquity, it is indeed improbable that it would look like this, and even more so that an outcast in the north of Britain would wear it. In an article for *Entertainment Weekly*, Tricia Johnson describes another example of what appears believable to audiences, saying that the most famous gladiators were often used to endorse certain products, similar to modern advertising using celebrities. Ironically, this historical aspect was ignored in *Gladiator* as those working on the film felt that modern audiences would not accept this as believable.[27] This again reinforces the idea of capturing the 'essence of history' and a desire to create and see something that is believable rather than authentic and accurate.

In the earlier analysis of the survey data the vast majority of respondents felt that it was to be expected that the true nature of events would be changed to suit the plot. In the same survey, ten people stated that they believed *Gladiator* gave an accurate representation. One comment received raised questions about how film should be framed:

> While I don't think that movies based loosely on history should educate, it's important that they at least acknowledge that only the names and dates (sometimes) are the same and everything else is simply for the audience's pleasure. Otherwise people who will never read a book or watch the history channel's 'what really happened?' will receive a very skewed portrayal that they take as fact.

A number of reactions to the idea that a film should therefore state clearly whether it has a fictional plot were also revealing:

> A: Claims to accurate historical representation are most likely to be made during the initial marketing of the film. The audience takes for granted that it is not factual due to its medium as a film as opposed to documentary.

> B: It should be, and usually is, the other way. Rather than make a statement that the film is fictional, if it's an attempt to make a truthful film, then they should say that it is based on real events.

> C: Definitely no, how would they do it effectively? You can't watch a film that starts by saying the following didn't happen! What's the alternative, putting a footnote at the end of the film? That would just make the past two hours a complete waste of time. If there is any place for telling a correct historical overview then stick it on the DVD extras. I fully believe that if the film is good enough then it will spark some interest for the viewer to find out more on their own. History is always more complex than a film could possible do justice too [*sic*].

> D: I find films that 'change' history really bug me. The example of *U571* is great. They changed history to make a story and people got upset. They then had to conclude the film saying 'this didn't happen, the Brits and the Poles found the Enigma first' which then shatters the whole illusion of the film. Makes me question why the film chose real events in the

first place if they have to say 'all of this is a lie' at the end. I appreciate sometimes real life doesn't make great cinema but surely that is the challenge of making great cinema?

Claims about historical representation are often made during the marketing of the film; Neil Marshall made it clear *Centurion* was his own interpretation of events and not an attempt to imply that the events of the film were 'historically perfect'.[28] This is an obvious problem for those who do not read all the marketing material, yet the implication is that film is a medium which will not provide accurate representations and should not try to maintain otherwise. This is expanded upon in the second comment; audiences should know that what they are seeing is entirely fictional unless they are told otherwise. This is backed up by my data, as only two people believed that historical film would not alter events to suit its plot. The third comment's reference to DVD's special features specifically relates to the *Centurion* DVD, which contains a mini-documentary entitled *The Lost Legion* in which Marshall offers explanations behind his decisions in making the film. One insight explains his choice of using Scottish Gaelic as the language for the Picts. The main theories suggest that the closest similar language to what the Picts spoke is Welsh; however, Marshall believed that Gaelic would seem more authentic. Despite the comments that there was no requirement for films to make a declaration of their fictitious nature, my survey showed that twenty-four people agreed that changes in events do not disrupt their viewing experience, yet forty agreed that changes do not concern them if the film makes a declaration of its fictitious nature from the outset.

The contention, therefore, arises through framing the film as fictional without disrupting the illusion and enjoyment of the film. The following comment links back to our earlier analysis of different forms of cinema. Here, a clear distinction is made between historical fiction and historical drama:

> I am generally bothered by any inaccuracy and inconsistency with the source material, but in the case of *Gladiator*, where there is no attempt to try and tell a truthful story, I am not bothered in the slightest. While I would like to see an accurate portrayal of ancient life in a big budget movie, I believe there is both a place for this and historical fiction on the market.

How *Gladiator* is framed could explain the perception of those who thought that the events shown were accurate. Peter Lamont's article 'Magician as Conjurer' presents Erving Goffman's theory about the frame in relation to magic and psychic fraud:

Figure 5.3 Etain (Olga Kurylenko) in *Centurion*. Respondents' rejection of make-up revealed differences between accuracy and plausibility in the historical film.

A frame analysis of magic and psychic fraud actually points up the fundamental differences between the two forms of fabrication rather than the superficial similarities. Magic clearly involves fabrication since there is an intentional effort to induce a false belief about what is going on, but this is typical only in the case within the frame of the trick itself. If asked what is going on, for example, an observer might state that a coin is in the magician's hand (when it is really up his sleeve) or that a box is empty (when it secretly contains a rabbit). Nevertheless, outside the frame of the trick there is no fabrication, since at that level the observer knows what is going on – i.e. that s/he is watching a magic trick . . . This is quite different in the case of psychic fraud, where the intention is to induce a false belief not only about the details of the event, but also about its authenticity.[29]

This theory can usefully be transposed onto historical epic through Goffman's concept of the frame.[30] Is the director trying to pass off their portrayal of events as a true representation, like the psychic frauds, or have they made it clear that the audience are watching a trick, an entertaining fabrication of events? Unfortunately it is not always so clear-cut. The opening narration to *The Fall of the Roman Empire* tries to explain the film's place within history while trying to establish its role in the collapse of the Empire. In reality the events shown were inaccurate and largely irrelevant to Rome's ultimate demise. A voiceover at the end was then needed to try to justify its title and opening narration. The introduction appears to frame the film as fact, which is surprising given Mann's take on his film:

> All we were trying to do was dramatize how an Empire fell. If everything [in such a film] is historical, then you don't have dramatic liberty . . .

inaccuracies from an historical point of view . . . are not important. The actual facts, only very few people know. The most important thing is that you get the feeling of history.[31]

This appears to contradict the film; the facts are not important, yet the film tries to use them to justify its plot. *Gladiator* offers a similar attempt to place itself within a historical timeframe. The opening title scroll reads:

> At the height of its power the Roman Empire was vast, stretching from the deserts of Africa to the borders of Northern England.
>
> Over one quarter of the World's population lived and died under the rule of the Caesars.
>
> In the Winter of 180 AD Emperor Marcus Aurelius' twelve year campaign against the Barbarian tribes in Germania was drawing to an end.

By defining the events within a specific year, the film established itself within a specific point in history involving a real historical figure. However, the historical chronology has already been changed; there was no battle under Marcus Aurelius in 180 ce, although it is the year of Marcus Aurelius' death and Commodus' ascension. The geographical references are inconsistent, 'Northern England' being a modern name and 'Germania' a Roman name. These are clear indications to the specialist, but would the non-specialist be aware that the campaigns actually ended in 179 CE? There is no indication that the film is framed as fiction, which raises new questions about whether it is possible to frame a film set within real events as fictional without shattering its illusion.

In *Inglourious Basterds* (Tarantino 2009), Adolf Hitler is killed in a French cinema in 1944. The film's title scroll reads 'Once-upon-a-time in Nazi occupied France'; the phrase 'once-upon-a-time' offers a clear indication of the fictitious plot which is to follow. *Inglourious Basterds* is obviously not an attempt to make a historically accurate picture, and there is no requirement for a title screen informing audiences that the events are fictitious or a postscript saying how the war really panned out. The audience should be well aware that what they are seeing is nothing more than pure fiction. Both *Inglourious Basterds* and *Gladiator* involve the interaction of fictional and historical individuals within a vastly altered chronological timeline, yet the respondents' reactions suggest that Tarantino's expression of artistic creativity is acceptable while Scott is criticised for adding fiction to the treatment of a period which is arguably less important on a contemporary global scale.

Thus, it is perhaps the *popular* understanding of the past which allows us a way out of this contradiction. It is fair to assume that the majority of people would know more about the Second World War than they do about ancient

Rome. This suggests that there is a relative scale of historical importance where a film based around events which are not common knowledge should be more accurate (or else more open about its inaccuracy) so as not to mislead its audience. The difference between *Gladiator* and *Inglourious Basterds* is, therefore, how they are framed, which influences how they are received. Tarantino's method would not fit with *Gladiator*, yet *Centurion* uses a different tactic entirely and, interestingly, only one participant believed its plot was accurate. *Centurion*'s title card sets the date and location of the film; however, the first dialogue is a voiceover from Quintus Dias, the film's protagonist and narrator, saying, 'My name is Quintus Dias. I am a soldier of Rome. And this is neither the beginning nor the end of my story.' Audiences will be familiar with the use of the narrator as a common device in telling fiction, and hearing Quintus Dias tell his story allows the audience to develop a bond with him. The importance of this is clear:

> I went into the film knowing that there was no record of what happened to the Ninth Legion and so this allowed me to accept several aspects of the story. [Though] the addition of the love story felt out of place, this was an acceptable addition to the story as after going on this journey I obviously didn't want to see him die. I knew that this addition to the story allowed the opportunity for him to survive and the film to still offer an explanation for the disappearance of the legion.

The use of the narrator frames the film as fictional, immediately setting the expectation of the viewer. An earlier comment said that if a film is based on real events it should state this as a requirement, otherwise it should always be assumed that it is fictitious. In theory this would work; however, the way in which films are presented is not always readily accepted. One film which came in for some criticism in this regard was *King Arthur* (2004):

> I recognise that films are there [sic] trying to provide entertainment and therefore it doesn't bother me when film makers change historical events in order to better present their story. What does bother me is when they change things for the sake of it or try to argue that their version is the truth. For example, as an archaeologist, I find *King Arthur*, with its claims of having been based on recent archaeological research, to be particularly annoying.

This would suggest that *Gladiator* and *King Arthur* are received differently; although it makes no statement about its fictional nature, *Gladiator* also does not claim to have any historical basis. This position is reinforced by other responses to the survey, which suggest that if a film makes no historical claims nor states that it is based on real events then it can be as creative as it likes:

> A historical frame is important for a historical film, but unless the film explicitly claims to be an accurate portrayal of events, I personally find artistic licence within that frame generally acceptable.

This represents an acceptance that any film is implicitly framed as fictional as long as it does not explicitly state otherwise. However, even a fictitious historical focus was also raised as a potential way in which film can educate:

> I believe that historical, or period films, have the ability to stir interest in human/world history which might otherwise go un-evaluated or un-researched by the lay public. It is in this function that cinema serves to provide a value to society today. For example, a film which takes place on Hadrian's Wall in antiquity would raise awareness of the importance of such an archaeological site today and assist in preserving such rich and informative sites. The same principle could be applied throughout the world.

Accordingly, film could serve to promote further relations between our society and our history. *Centurion* depicts the savage nature of the war with the Picts that brought about the construction of Hadrian's Wall, so instead of just encouraging individual research the film could potentially attract attention to and interest in British archaeology. In light of this suggestion the disparagement of *King Arthur* can be re-evaluated and, instead of criticism, perhaps praise could be offered instead. This idea offers a challenge to the academics who bemoan the lack of accuracy in historical films' plots; rather than experts analysing everything historical films do wrong when it comes to educating non-specialists, the film challenges them to look to see what they do right. My research has highlighted the fact that there are audiences out there who, while primarily wanting to be entertained, have identified numerous ways in which cinema can potentially educate and inspire them to be interested in the ancient world.

CONCLUSIONS

In analysing non-specialists' perceptions of the historical epic I have encountered a wide range of results and, while there are extreme points of view at each end, there has generally been a consistent set of views provoking pertinent debate. Audiences tend to absolve the historical film of any responsibility for maintaining a level of accuracy, the general consensus being that the creation of a *believable* world on screen, which meets prior conceptions and expectations, is far more important than the creation of an *authentic* world. This was backed up by discussion of how the genre, and cinema, can educate in alternative ways. The main debates about the genre consequently form around the level of detail which is required to capture this believable feel, referred to as 'the essence of history', and what impacts on and influences it. There appears to be a common understanding between directors and audiences of the genre in its current guise, with both Scott and Marshall consciously making changes which alter the authenticity and accuracy of their film in the aim of creating a more believable picture. There appears to be a clear preconception about what films exploring the time period termed 'ancient Rome' should be like. These preconceptions can, however, be counter-productive; one participant revealed how they thought the events of *The Fall of the Roman Empire* were inaccurate purely because they had seen *Gladiator* first and that is how they expected and understood Marcus Aurelius' death and Commodus' reign to have happened. Such seemingly throwaway comments therefore reveal an important secondary hypothesis which, in retrospect, was evident throughout all my research: that what audiences want to see is becoming heavily influenced by what they have come to expect to see. On this basis, given the resurgence of popularity of these films, the likelihood of a historical film being as accurate as possible is, if anything, liable to become more and more remote.

NOTES

1. See, for instance, Martin M. Winkler (ed.), *Troy: From Homer's Iliad to Hollywood Epic* (Oxford: Blackwell, 2007); Martin M. Winkler (ed.), *Gladiator: Film and History* (Oxford: Blackwell, 2005); Martin M. Winkler (ed.), *Classical Myth and Culture in the Cinema* (Oxford: Oxford University Press, 2001); Martin M. Winkler (ed.), *The Fall of the Roman Empire: Film and History* (Oxford: Wiley-Blackwell, 2009); Monica S. Cyrino, *Big Screen Rome* (Oxford: Wiley-Blackwell, 2005); Maria Wyke, *Projecting the Past: Ancient Rome, Cinema, and History* (New York: Routledge, 1997); Jon Solomon, *The Ancient World in the Cinema* (New Haven, CT: Yale University Press, 2001). For an excellent overview of the field, see Joanna Paul, 'Cinematic Receptions of Antiquity: The Current State of Play', *Classical Receptions Journal*, 2 (2010), pp. 136–55.
2. Pierre Sorlin, *The Film in History: Restaging the Past* (Oxford: Blackwell, 1980), pp. 19-22.
3. For specifically historical analysis of *Gladiator*, see Winkler, *Gladiator: Film and History*, and Cyrino, *Big Screen Rome*, pp. 207–57.
4. For a more detailed discussion of this see Chapter 6 of Jeffrey Richards' *Hollywood's Ancient Worlds* (London: Continuum, 2008), pp. 157–90.
5. See in particular Robert A. Rosenstone, *Visions of the Past: The Challenge of Film to Our Idea of History* (Cambridge, MA: Harvard University Press, 1995); Robert A. Rosenstone, *History on Film/Film on History* (Harlow: Longman/Pearson, 2006).
6. Winkler, *Gladiator: Film and History*, p. 17.

7. Ibid., p. 17.
8. See Kathleen M. Coleman, 'The Pedant Goes to Hollywood: The Role of the Academic Consultant', in *Gladiator: Film and History* (Oxford: Wiley-Blackwell, 2005), pp. 45–52.
9. Coleman, 'The Pedant Goes to Hollywood', p. 47; p. 49.
10. Ibid., p. 48. Coleman's experiences are also eloquently echoed by Kristina Milnor in her essay 'What I Learned as Historical Consultant for *Rome*' in Monica S. Cyrino (ed.), *Rome Season One: History Makes Television* (Oxford: Blackwell, 2008), pp. 42–8.
11. Winkler, *Gladiator*, p. 17.
12. Robert Stam and Alessandra Raengo, *Literature and Film: A Guide to the Theory and Practice of Film Adaptation* (Oxford: Blackwell, 2005), p. 14.
13. Allen Ward, 'Gladiator in Historical Perspective', in Winkler, *Gladiator: Film and History*, p. 32.
14. Stam and Raengo, *Literature and Film*, p. 22.
15. Ibid., p. 23.
16. Ward, 'Gladiator in Historical Perspective', p. 34.
17. 'I've read a brief history of Commodus the Emperor . . .', comment made by Kronos251 on 14 August 2009, http://imdb.com/title/tt0172495/bcard/thread/137326679?d=1451 71005&p=1#145171005, last accessed 14 July 2010.
18. 'Joaquin Phoenix delivered one of the most perfect depictions of . . .', comment made by Rorysfirstkiss on 6 May 2009, http://imdb.com/title/tt0172495/board/thread/13732667 9?d=137326679&p=1#37326679, last accessed 14 July 2010.
19. Cyrino, *Big Screen Rome*, p. 1.
20. Sandra R. Joshel, Margaret Malamud and Donald T. McGuire Jr (eds), *Imperial Projections: Ancient Rome in Modern Popular Culture* (Baltimore, MD: Johns Hopkins University Press, 2001), p. 6.
21. Cyrino, *Big Screen Rome*, p. 1.
22. *U571* told the story of the capture of the German Enigma machine by an American submarine crew. The Enigma machine was actually captured by a British submarine crew in August 1941, four months before America joined the war. A title card was added at the end of the film explaining the truth after heavy pressure from British veterans.
23. Diana Landau (ed.), *Gladiator: The Making of the Ridley Scott Epic* (New York: Newmarket Press, 2000), p. 28.
24. Richard Koszarski, *Hollywood Directors, 1941–1976* (Oxford: Oxford University Press, 1977), p. 336.
25. Juklemann, 'Familia Gladiatoria: The Heroes of the Amphitheatre', in E. Kohne and C. Ewigleben (eds), *Gladiators and Caesars: The Power of Spectacle in Ancient Rome* (Berkeley, CA: University of California Press, 2000), pp. 31–74.
26. Ward, 'Gladiator in Historical Perspective', p. 40.
27. Tricia Johnson, 'Far From Rome', *Entertainment Weekly*, 19 May 2000, pp. 8–9 (p. 9) (cited in Monica Cyrino, 'Gladiator and Contemporary American Society', in *Gladiator: Film and History*, pp. 124–49 (p. 138)).
28. Jeff Otto, 'Interview with Neil Marshall for *Centurion*', Dark Horizons.com, http://www.darkhorizons.com/features/1560/neil-marshall-for-centurion (8 August 2010), last accessed 20 August 2010.
29. Peter Lamont, 'Magician as conjuror: a frame analysis of Victorian mediums', *Early Popular Visual Culture*, 4.1 (2006), pp. 131–42.
30. Goffman, E., *Frame Analysis: An Essay on the Organisation of Experience* (London: Harper Row, 1974).
31. Koszarski, p. 336.

PART II
Epic Aesthetics and Genre

CHAPTER 6

Colour in the Epic Film: *Alexander* and *Hero*

Robert Burgoyne[1]

Charged with symbolic meaning and laden with cultural associations, colour is one of the emblematic devices of the epic film, conveying stylised messages of sexuality, race, and power in ways that sometimes overwrite the genre's ostensible themes. A key feature of the genre since the appearance of the tinted and stencilled Italian epics of the 1910s, colour technology and design constitute a direct line of formal innovation that extends from the earliest iterations of the genre to the exalted colour symphonies of the present. The significance of colour in the epic, however, has largely been ignored. Although chromatic design communicates emotion, cultural value and technological sophistication, it has to date been discussed in very limited ways – as if the aesthetic language of colour in epic film were superfluous or incidental, having little to do with the deeper meanings and pleasures of the form.

When we consider the unusual persistence and importance of colour throughout the history of the epic genre, the absence of critical discussion is even more noteworthy. Although the striking chromatic values of early film history – the majority of films were tinted, stencilled, or toned in multiple vivid hues – were actively suppressed from about 1908, colour remained an expressive and significant feature of epic form.[2] Associated most immediately with prestige, exoticism and the projection of cultural and cinematic achievement, the chromatic features of the epic film also helped shape the large thematic questions of the genre – the conflicts between barbarism and civilisation, carnality and reason, masculine and feminine.

The recent appearance of critical works that consider the cultural significance of colour in painting, literature and film may provide a new way of approaching the subject of colour in the epic film. In this chapter, I consider Oliver Stone's *Alexander* (2005) and Zhang Yimou's *Hero* (2003) as films that bring several new perspectives into frame. I argue that colour design in both films provides something like a subversive counterpoint, an internal critical commentary. Counterposing the narrative patterning that dominates these films – the rise and fall of the hero, the unfolding of a heroic destiny – colour asserts a kind of alternative vision of history, centred on the triumph of emotion and desire, a message conveyed in sensual form. The formal articulation of these messages, moreover, expressed in the films' vivid chromatic designs, conveys an overtonal message that contrasts with the overarching 'critical-ethical' horizon of epic form.[3] In *Alexander*, for example, the florid tints and hues long associated with barbarism, carnality and the feminine seem to surge from the screen to challenge and reorder the colour palette traditionally associated with classical civilisation. In *Hero*, similarly, the exorbitantly coloured memory sequences, rendered in intense red, green, blue and white, are juxtaposed with the sober discourse of sacrifice and martyrdom for national unification that dominates the present-tense sequences, rendered in muted tones of black and grey. The lavish coloration of these memory scenes, most of which emphasise female knights, or the *nuxia pian*, might be read as a kind of alternative history to the film's ostensible message of individual sacrifice for collective purpose. By highlighting the role of colour as a symbol of cultural meaning, both films bring the seeming ephemera, the ornamental and the decorative dimension of epic film, the colours of costume and the symbolism of set design into thematic focus.

In a provocative study of the ideological encoding of colour in Western art and theory, David Batchelor writes that colour is understood as 'the mythical, savage state out of which civilization, the nobility of the human spirit, slowly, heroically, has lifted itself'.[4] Moreover, he writes that 'colour is often close to the body and never far from sexuality, be it heterosexual or homosexual. When sex comes into the story, colour tends to come with it.'[5] The history of the epic film would seem to bear this out. Among the innumerable associations of savagery, sex and colour in epic films – and the corresponding absence of colour to depict the noble realm of a higher spiritual plane – I will cite here only two or three of the most ready examples. In *Gladiator* (Scott 2000), Maximus' body is drizzled with blood as he descends for the first time into the underworld of the arena. 'Red is the colour of the gods', his fellow gladiator informs him, 'you are in their favour.' Maximus' long travail as a gladiator is marked by increasingly vivid colour cinematography, highlighted by the golden sand of the Colosseum, the gleam of armour, the dazzling white, red and purple of the décor. The barbaric richness of Maximus' life among the mongrel nation of gladiators, the subalterns of the empire, is in striking contrast to his frequent flash-forwards to the mystic land of Elysium, which appears initially as a grey wall with a gate, and later as an idealised landscape from which most colour has been drained. Elysium, in the film's chromatic scheme, is painted in faded, muted tones, lightly tinted with blue. The afterlife – the location of Maximus' long-awaited reunion with his wife and son – is curiously pictured here in almost dismal colours, an enfeebled palette that has a twilight gloom about it, perhaps to signify a kind of elevation or transcendence from the fleshly realm.

Similarly, in *Ben-Hur* (Wyler 1959) the hero's sojourn in Imperial Rome and in Palestine unfolds as a kaleidoscope of colours. Rugs, tapestries and costumed characters abound, as Ben-Hur's Roman benefactor offers him a noble lineage and the riches that go with it, and his Arab benefactor offers him the opportunity to drive his horses in the Circus. Ben-Hur's visit in the Arab tent is replete with the trappings of luxury, a spectacle of saturated colour, providing an emphatic shorthand for the delights of the Eastern world. At the film's conclusion, however, as the crucifixion and death of Christ unfolds, the film shifts chromatic keys dramatically, darkening the sky, muting the set in greys and blues, clothing Ben-Hur, his sister and his mother in drab cloth. The release of Ben-Hur's family from the curse of leprosy, and the symbolic redemption of the world that is suggested here with a lightning bolt, is rendered by flooding the screen with the red of Christ's blood, and then, oddly, constraining the colour, reducing the palette, suppressing the chromatic range to brown, grey and shadow, a decisive subduing of the vitality and energy communicated in the film's earlier scenes.

Perhaps the most striking example of the cultural messages embedded in colour in the epic film can be found in recent Chinese epics, a genre in which striking hues are dominant. In the extraordinary films *Hero, House of Flying Daggers* (Yimou 2004) and *Red Cliff* (Woo 2008), for example, colour defines cultural values that are strongly associated with aesthetic traditions of painting, theatre and philosophy. The design-intensive mise-en-scène featured in these films foregrounds colour almost as a kind of metalanguage, registering both nation and historical tradition as well as communicating what Batchelor calls an 'ahistorical, extra-linguistic, sensual embrace . . . that ravishing intimation of paradise'.[6] Taking on a specifically art cinema quality, the epic here can be characterised explicitly as a colour genre, one in which the rich palette, the sumptuous display of a series of enamelled frames, functions as an aesthetic language that is overpowering and seductive, and that often works in counterpoint to themes of duty and sacrifice. Rather than a threatening state of savagery, colour here signifies the meeting place of national feeling and aesthetic form.

In Oliver Stone's *Alexander*, the eponymous hero embraces the alternative modes of life symbolised by colour, adopting the colours and clothing of the East in order to embody in his person the antinomies of ancient and modern, masculine and feminine, West and East. Painting his face, costuming himself in a lion headdress, adopting the ornamental style of the East, the titular hero of *Alexander* conveys a very different heroic narrative of the Macedonian conqueror from what we might expect, bringing to light the virtual narrative immanent in the story, a possible world of absorption and crossing over. In this regard, the film can be read as a sustained reconsideration of one of the central tropes of epic film. Typically, the epic hero gains the authority, the mandate to complete his quest only after becoming one with the multitude – falling into slavery, becoming a nomad – drawing from the multitude a sense of purpose and nobility. Forced into a period of wandering, exile, and nomadism, the hero in many epics becomes one with the mongrel and subaltern worlds – a crucial motif in films such as *The Ten Commandments* (De Mille 1956), *Spartacus* (Kubrick 1960) and *Ben-Hur*. The encounter with the refugee and the dispossessed, the slave and the subaltern, provides the hero with strength of purpose; by becoming a nomad, the character discovers his true course.

In *Alexander*, however, the radical dissolution of boundaries and the incorporation of the Other become the entire point and purpose of the hero's narrative, a theme that is conveyed most effectively through colour. Rejecting the world of Macedonia, a domain riven by hierarchy, jealousy and rivalry, Alexander embraces the 'barbaric' styles of Babylon and India, a theme rendered emphatically in the changing colour schemes of the film, with its most elaborate sequences of chromatic invention occurring in scenes that are set in explicit contrast with Macedonia. The film juxtaposes three major colour movements defining the three principal settings of the film: Macedonia, Babylon and India. Each communicates a set of messages through colour, messages that are underlined and amplified by juxtaposition. Cutting from Macedonia to Babylon, and from India to Macedonia, Stone constructs a kind of intellectual montage of colour contrasts that augments and to some extent shapes the larger messages of the film.

The cinematographer for the film, Rodrigo Prieto, has discussed the use of coloured filters in *Alexander*, and stated in an interview that Stone wanted the Macedonia sequences to have a pellucid, 'innocent' look filled with primary colours.[7] Indeed, the diurnal, exterior scenes set in Macedonia are exceptionally crisp compositions, almost abstract in their bleached clarity. The 'innocence' that Stone wishes to achieve, however, is deceptive; the whiteness of the Macedonian scenes seems to me to be aggressively white; as Batchelor says, 'There is a kind of white that is more than white . . . that [doesn't] really admit the presence of other worlds. Or it [does] so grudgingly, resentfully, and absolutely without compassion.'[8] The transparent air of Macedonia, without viscosity or weight, produces whiteness not as the innocent mark of a new world, but as the sign of a civilisation that Alexander must cast off, a civilisation which, as Batchelor writes, 'did its work on everything around it, and nothing escaped'.[9]

The cave scene in Pella is exemplary. After brilliantly taming the wild stallion Bucephalus, the boy Alexander is ushered to the caves by his father, who instructs him on the duties of kingship and the costs of pride and ambition. Archaic illustrations on the walls, nearly monochromatic, are incised in black silhouette on dull stone, illustrating the fates of Prometheus, Oedipus, Heracles and Achilles, heroes whose ambition, Phillip asserts, offended the gods. The dialogue here is of overreaching and punishment, and the colour scheme is a muted, burnt shade that is drained of all lustre. The one colour that stands out, illuminated by Philip's torch, is the red of the heroes' blood seemingly flowing down the rock. Although these illustrations are not based on the artistic forms of the known historical past, but rather are inventions on Stone's part, they serve a distinct narrative and symbolic role, setting Philip in the position of an intimate but also in the role of punisher of youthful ambition. It is not by accident, it seems to me, that the first illustration Philip explicates in this scene is a primitive drawing of Prometheus being attacked by the eagle, a scene illuminated by Philip's flaming torch thrust tellingly towards the wall painting as he describes Prometheus' fate. Here the world of the mythic past is reduced to two colours, and two emotions – ambition and suffering. Deeply ambivalent, the scene begins as Philip's introduction into the hard responsibilities of kingship and the sacrifices it entails, but ends with Alexander proclaiming, to his father's unease, his determination to one day appear upon this wall, to challenge the gods and have his name proclaimed among the greats. Concerning the wall paintings in this scene, Oliver Stone writes:

> In that cave in Pella, Philip brings the full weight of his Greek classical pessimism to bear on his son's idealism . . . This one-eyed Cyclops brings us back to the archaic age of Titans and Olympians when fathers ate their sons, and sons murdered their fathers, and committed incest with their mothers . . . He implies that the human race, as in tales of the Garden of Eden, is cursed from its inception.[10]

In striking contrast, the sequence of Alexander's entry into Babylon is depicted as a cornucopia of colour, movement, and blissful sensation. Dazzling blues, greens, pinks, and whites greet the hero, lavishly dressed Babylonians offer tributes of jewels and gold, floral petals of pink and white rain down upon the hero. As Ptolemy says in voiceover, 'at this one glorious moment in time, Alexander was loved, by all'. With the scene overflowing with colour, as Batchelor reminds us, sex can't be far behind. Once he arrives at Darius' palace, Alexander and his men discover the harem, a study in styles of physical beauty, with men, women and eunuchs seemingly equally dispersed among the swaying multitude. Here, Alexander is introduced to Bagoas, in a scene that condenses sexual freedom with the freedom from constraint implied by colour.

Lloyd Llewellyn-Jones has written a lengthy and critical analysis of the harem sequence in *Alexander*, describing it as an Orientalist fantasy, a negative judgement with which Stone concurs.[11] The long tradition of Orientalist

Figure 6.1 The hero's (Colin Farrell) entry into Babylon in *Alexander* (2005): 'at this one glorious moment in time, Alexander was loved by all'.

projections in art, literature and film centring on harem sequences, from Delacroix and Ingres to D. W. Griffith's *Intolerance* (1916) – which Stone screened for his production team – is more or less summarised in Stone's admittedly retrograde treatment. Nevertheless, the specific dimension of colour serves here to communicate a larger meaning. In an essay on Giotto's colour style, Julia Kristeva associates colour with escape: 'colour escapes censorship'; through colour, the subject escapes its alienation.[12] Alexander's 'escape' from Macedonia is registered, I argue, as an escape into colour. Cutting directly from the dark foretellings in the cave at Pella to the plenary earthly delights in Babylon, Alexander as conqueror also reveals a nobility of mind and spirit, offering freedom to all of Darius' slaves and preserving the noble status and position of Darius' sister. Here, colour enlarges the character; far from being coded as savage, it is a sign of civilisation – the older, more magnificent civilisation of Babylon that Philip never saw, and that Alexander and Hephaestion both admire. It speaks, as Batchelor writes, 'of nobility'.[13]

The death scene of Philip, rendered in the primary, 'innocent' colours Prieto describes, serves as the core of Stone's drama and establishes the conundrum that plagues Alexander throughout his life. In the detailed commentary Stone makes about the film, he writes that the murder of Philip casts suspicion on both Alexander and on Olympias. Crediting Joanna Paul with keen insight into the 'single action' of narrative called for by Aristotle,[14] Stone remarks that 'the theme, the main action of this piece was always murder – the murder of Philip – and whether Alexander was involved or not'. And further:

> Is he complicit because of his mother's hate? Can he bring her to justice, as Orestes did his mother? What a horrible twist of fate to have to choose between matricide and patricide . . . And because of this dishonourable desire in himself for power at any price, we are suggesting that Alexander will always feel complicit.[15]

The scene unfolds in the clear light of the Mediterranean afternoon, in lightness and clarity. It is vivid colour, however, that organises and shapes our perception of the sequence. From the very first glance, the spectator is put on the alert: the whites are too white; the red of Olympias' shift is too red; the primary, saturated colours are so intense that they function almost as a series of caution signs, shouted warnings, a mood reinforced by the near-toppling of the god statue that Philip erects to himself. As Philip prepares to celebrate his victory over the Greeks by staging a tribute to himself, a celebration that takes place in a theatre, Alexander asks to stay by his side, as if he has a premonition. Philip rejects his offer, accusing Alexander of political motivations, and sends him out of frame. But as Philip steps into the ante-room of the theatre, the shadows of the room engulf him, and the scene shades to black. When he emerges from the ante-room into the main arena, Olympias, clothed in scarlet, is situated in the centre of the frame. Philip raises his arms, and the camera follows, providing a brief shot of sky and then a blinding image of the sun that seems to wash all colour from the frame. As a young soldier approaches to begin the honours, clothed in a scarlet cape, he kisses Philip on the lips; the scene then cuts to Alexander, who now remembers the soldier as a youth, a young man who Philip had allowed to be abused. The man breaks off the kiss, spits on Philip, and runs him through with his sword, with the red of his assassin's cape nearly blotting out the scene.

For the spectator, the violence of the scene is already foreshadowed and encoded in the colour imagery. The black and white frames that bracket Philip's murder, the wild red of Olympias' costume and the assassin's cloak, the bleached backdrop of the theatre and the garish colours of the statues of the gods: the colour details stand out as a kind of visual punctuation against the chalk white of the amphitheatre. And as Philip steps into the dark cave of the ante-room, it recalls the cave scene at Pella, where dark and light cohabit. The colour that has historically been dialled back in narrative films, seen either as a distraction or as a spectacle that would lead the viewer's attention away from the loftier goals of narrative, goes underground in epic films, and reappears in scenes of violence or sex.

The summit of the film's colour design is in the use of colour infrared film stock in the massive battle scene set in India. With the Macedonian cavalry ranged against Indian elephants in a dense forest, the battle turns against Alexander's troops. He charges directly in to wage single combat against the Indian king riding on an elephant. In the words of Oliver Stone, 'Alexander's action is a classic heroic sacrifice, meant to motivate his lagging men into action – as was historically true at the battle of Multan, when this suicidal heroism in fact turned the tide of battle in favour of the Greeks, but led to Alexander's most grievous wound'.[16] He is cut down with an arrow to the chest, and falls from his horse. Directly after his fall the film shifts chromatic keys, shading to bright, voluptuous red. At various points in this sequence, colour overwhelms form entirely; reddish hues flood the screen, colouring the sky, the leaves of the trees, the flesh and armour of the human figures. Blood appears yellow. Here, in some shots, differentiated mass and volume almost disappear; the distinction between surface and depth, near and far, positive and negative space nearly evaporates. The operatic intensification of colour, form and movement, with the shots alternating between frantic montage and long, slowed, stylised movement is reinforced by the sound track, which combines an orchestral accompaniment of tragic power with the sounds of human struggle in battle.

Rodrigo Prieto says about this scene that 'in the ecstasies of near-death, Alexander might see things that aren't normally visible to the eye, and in turn, the Macedonians might see things in him they hadn't seen before ... perhaps in a moment of enhanced perception, you can "see" the invisible and understand another reality'.[17] Roland Barthes writes, 'If I were a painter, I should paint only colours: this field seems to me freed of both the Law ... and Nature.'[18] The quotations, like the sequence, are revealing. The 'ecstasy' of Alexander, in Prieto's view, is expressed in colour, free of what Barthes calls the Law, and also free of Nature, of photography's supposed ontological responsibility to imitate nature. In this scene the film pushes through both narrative convention and pictorial form to give free rein to the colourist, fauvist impulse, an expression of primary emotion.

The expressive, primal dimensions of epic form, so often buried in the linear order of narrative, can be found, I have argued, in the colour, in the violence, and in the vertiginous camera movements that depart from convention – from the law and from nature – and that express the deepest messages embedded in the genre. Vivian Sobchack has written of the 'surge and splendor' of epic form as reproducing a sense of the spectator's 'being in history', of experiencing the sweep, majesty, and sense of meaningfulness that historical experience confers.[19] I would like to take this one step further and describe the surge and splendour of epic form as a primary experience of somatic empathy, of emotional arousal concentrated in form, in the phantasmagoria of colour and movement which serves here as an emotional container of meaning.[20]

HERO (2003)

In Zhang Yimou's *Hero*, the use of colour as an emotional container of meaning is perhaps even more pronounced than in *Alexander*. The primary conflict of the film, which centres on the opposition between unity and freedom, is explicitly displaced from the narrative structure to the colour register; in other words, displaced from the 'core' of the film to the surface, coded into expressions of hue, shade and saturation. Primarily a director of surfaces, Zhang, in the words of Rey Chow, shifts attention away from message to the form of the utterance:

> 'meaning', she writes . . . is displaced onto the level of surface exchange. Such a displacement has the effect of emptying 'meaning' from the conventional space – the core, the depth, or the inside . . . and reconstructing it in a new locus, the locus of the surface, which not only shines but 'glosses', which looks, stares, and speaks.[21]

In this essay, Chow traces and describes a deep-seated cultural hierarchy in Chinese philosophy based on oppositions of surface and depth, shallowness and profundity. The filmmaker Zhang, although renowned for his colour cinematography in films like *Raise the Red Lantern* (1991), *House of Flying Daggers* and *Hero*, and for his ethnographic appropriation of the artefacts and surfaces of the past, has often been labelled a superficial director, an artist whose visual flair sacrifices depth for surface design, alluring cinematography and, not least, fetishistic images of women. Chow argues that critiques of Zhang, however, mostly reiterate the traditional hierarchy of surface and depth in Chinese culture, and are thus folded into a conservative, traditional stance that regards visual brilliance, arresting images and surface style with suspicion.

To my mind, the analysis she provides can be compared to the suspicions regarding vivid colour in the West – what Batchelor calls the 'chromophobia' that characterises Western philosophy and aesthetics. Vibrant colour, as Batchelor writes, is associated with instinct and barbarism, but also with a kind of infantile shallowness. Restricted and subdued in early film in favour of narrative absorption and aesthetic uplift, and further restricted directly after the transition to Technicolor, vivid colour in Western film has historically been regarded with suspicion, and as a distraction from the depths of narrative content. And in critical reactions to the work of Zhang, it appears a comparable 'chromophobia' persists in a contemporary Chinese context.

The suspicions concerning Zhang as a superficial, sensational director extended, for some critics, to the narrative content of *Hero* as well. *Hero* has been critically condemned for its seeming acceptance of totalitarian rule, its apparent endorsement of the sacrifice of the individual for the sake of unity.[22]

Figure 6.2 *Hero* uses the traditional forms of Chinese culture, such as martial arts, music, calligraphy and painting, to attract a global audience.

The treatment of the first emperor of China as a figure of enlightenment in the film has proven particularly problematic, as the historical figure is known in history as a tyrant who insisted on conformity. Critical debate over *Hero* has been polarised, ranging from condemnation for its seeming support of despotism, to a keen appreciation of its use of Chinese idioms – martial arts, music, calligraphy and painting – to fashion an international art-house success, using the traditional forms of Chinese culture to attract a global audience.[23]

In my view, however, the film's extraordinary colour design invites us to consider an altogether different reading of the work, and to shift our focus from the narrative of sacrifice and conformity to the utopianising effect of cinematic aesthetics. As I have argued elsewhere, the magnifications of scale, the virtuosity of special effects, the detonations of violence and, especially, the climaxes of colour so characteristic of epic film create what Sobchack calls a 'carnal experience of history in film'.[24] Reading *Hero* in this light, as a carnal experience of history accessed through colour and movement, provides a way of understanding the film that overwrites the ostensible narrative message of unity over freedom.

Set in the Qin dynasty of 2,200 years ago, the framing story concerns a Chinese king who sets out to unite China's warring states. A possible assassin, Nameless, has been granted an audience with the king because of his claim that he has slain three of the king's sworn enemies, the legendary fighters Sky, Broken Sword and Flying Snow. The king asks Nameless to tell the story of his conquests, and to provide proof of his valour, as he is dubious that Nameless could be so skilled as to defeat all three. Nameless narrates the stories of his various encounters with the three warriors, each of which is expressed in a different colour, after which the king narrates his own version of what happened on the basis of what he knows of the protagonists. The principal colours of the narrations are white, red, blue and green. The film's cinematographer, Christopher Doyle, provides a brief allegorical reading of the colour scheme, essentially trying to deflect more elaborate interpretations of the 'meaning' of the colour narrations, which he says has been overdone: 'White', he writes, represents the 'truer sequence, and we chose red to suggest that passion has a different truth.'[25] Further:

> like the West, from Aristotle to Newton, Chinese conceptual systems associate colour with elements, objects, parts of the body and sounds ... I guess someone deserves a Ph.D. if he applies all of those concepts to *Hero*. As far as I'm concerned, these colours are nothing more or less than what they are.[26]

In this essay, Doyle seems to dismiss the idea of symbolic correspondences between the colours of the scenes and any larger philosophical tradition or specific coded meaning. Rejecting the notion of an iconography of colour, which would reduce the sensual style of the film to a conventionalised programme, the cinematographer insists that the colour values of the film are not reducible to an external system of symbolic expression. While I sympathise with Doyle's impatience with any kind of programmatic reading, I am not convinced that the colour design of *Hero* is simply a ravishing form of spectacular imagery devoid of semiotic importance. Rosalind Galt's recent work on the ornamental and the decorative in film, for example, has shown how the cosmetic surfaces of cinematic form serve expressive purposes that are often ignored or suppressed in critical analysis and evaluation.[27] Indeed, it seems to me that Zhang's powerful use of colour throughout his oeuvre might be read as a key device in his work, with vivid colour serving paradoxically as kind of camouflage or concealment, or perhaps better, a kind of masquerade. I will elaborate this point in the paragraphs below.

First, however, I would like to consider the film's use of colour in terms of epic form. Derek Elley's definition of epic as a work that 'transfigures the accomplishments of the past into an inspirational entertainment for the present, trading on received ideas of a continuing national or cultural consciousness' seems relevant here.[28] Moreover, the distinguishing formal characteristics of the film, its colour design, its use of martial arts, and its choreography, can be compared, I believe, to the central characteristics of epic cinema as set forth by Gilles Deleuze. Describing the epic film in terms of three horizons or perspectives – the monumental, the antiquarian, and the critical-ethical – Deleuze writes about the antiquarian aspects of epic form in ways that resonate with Zhang's films: 'Antiquarian history must reconstitute the forms which are habitual to the epoch: wars and confrontations ... actions and intimate customs, vast tapestries, clothes, finery, machines, weapons or tools, jewels, private objects'. The antiquarian horizon includes what he calls the 'colour-image' in epic film, where fabrics become a fundamental design element: 'In *Samson and Delilah* ... the display of cloth by the merchant and Samson's theft of the thirty tunics, constitute the two peaks of colour.'[29]

In *Hero*, the antiquarian and the monumental aspect of epic are plainly visible in the exotic mise-en-scène and in the elaborate choreographies of the duels. Where the film departs from and deepens the coded characteristics of epic, however, is in its rethinking – as in Stone's *Alexander* – of the critical-ethical horizon, the key dimension of epic form for Deleuze, the dimension that 'supervises and organizes' the rest.[30]

The critical-ethical horizon, I suggest, is articulated in the stories of the female knights, which are rendered in the exquisite colour sequences for which the film is famous. The film's use of the traditional narrative-folkloric form of the *wuxia pian*, or wandering knights-errant, is instructive – for this traditional form also includes stories of female knights, or the *nuxia pian*.[31] With the female knights Flying Snow and Moon carrying central importance, and the male character Nameless serving as the primary narrator of the framing story, the film combines the two narrative traditions. And in the scenes featuring female knights, exorbitant colour and movement reign. Here the film foregrounds the connection between emotional truth and a different kind of historical truth. In its emphasis on the *nuxia pian*, and in the elaborate orchestration of colour frequencies associated with the female knights, *Hero* presents a fascinating variation on typical epic themes, variations that are particularly interesting in light of Zhang Yimou's oeuvre. I suggest that the stories of the *nuxia* in *Hero*, and by extension the stories of several of the female protagonists in Zhang's films, may be read as coded representations of Zhang's authorial perspective, channelled and to some degree disguised in the female knights.

The framing story of the male 'hero' Nameless, by contrast, narrated in the present tense, unfolds with Nameless and the king seated in static poses in the king's chambers, a scene that is returned to several times in the course of the story. The framing scene is rendered in sombre colours of burnished black and shadow, with the only chromatic accent consisting of an array of candles and a large scroll bearing the crimson character for 'sword'. And colour is all but excluded from the first duel that features two male knights, Nameless and the warrior Sky. Set in a chess house, a kind of open air pavilion with rain

COLOUR IN THE EPIC FILM: *ALEXANDER* AND *HERO* 107

Figure 6.3 In its elaborate use of colour frequencies associated with female knights, *Hero* presents a variation on typical epic themes.

falling onto the chessboards, the floor, and the warriors, the duel is filmed in what is nearly a black and white palette, with only the subtlest tints of colour. Although this episode is defined by dramatic movement and sound, and is choreographed in the expressive, weightless style we have come to associate with Asian martial arts films, colour has been almost entirely drained from the scene.

Perhaps the contrast between the peaks of colour associated with the female knights and the subdued colour palette in the scenes that feature male characters – which foreground self-sacrifice in the name of an authoritarian collectivity – can be read as a coded protest, a symbolic form of resistance. The conflict between 'unity' and 'freedom' that structures the film's ostensible theme might be summarised not in the film's narrative progress but rather in the languages of emotion that pervade the film's colour design – in the opposition of the menacing black-clad armies and faceless masses of the king's nation versus the spectacular chromatic worlds associated with the *nuxia pian*. The film's surface design might then be read politically, with brilliant colour serving as a paradoxical form of camouflage, a masquerade that conveys messages of freedom and desire through the stylised registers of cinematic form.

CONCLUSION

Colour has begun to be addressed in film studies in ways that have illuminated the history of the medium in new ways. Far from being a rare and specialised technology, various colour techniques were applied to film from the very earliest period of filmmaking, indeed, from the medium's inception. Recent studies have also traced the broad implications of colour strategies in film, its role in shaping discourses of national identity, and its importance in framing narratives of modernity. Resistance to colour, however, has also been a prominent characteristic of Western modernity, as competing claims of social authority and cultural taste have often coalesced around colour as an emotional language, one that moves spectators along a continuum that includes sensual excitement and moral refinement.

In this chapter, I have considered colour in film from the perspective of genre studies, exploring the epic film as a case study. Vivid chromatic design has been a prominent feature of the epic from the first iterations of the genre form. Yet colour has been nearly ignored in critical discussions. By analysing the colour schemes of two exemplary works of film colour design, I have tried to show how the thematic and narrative registers of these two films is complicated and enriched by codes of colour. Often considered simply as spectacle or as merely decorative, colour asserts itself in these works as a primary strategy for rendering character, for articulating plot, and ultimately, for linking the historical past with ongoing critical and ethical issues in the present.

NOTES

1. A version of this chapter also appeared in *rebeca*, the journal of the Brazilian Society of Cinema Studies SOCINE, issue 2.2 (2012), pp. 14–39. We would like to thank the editorial board for their generosity in kindly allowing us to reprint it here.
2. The intense emotion associated with colour was thought to work against the goals of narrative absorption and moral uplift, and was actively dialled down during the second early period from about 1908 onwards so that colour would not distract from narrative meaning. Joshua Yumibe provides an excellent study of this process in *Moving Color*: 'The attempt to subdue color during this period also registers a genuine alarm at the sensual effect of color on the spectator. The supposedly black-and-white, American style of Biograph . . . and the significance of light tints and tones . . . can be thought of as an effort to keep color in its place, in the background subservient to narration.' Josh Yumibe, *Moving Color: Early Film, Mass Culture, Modernism* (New Brunswick, NJ: Rutgers University Press, 2012), pp. 121–2.
3. Gilles Deleuze, in *Cinema 1*, considers the epic in terms of the monumental, the antiquarian, and what he calls the critical-ethical horizons: 'Finally, the monumental and antiquarian conceptions of history would not come together so well without the ethical image which measures and organizes them both . . . The ancient or recent past must

submit to trial, go to court, in order to disclose what it is that produces decadence and what it is that produces new life; what the ferments of decadence and the germs of new life are, the orgy and the sign of the cross, the omnipotence of the rich and the misery of the poor.' *Cinema 1* (London: Continuum, 2005), pp. 155–6.
4. David Batchelor, *Chromophobia* (London: Reaktion Books, 2000), p. 23.
5. Ibid., p. 63.
6. Ibid., p. 79.
7. Rachel K. Bosely, 'Rodrigo Prieto, ASC, AMC Details His Battle Plan for *Alexander*, a Vivid Account of Alexander the Great's Remarkable Reign', *American Cinematographer* (November 2004). Available at: http://www.ascmag.com/magazine/nov04/alexander/page1.html, p. 3, last accessed 26 October 2012.
8. Batchelor, *Chromophobia*, p. 10.
9. Ibid., p. 10.
10. Paul Cartledge and Fiona Rose Greenland (eds), *Responses to Oliver Stone's* Alexander: *Film, History, and Cultural Studies* (Madison, WI: University of Wisconsin Press, 2010), p. 343.
11. Ibid., pp. 243–81.
12. Cited in Batchelor, *Chromophobia*, p. 82.
13. Ibid., p. 55.
14. Cartledge and Greenland, *Responses to Oliver Stone's* Alexander, p. 343.
15. Ibid., p. 350.
16. Ibid., p. 350.
17. Bosely, 'Rodrigo Prieto', p. 2.
18. Cited in Batchelor, *Chromophobia*, p. 55.
19. Vivian Sobchack, 'Surge and Splendor: A Phenomenology of the Hollywood Historical Epic', *Representations*, 29 (winter 1990), pp. 24–49 (p. 37).
20. Robert Burgoyne, 'Bare Life and Sovereignty in *Gladiator*', in Robert Burgoyne (ed.), *The Epic Film in World Culture* (New York and London: Routledge, 2011), pp. 82–98 (pp. 93–4).
21. Rey Chow, 'The Force of Surfaces: Defiance in Zhang Yimou's Films', in John Orr and Olga Taxidou (eds), *Post War Cinema and Modernity: A Film Reader* (New York: New York University Press, 2000), pp. 384–98 (p. 389).
22. As Ian Christie once said to me in conversation regarding *Hero*, 'Leni Riefenstahl would have wept!'.
23. See Jenny Kwok Wah Lau, '*Hero*: China's Response to Globalization', *Jump Cut*, 49. http://www.ejumpcut.org/archive/jc49.2007/Lau-Hero/2.html, last accessed 26 October 2012.
24. Sobchack, 'Surge and Splendor', p. 24.
25. Christopher Doyle, 'A Fantastic Fable', *American Cinematographer*, 84.9 (September 2003), pp. 32–45 (p. 33).
26. Ibid., p. 33.
27. Rosalind Galt, *Pretty: Film and the Decorative Image* (New York: Columbia University Press, 2011).
28. Derek Elley, *The Epic Film: Myth and History* (London: Routledge & Kegan Paul, 1984), p. 13.
29. Deleuze, *Cinema 1*, p. 154.
30. Ibid., pp. 150–1.
31. Lau, '*Hero*'.

CHAPTER 7

Defining the Epic: Medieval and Fantasy Epics

Paul B. Sturtevant

Before embarking on a discussion of the contemporary epic, its characteristics, tropes and sub-genres, it is crucial first to define what we mean when we call a film an 'epic'. Taking examples only from the medieval and fantasy sub-genres from the period roughly drawn between *Fellowship of the Ring* (Jackson 2001) and *The Hobbit* (Jackson 2012), we can see that there exist a handful of clear, easily agreed-upon examples of the genre: *The Lord of the Rings: Return of the King* (Jackson 2003); *King Arthur* (Fuqua 2004); *Kingdom of Heaven* (Scott 2005); *Arn* (Flinth 2007–8); and *Robin Hood* (Scott 2010). But which attributes make these films fit to wear the label 'epic', either in scholarly works, marketing materials or casual conversation? And what causes other cases – for example, *Beowulf* (Zemeckis 2007) or *Outlander* (McCain 2008) – to be only debatably epic when both are adaptations of *Beowulf*, one of the defining epics in the literary canon?[1]

One difficulty which arises when seeking to answer these questions is the relative lack of discussion within the academy of the epic film genre until recent years. As a result of this recent interest, a few tentative definitions of 'epic film' have emerged. This question is still under such debate that Constantine Santas begins his monograph, *The Epic in Film: From Myth to Blockbuster*, by asking 'What is an epic?'.[2] He then proceeds to focus his definition on a concept of size and scope, as well as on what he calls the epic's 'mythic dimensions'. Epic, to Santas, is a category which encompasses more than just film:

> Any venture of large proportions, a war, a trek, an exploration, a social struggle, a trial, a lengthy football game that went into overtime, an election campaign of unusual length – all of these endeavours associated with size, lengthy, complexity and heroic action could be categorized as epics.[3]

More poetically, he describes epic as 'the apotheosis of human action, an escape from pedestrianism to an ideal fashioned by tribal struggles'.[4] Grand and (perhaps) appealing as this definition is, its all-encompassing verbiage makes it unhelpful in defining what specifically makes an epic film. Similarly, Gary Allen Smith, in his catalogue of the epic, defines the genre by saying only that 'all epics are concerned with momentous events and larger-than-life characters'.[5] But it seems that these definitions, when reduced to their bare components, rely only upon scope of action and suitably impressive protagonists – traits shared by a great many action and adventure films which are not *necessarily* epics themselves. The *Indiana Jones* series of films, for example, certainly contain larger-than-life characters and depict momentous, if fictional, events. But they are not regularly categorised or discussed as epics.

When Santas continues to discuss the 'mythic dimensions' of the epic, a clearer focus is revealed. He continues, 'epics can be seen as the embodiments of collective myths and symbols that enable a society to establish its own identity and face its severest tests . . . the epic film can be seen as an embodiment of aspirations, hopes, fears and other collective emotions and feelings [of a society]'.[6] Robert Burgoyne echoes this focus, pointing to the relationship between epic and 'the imagined community of nation' which, in the epic, is 'traditionally framed as an expression of national emergence and national consciousness'.[7] Burgoyne then continues to question the centrality of nation to the epic film within the context of contemporary global/transnational cinema production and reception. This framework may be overly narrow in scope. 'Myth' and 'collective identity' – when not limited only to nation, but to *any* group identity which is infused with meaning by a contemporary audience – may help us better to begin to define the qualities of an epic film. Relying upon this definition, we can then argue that the question of defining the epic film genre is not a question of production, marketing, industry or aesthetics, but one of audience reception. Films are not produced by 'society' (however one wishes to define that), but only by a certain few of a society's members. They are, however, consumed by entire societies – or at least, the filmmakers hope, by a wide subsection of societies. And, as elucidated by Burgoyne, in today's age of global markets, many films are consumed by a range of societies across the world. As Santas suggests, each society has its own 'aspirations, hopes, fears and other collective emotions'.[8]

This requires epics to be particularly attuned to the world-view of their audience. As a result, epics – particularly successful ones – can be viewed as especially sensitive barometers of the gestalt of their age. Of course, there is not one 'audience', but many. Every film must position itself to engage with different audiences in different ways. Interestingly, for many epic films, the primary target audience is not the group whose identity is depicted in the film.

Take, for example, *El Cid* (Mann 1961). By the above definition, *El Cid* is certainly an epic – it is the story not only of one Spanish hero, but of a crucial (if largely fictional) moment in the formation of Spain through cooperation between Moors and Christians. Thus, the film is a statement of what it means to be Spanish, both in the eleventh century and in 1961. This is a problematic interpretation of the medieval past, since the film is shot through with the ideology of the Franco administration.[9] It includes powerful, specifically Spanish, statements of national, ethnic, religious and cultural identity. Yet, while Spaniards were certainly expected to view the film (and did so), its largest single national market was the American audience. The filmmakers clearly sought this audience in the casting of bankable Hollywood stars (Charlton Heston and Sophia Loren) in the leading roles, who performed in English rather than Spanish. But what makes the film appreciably an epic within the USA? Why would this film resonate with an American audience who hold few particular feelings about Spain?

The answer may be that *El Cid*, and similar epics, are interpreted allegorically by audiences. Audience members do not need to be Scottish to be moved by the Scots' struggles for 'freedom' in *Braveheart* (Gibson 1995), to cheer their victories and lament their defeats. They do not need to be Roman slaves to empathise with Maximus or Spartacus and their followers, nor do they need to be riders of Rohan to consider *Return of the King* suitably epic. And, thus, without a sympathetic and empathetic allegorical engagement with the group struggle on the part of the audience, fantasy epics like *Lord of the Rings* or *The Chronicles of Narnia* would be ludicrous. Moreover, epics set in classical, medieval and medievalesque worlds – so emblematic of the genre – would not prove popular, owing to their distance from the present. Instead we find the reverse. This implies that there is something to be gained, rather than lost, when setting an epic film in a past that is distant, imaginary, or both.

This chapter will explore this new way of defining the epic film. Central to this definition is the degree to which an epic film inspires 'collective compassion' within its viewers. This compassionate response – including both sympathy and empathy – is collective insofar as it is not restricted only to the protagonists as individuals, but extends to the larger group whose struggles are depicted by the film – and which define it as an epic. To demonstrate this I will examine, in particular, a handful of the medieval and fantasy films released from the period 2001 to 2012. This sub-genre has been one of the most productive strands of epic film as a result of the successes of *The Lord of the Rings* franchise, despite the great distance between audience and subject. This distance makes the collective identification with the group struggles in these films all the more interesting, as it requires the audience to empathise with the struggles of people who are, in many ways, fundamentally unlike themselves. That does not mean that the establishment of compassion with the struggles of a group in a film is a simple cipher, where the group represented in a film is an obvious stand-in for a real-world, contemporary group. Instead, there seems to be a plastic, indexical relationship between the group depicted and real-world identities. This malleability of interpretation allows a range of audiences, and a multitude of individuals, to recognise themselves, and people like them, within these films. The individual viewers make the film specific to their own contexts. An epic's ability meaningfully to accommodate this multiplicity of viewing positions, while retaining its affective and narrative power, is a key to success.

But before we begin in earnest, let us briefly explore the concepts of empathy and sympathy within the context of historical fiction, film and audience reception. Empathy has been a cornerstone of some approaches to history and sociology since the late nineteenth century, often through the use of the term '*Verstehen*'. *Verstehen* roughly translates as 'meaningful understanding'. The word has long been employed by historians and social scientists to describe an empathetic approach to individuals or cultures separated from the viewer by time or space – imaginatively meeting them on their own terms. According to Michael Martin:

> In its strongest forms, *Verstehen* entails reliving the experience of the actor or at least rethinking the actor's thoughts, while in its weaker forms it only involves reconstructing the actor's rationale for acting.[10]

Empathy is also a central concept in morality, both for philosophers such as Michael A. Slote and Patricia Churchland (who argue that empathy should be the foundation of ethics and morality) and for cognitive psychologists such as Simon Baron-Cohen, who defines '"evil" in terms of the erosion of *empathy*' [his emphasis].[11] Baron-Cohen also differentiates between 'cognitive' and 'affective' empathy; in short, cognitive empathy is the ability to correctly identify the emotions of another, whereas affective empathy is the degree to which a person's emotions are affected by those of others.[12] People with autism spectrum disorders often suffer from a lack of the former, whereas psychopaths suffer from a lack of the latter. A crucial point is that all of these responses are automatic, not voluntary, acting upon the unconscious rather than the conscious mind.

Refocusing on the topic at hand, we observe that audience engagement had previously been viewed by academics in terms of *sympathy* – which Alex Neill distinguishes from empathy thus:

> with sympathetic response, in feeling *for* another, one's response needs not reflect what the other is feeling . . . Your happiness may make me

happy for you, but it also may irritate me . . . In contrast, in responding empathetically to another I come to *share* his feelings, to feel *with* him; if he is in an emotional state, to empathize with him is to experience the emotion(s) that he experiences.[13]

Sympathy might sufficiently describe reactions to suspense or horror films where, to use Neill's example, the audience can see (and are caused to fear) perils of which the characters on screen are unaware. That being said, Neill argues that empathy, a compassionate response evoked by imagining the experience of the characters from their point of view, 'plays a critical role in our response to, and understanding of', dramatic films.[14]

Epic films also rely upon empathy. But their defining characteristic, as discussed above, is that these films tell the story of a group rather than an individual. Is it possible to empathise with an entire group?

DEFINING THE EPIC MODE

Of course, some medieval films are not epics. And by the above metric, in some examples only part of a film should be considered epic. This distinction can help us understand why defining the epic as a genre, or even circumscribing a cogent corpus of epic films, is fraught with difficulties, as we saw in the introduction. Many films have sections which bear all the hallmarks of an 'epic', but freely mix with other genres as well. The sections of a film which can comfortably be called 'epic' are defined by the point at which the story involves the actions of the hero within the actions of a larger group. Furthermore, these films often contain scenes of group suffering, effort, and triumph in order to evoke a compassionate response.

Take, for example, Ridley Scott's 2005 film *Kingdom of Heaven*. The film begins in France, where the protagonist Balian is confronted by a baron and Crusader who reveals himself to be Balian's father. After learning this, Balian reluctantly leaves France to take up his father's life in Outremer. Along the way he is trained in how to be a good knight, both by improving his martial prowess, and also by learning his father's chivalric ideology (laced, as it is, with the film's overarching pacifistic/humanitarian morality). If we were to divorce these introductory acts of the film from the remainder, they do not, themselves, constitute an epic – Balian's story could very easily become that of a solitary questing hero. It is only when Balian's actions become part of a context greater than himself, when he becomes a leader of men in the Holy Land, that the film becomes an epic. This manifests itself most in the scenes where Balian acts as a leader in peacetime and at war. Balian is the figure of good stewardship of his land when he (in a much-derided scene)

Figure 7.1 *Kingdom of Heaven*'s defence of Jerusalem: when Balian (Orlando Bloom) acts with and for larger group causes, the film acquires a mythic dimension and becomes an epic.

teaches the Arabs on his father's land how to dig for irrigation water (and thus, in an orientalist fantasy *par excellence*, 'makes the desert bloom'); a medieval man of the people, he even jumps into the hole to dig alongside his peasants.

In war, Balian leads a suicidal charge against a vastly superior Muslim cavalry in order to preserve the lives of the peasants fleeing the oncoming army; he also leads the garrison of Jerusalem to a stalemate with Saladin in the climactic scenes of the film. It is at this point, when Balian acts with and for larger group causes, that the film acquires the 'mythic dimension' described by Burgoyne and becomes an epic. It is perhaps unsurprising that the pacifistic, humanistic, secular and humanitarian ideologies of the film are most evident in the scenes of group action.

It is interesting, however, that the group which Balian represents, leads and fights for is never clearly defined. Balian's eve-of-battle speech (which, along with the opening and closing title cards, is often one of the places where a medieval epic film's ideology is made most clear) does little to rectify this:

> It has fallen to us to defend Jerusalem, and we have made our preparations as well as they can be made. None of us took this city from Muslims. No Muslim of the great army now coming against us was born when this city was lost. We fight over an offence we did not give, against those who were not alive to be offended. What is Jerusalem? Your holy places lie over the Jewish temple that the Romans pulled down. The Muslim places of worship lie over yours. Which is more holy? The wall? The Mosque? The Sepulchre? Who has claim? No one has claim. All have claim! . . . We defend this city, not to protect these stones, but the people living within these walls.

This lack of specificity is further reinforced with the scenes of collective suffering in *Kingdom of Heaven*. For example, during the siege of Jerusalem, the camera pans over the faces of peasants huddling within the walls, while mournful music plays. But 'the people' are rarely elevated above the level of a humanitarian cause undertaken by outsiders. Balian rarely interacts with them, and he is not one of them; his leadership is paternalistic rather than grass-roots. As a result, it feels inauthentic.

Additionally, Balian's secular, humanitarian cause does not resonate well because he is not fighting *for* a cause, but against one. He is shown fighting against the war-mongering Templars as often as (if not more often than) he fights against Muslims. He is an anti-holy warrior, but his goals, and the group he represents, are vaguely defined – either within the context of the film or as an allegorical stand-in for contemporary groups. Their definition in the film relies only upon Balian's (along with Baldwin IV and his supporters') secular, humanistic and peaceful rhetoric. The final title card even reveals the fruitlessness of their efforts: 'Nearly a thousand years later, peace in the Kingdom of Heaven remains elusive.' The group whose story is here told is simply 'those who want peace in the Middle East', but the problem in the film is not unlike the problem in reality. The peacemakers are not a cohesive group with a history or leadership; while many individuals have worked to reconcile the conflicts in that region, they do not represent a sustained movement. They are usually not participants in the current conflict, but outside observers. An epic mythology for this non-group thus falls flat.

Kingdom of Heaven may then be compared to the lesser-known Swedish Crusader-epic *Arn*.[15] At first, *Arn* follows a similar pattern to *Kingdom of Heaven*; the protagonist, Arn, is forced to leave home and take up the mantle of a templar knight owing to complications arising from a feud that his clan, the house of Folkung, has with a powerful rival clan, the Sverkers. In the Holy Land he has adventures, such as meeting and befriending Saladin, successfully leading an ambush of the Saracen army, and participating in the disastrous defeat of the Crusaders at the Battle of Hattin. But it is only when Arn returns home that the film becomes an epic. Arn brings with him craftsmen and doctors drawn from the Holy Land and Europe, and proceeds to build a new home with this multicultural expertise. When war returns as a result of the Sverker clan taking the throne, Arn trains and arms the Folkung clan with the help of his multicultural coterie.

Arn goes to battle, and defeats the Sverkers and their Danish allies. Upon his doing so, his legacy is revealed in the closing title card: 'Arn Magnusson's victory secured the peace for many years. Thanks to him, the country was soon united as the Kingdom of Sweden.' The group central to the epic portion of this film, while perhaps not recognised at first by those outside Sweden, is the Swedish nation itself. The film is a myth of national foundation. When it is examined closely, similarities emerge between the myth depicted here and the contemporary Swedish self-image. As depicted in the film, contemporary Sweden sees itself as a society built upon multicultural cooperation. Furthermore, contemporary Sweden takes pride in its history of neutrality and pacifism.[16] This is reflected in the film when Arn claims, without a hint of irony, that his goal in going to war is to achieve peace. For example, in his eve-of-battle speech, Arn says:

> Listen to me! Have no doubt. Believe! Believe in our victory. We chose this place. Not the Danes, and not the Sverkers. We chose this time, not the Danes and not the Sverkers. Believe. God stands by those who are strong in faith. That is why we shall win *and peace shall reign*. [my emphasis]

When Arn dies at the close of the film, he is depicted as the founding father of the unified Swedish Kingdom; while Arn himself is fictional, the film claims that his grandson was Birger Jarl, a well-known real-life Swedish statesman who played a crucial role in the thirteenth-century consolidation of Sweden. As a result of this link, *Arn* is a more satisfying epic narrative than *Kingdom of Heaven*, despite a similarity in their narrative forms and the events portrayed. *Arn* is arguably a more traditional epic, insofar as it presents a straightforward national-foundational myth. While the group the protagonist represents may be unfamiliar to those without knowledge of medieval Swedish history, by the final act of the film it becomes clear that Arn is forging the Swedish nation and identity.

SEPARATING THE STRANDS: *THE LORD OF THE RINGS*

But what of more complicated epics like *The Lord of the Rings*? If we, for a moment, regard the three-film trilogy as one contiguous whole, the narrative bears two complementary strands: one that fits within the 'adventure' genre and one that fits the 'epic' genre. The first film opens with a prologue in an epic mode: the story of the rings and the battle against Sauron. The battle is presented as a grand history that threatens all the people(s) of Middle Earth and requires their participation. However, after the introduction, the story begins again in the Shire, and the film adopts a quest-adventure mode. The introduction has given the audience the context and the stakes, but it is only when the hobbits reach Rivendell that the wider participation of the people of Middle Earth is again required by participation in the Fellowship of the Ring.

At the end of the first film, the narrative then splits into two strands: one an adventure-quest, and one an epic. These pieces are complementary; the epic strand (which we could call the *King* strand) takes the viewer to Edoras and the siege of Helm's Deep, then to the siege of Gondor, the Pellenor fields, and finally to the Black Gates of Mordor. The quest-adventure strand (which we could call the *Ring* strand) follows the hobbits and Gollum through Emyn Muil and to the Black Gates, across the Dead Marshes, to Ithilien, up the Stairs of Cirith Ungol, through Shelob's lair, and across the wastes of Mordor, and ends in the fires of Mount Doom. It is entirely possible that an enterprising editor could create two separate films from these strands which would be entirely comprehensible and satisfactory, but of which only the film of the *King* strand would be an epic.[17]

The two narrative strands, as they exist within the films, are complementary. The epic *King* strand situates the struggle within a larger group context – the fight against evil, in this case, involves the struggle of large numbers of people who suffer and sacrifice for the survival of themselves, their friends, and their world. The adventure-quest *Ring* strand makes the struggle personal: it offers to the audience ordinary protagonists who seem like us, and with whom the audience is asked to empathise. The struggles of Sam and Frodo are largely interpersonal and psychological, and the story becomes one of good and evil on an individual level. The struggles of Aragorn and his fellows are mythic precisely because they centre on group values and existential struggles, including how an individual must act as a member and as a leader of a good society. Aragorn and Frodo are different types of heroes, who demand a different sort of engagement from their audience. We cheer Aragorn on because we know that he will succeed – he being an epic hero, it is inconceivable that his actions will not result in the success of his cause. Even if the struggle results in his death (as for example, in *El Cid*, *Gladiator*, *300*, *Braveheart* or *Arn*) making him a martyr, the story can end satisfactorily if his efforts result in success for the group. However, we cheer Frodo because it is entirely reasonable to fear that he will fail and that his vulnerabilities (far larger than Achilles' heel) will overcome him. It is reasonable to expect that Frodo, as an everyman-hero, may not survive his quest unscathed. And that indeed comes to pass; Frodo is broken by the experience and scarred for life. Not only does he lose a finger, he is forever changed by the experience.

It is easy to see the difference between an epic and adventure film when comparing these two strands of *The Lord of the Rings*. Frodo's quest is solitary; it involves only collaboration from Sam and Gollum, and takes him through liminal spaces away from society. The effort exerted, successes achieved and suffering endured are limited to the three adventurers; their battles, whether against orcs, giant spiders or each other, are always one-on-one, duels of individual will. By comparison, the *King* strand revolves around the recruitment of groups to help in the battle against Sauron, whether those groups be the Rohirrim, the Ents, the Army of the Dead or the Gondorians. This strand contains the scenes of group effort and suffering which extend beyond the protagonists. During the siege of Helm's Deep, brief scenes show the women and children cowering in the caves below the fortress. Similarly, in the scenes of the siege of Gondor, the camera lingers upon the faces of the people of Gondor in addition to the heroes. And the battles herein are 'epic' not because of their length or cinematographic style, but because they depict the pinnacle of group effort, suffering, and, in this case, triumph.

REMAKING *ROBIN HOOD* AND *KING ARTHUR* IN THE EPIC MODE

It is perhaps the runaway financial success of *The Lord of the Rings* trilogy that inspired filmmakers to create new versions of Robin Hood and King Arthur – the most perennially popular medieval heroes in the English-speaking world since the nineteenth century – as epics.[18] The story of King Arthur lends itself readily to this, since the Matter of Britain is, as the name might imply, already centred on the formulation and definition of a national/cultural group identity. Boorman's *Excalibur* (1981) accomplished an epic retelling of the Arthurian legends within a more or less entirely mythological context. The Britain for which Boorman's Arthur fights is not one of our world, but a mythological parallel universe replete with monsters and magic. This world is more or less indistinguishable from the other medievalesque fantasies popular in the 1980s and 1990s such as *Ladyhawke* (Donner 1985), *Willow* (Howard 1988) or *DragonHeart* (Cohen 1996), and a similar tack has been taken for recent TV adaptations of the legends such as *Merlin* (2008–12), and *Camelot* (2011). Fuqua's *King Arthur* (2004), on the other hand, places the action within a specific – if flawed – historical context, and strips away the supernatural in favour of what Umberto Eco calls a 'shaggy medievalism'.[19]

King Arthur thus, as an epic, makes claims towards what it means to be British – not a kaleidoscopic fairy-tale British, but real-world historical British. At its heart, it defines the British as a liminal people, born of a marriage between idealistic remnants of a crumbling Empire and a proud, native people living in tune with the land – a fusion between the noble savage and savage nobility. The film defines these Britons – represented by Arthur's Romano-Sarmatian knights and the quasi-Celtic 'Woads' north of Hadrian's wall – against truly savage Saxon invaders. When compared with previous iterations of the Arthurian legends, this is a curious turn. The conflict central to this film is not within Arthur's court – either in conflict with Lancelot as a result of his affair with Guinevere (as in *First Knight* (Zucker 1995)) or due to the betrayal by his treacherous son Mordred (as in *Camelot* (Logan 1967), *Excalibur* or *Merlin*) – but rather from an invasion of foreign savages. This

Figure 7.2 *King Arthur* (2004) defines the British as a liminal people, born of a marriage between idealistic remnants of a crumbling Empire and a proud, native people living in tune with the land.

externalisation of the source of conflict can be read as an example of psychological projection (the defence mechanism first described by Freud wherein a person unconsciously rejects their own negative attributes and instead sees them in others in order to, as Freud put it, 'fend off an idea that was intolerable to [the] ego') in which internal sources of conflict and fault are externalised.[20] It is easy to see how a new myth of our group identity, which places the blame for the problems in our society on external sources, would have broad appeal, particularly in a xenophobic post-9/11 world. Seen within a post-9/11 context, Arthur's eve-of-battle speech to his knights is curious:

> Knights! The gift of freedom is yours by right. But the home we seek resides not in some distant land, it's in us, and in our actions on this day! If this be our destiny, then so be it. But let history remember, that as free men, we chose to make it so!

Fighting the Saxons is reshaped as a fight for 'freedom'. Freedom as used here is an empty sign, into which any vaguely patriotic meaning can be poured; when read closely, the speech means little, but is intended to resonate with an audience who associate the concept of freedom, no matter how hazily understood, with a good thing.

Unlike those fighting for the 'freedom' bellowed by William Wallace in *Braveheart*, these people are not fighting against subjugation or oppression, but extermination. The savagery of the Saxons in *King Arthur* also bears a specific tenor intended to resonate with contemporary audiences, particularly those in Britain and the USA. Their barbarism manifests itself most in a scene in which the Saxon leader, Cerdic (apparently a reference to Cerdic, the putative founder of the Saxon Kingdom of Wessex), kills one of his soldiers for raping a local woman. This moment of apparent mercy and justice is quickly dispelled as Cerdic then orders the woman to be killed as well. He gives his reason:

> Don't touch their women. We don't mix with these people. What kind of offspring do you think that would yield? Weak people. Half people. I will not have our Saxon blood watered down by mixing with them.

This frames the invading Saxons as proto-eugenicists, and the conflict over Britain as an existential struggle between ethnicities. Furthermore, Germanic eugenicist invaders of Britain evoke similarities with the Nazis, which reframes this conflict as a historical echo of the Second World War. More generally, this relates the conflict in the film to grand narratives that contribute to the identities of many contemporary Americans and Britons. In terms of their collective ethnic and cultural identities, both of these nations are multi-cultural nations comprising Cerdic's 'half-people': offspring of different ethnic and cultural groups. Arthur's army of multicultural misfits ultimately proves itself superior to Germanic savage homogeneity, a point further emphasised as the film closes with a wedding between the Romano-British Arthur and the native Woad Guinevere. This very success is a strange turn on the Arthurian legend. In other iterations, the death of Arthur (as in *Le Morte d'Arthur*) is not only necessary but central to the myth of England; its heroes are dead but not gone, awaiting the moment of need to return. Here, in the reverse of Malory, Lancelot dies but Arthur lives. Arthur is not a martyr for the group, but lives on as a literal founding father.

By contrast with King Arthur, Robin Hood is a less obvious candidate to be rendered into an epic. Previous film and TV iterations of Robin, starring Douglas Fairbanks, Errol Flynn, Richard Greene, Brian Bedford, Kevin Costner or Cary Elwes, have followed an adventure-film structure, typically in a jolly Technicolor. But Ridley Scott's recent *Robin Hood* places Robin Hood within an epic context, owing more, perhaps, to the director's earlier *Gladiator* and *Kingdom of Heaven*. By the above definition, if *Robin Hood* is to be considered an epic, it requires a group with which the audience can identify. While previous iterations of the tale have always placed Robin as a leader of his band of merry men, they only occasionally place his struggle within a broader cultural context. For example, in *The Adventures of Robin Hood* (Curtiz 1938), Errol Flynn's Saxon Robin struggled to throw off the 'Norman Yoke' – a feature implanted into the Robin Hood myth by Walter Scott's *Ivanhoe* but omitted from recent film and TV adaptations.[21] However, even in the *The Adventures of Robin Hood*, this context is not central to the story – Robin's is not the story of the Saxons throwing off the oppression of Norman rule, nor was the return of Richard at the end shown to be of any great consequence to those aside from Robin and his men. The focus, until the end, remains very much on the hero and his compatriots rather than a greater group struggle.

By contrast, Ridley Scott's *Robin Hood* discards the adventure-film trappings of previous versions of Robin Hood, choosing to 'reboot' the legend in the context of popular politics surrounding the establishment of Magna Carta, with a secondary narrative about what it means to be working-class and English. The villains in this *Robin Hood* are not internal, but external. The Sheriff of Nottingham, for example, rarely appears in this version. When he does, he is relegated largely to the role of a sneering romantic foil for Robin. Prince John, too, is not really the villain. He is shown to be immature and stupid, but until the final scene, in which he reneges on his promise to sign Magna Carta and declares Robin to be an outlaw, he works in tandem with the heroes more often than he works against him. The real villains are the French, particularly in the figure of the traitorous Sir Godfrey. Godfrey's chief sin is treachery; he is a close friend of and advisor to King John, but secretly works against John and aids King Phillip II. His dual national loyalty makes him suspect; he speaks English and French fluently, and when asked if he is English he replies, 'When it suits me.' His motives for betraying John, and England, are never revealed. He leads an attempt to assassinate King Richard on the road back to England, and then later, after John's coronation, he leads a secret guerrilla army of Frenchmen, bearing English colours, to despoil the north of England. He does this in an attempt to provoke the northern barons against King John (all the while announcing their Frenchness to the viewing audience by continually shouting in French during their attacks). All of this is done in order to set the country in disarray, allowing the French to invade while the country is weak. This naturally fails. Despite what disunity lay in the county, as William Marshal says to John, 'when the French come, we are all Englishmen.' In the face of foreign invasion, whatever disunity the country may face must be relegated to secondary importance – loyalty to nation is above all. This is, perhaps predictably, historically inaccurate; the First Baron's War began in 1215 after John refused to abide by Magna Carta. The Barons invited Prince Louis of France to invade England and take the throne. This inaccuracy further highlights the nationalistic ideological underpinning of Scott's film.

It is remarkable how different this film is from previous Robin Hood films in terms of the filmmakers' interpretation. Here, the aristocracy are not defined as outsiders by the association with their Norman-Frenchness, but rather the 'evil' French are instead fashioned as insidious invaders and fifth-columnists within England. Subversiveness, stealth and treachery are the chief tools of the French enemy, in direct contrast to the good, simple, honest English. It is a paranoid, xenophobic refashioning of Robin Hood, fit for an ideology that wishes to see all origins of internal problems as lying in external sources (similar to *King Arthur*, above). The historical ludicrousness of this scenario only serves to further emphasise the ideology at work: while the Norman/Saxon divide did not exist at that time to anywhere near the degree that Sir Walter Scott presented it in *Ivanhoe* (and Anglo-Norman French was spoken by all the English aristocracy at that time), the nationalistic sentiments which pervade in this version of Robin Hood would have also been alien at the start of the thirteenth century. Modern 'English' and 'French' identities are markedly different from their late-medieval counterparts.

Despite this, the film creates a myth about the English in contradistinction to the French. King Richard enumerates the virtues of the English when he describes Robin as: 'Honest, brave, and naive. There is your Englishman.' This simple honesty evokes a deep-seated cultural metanarrative which forms part of English, and particularly northern English, identity, where honesty, bravery and simplicity are chief cultural virtues. The depiction of the English and French in the film supports Richard's assessment. For example, in every battle fought by the French, at least one Frenchman is shown fleeing – which clearly originates in the contemporary Anglo/American nationalistic stereotype of French battlefield cowardice. Furthermore, the French rely upon ambush and trickery, attacking twice while their opponents are asleep and once as an ambush in the forest.

The other group central to this film is a hazily defined mass of 'common people', often described in the film as 'the people'. The film's opening title card sets the context for this conflict: 'In times of tyranny and injustice, when law oppresses the people, the outlaw takes his place in history. England at the turn of the 12th century was such a time.' Marion is the first to specifically define the struggles of 'the people' in castigating the Sheriff of Nottingham:

> In the name of King Richard you have stripped our wealth to pay for foreign adventures. Whilst at home, the church, in the name of a merciful God, has reaped, without mercy, the larger share of what we have set aside to feed ourselves. Between the sheriff and the bishop, I wouldn't care to judge who's the greater curse on *honest English folk*. [my emphasis]

This statement is ironic, considering that Marion is depicted in this film as a local aristocrat, the wife of Sir Robert Loxley. But, predictably, she is no ordinary aristocrat: in the film she is first shown attempting to scare off raiders by firing flaming arrows at them, and the above-quoted scene with the sheriff takes place while she takes a break from ploughing the fields. She meets Robin while wearing rags and digging dirt out of a horse's hoof, and, in the climactic battle, dresses as a man and takes up arms against the French (in a turn perhaps inspired by Eowyn in *Return of the King*).

Robin also occupies a space between commoner and aristocrat. He and the merry men escape France by impersonating knights (with the aid of some looted armour and equipment), and Robin continues this ruse by impersonating Robert Loxley at Robert's father's request. But Robin is no Wat Tyler or John Ball; he makes no demands against serfdom or aristocratic privilege. His definition of 'common people' is extended to include roughly anyone not in (or representing) central government or a central church authority. This exception includes local clergymen like Friar Tuck, and local aristocrats as lofty as the Barons of the North, who take a surprisingly positive attitude towards the egalitarian, democratic, populist movement begun by Robin's father and continued by him. It is this movement of 'the people' that results in the film's proto-Magna Carta, which Robin refers to as a 'charter of liberties' for all Englishmen in his climactic speech to John:

> If you're trying to build for the future, you must set your foundations strong. The laws of this land enslave people to its king: a king who demands loyalty, but offers nothing in return. I have marched from France to Palestine and back, and I know, in tyranny lies only failure. You build a country like you build a cathedral, from the ground up! Empower every man, and you will gain strength! . . . If your majesty were to offer justice, justice in the form of a charter of liberties, allowing every man to forage for his hearth, to be safe from conviction without cause or prison without charge, to work, eat and live on the sweat of his own brow and be as merry as he can, then that king would be great. Not only would he receive the loyalty of his people, but their love as well . . . What we would ask, your majesty, is liberty. Liberty by law!

The distrust of central authority is rife throughout the film: the conflict with the Church over the seed-grain is blamed on 'politics out of London', and Tuck describes the church authority in York as 'wolves . . . voracious wolves'. He excuses himself from condemnation by pleading 'I'm not a Churchy Friar. Never was!' William Marshal is derided by the Northern Barons, who say 'You've spent too long in the palace, William'.

In a particularly telling scene, Marion, in the forced tax census that occurs when the French marauders take Nottingham, says she owns 'five thousand acres'. After this, she is escorted to a locked barn where she is joined by a French soldier who says, as he advances on her, 'no one should have four thousand acres'. As Marion corrects him, the scene cuts to his belt dropping on the floor. The man then undresses himself as he advances on her, clearly intending to rape her. This dialogue reveals another nuance to the politics of the film. The soldier-rapist implies that his assault is a punishment for her wealth, and thus becomes the worst caricature of Bolshevik or French revolutionaries, transplanted onto medieval France. The politics latent in the film therefore are not revolutionary; the virtuous Baronial revolt and Robin's egalitarianism are not espousing economic equality and a banishment of the aristocracy, but a medieval version of small-government conservative libertarianism.

However, a question remains: is *Robin Hood* an epic? It certainly fashions itself as such, both visually (owing to its similarities to Ridley Scott's previous epics *Gladiator* and *Kingdom of Heaven*), and more fundamentally owing to the incorporation of large-group narratives. That said, *Robin Hood* is not a very effective epic because of the failure of these very narratives. Robin's social revolution fails; John burns the charter of liberties and declares Robin an outlaw. Moreover, the conflict at the centre of this film is not a formative or pivotal struggle for the groups presented – the English are not significantly changed at the end of the film. Furthermore, the struggle is not even seen to be especially difficult. Even in the final, climactic battle on the beach, the English are shown to have every advantage and are in little danger of losing. Seen in these terms, the group's struggle against such paltry adversity seems uninspiring. In the end, Robin's actions have little meaning for those outside himself and his friends, which makes this an unsatisfying epic. That does not mean that it is not an epic, but it may serve to explain why the film opened to mixed reviews and none of the critical and financial success enjoyed either by *Robin Hood: Prince of Thieves* or *Gladiator*.

CONCLUSIONS

Looking back, then, we see that Santas' definition of epic encompasses 'Any venture of large proportions, a war, a trek, an exploration, a social struggle, a trial, a lengthy football game that went into overtime, an election campaign of unusual length . . .' However, I find that his definition lacks a crucial component.[22] In my view, any of these things could be rendered into an epic film, but only if the filmmakers forge a formative or definitive moment for a group with which the audience can identify either directly or allegorically. The hero of an epic is a different sort of hero from an action hero or an adventure hero: his (or all too infrequently, her) actions have greater meaning because they have an impact upon the success or failure of the group. For an epic, the filmmakers thus attempt to evoke compassionate empathetic and sympathetic responses within their audiences. Furthermore, the audience identifies with the group rather than the hero; when the hero makes his or her eve-of-battle speech, they are justifying their struggle simultaneously to their followers in the film and to the audience in the theatre. The mise-en-scène often reinforces this: the hero stands above the listeners – Arn and Arthur are on a horse, Robin is on a hill, and Balian upon the city ramparts. The shot of the hero is often from a low angle, from the perspective of the group. In *Robin Hood*, the shot even tracks within the listeners, giving the impression that the perspective is as a listener within the group. The hero is depicted with a medium shot, whereas the camera lingers upon each listener's emotive, attentive face in close-up. The viewers are meant to respond as the listener responds, and place themselves as members of the group.

The recent spate of medieval epics are not fundamentally different from their predecessors. This is because of the relationship between the hero and the wider movement they represent, which moves them away from the individually significant exploits of the hero of an action-adventure film and into the 'mythical' realm of group identity foundation and definition. However, these interpretations of the past, contingent as they are upon the audience understanding and empathising with the group presented in the film, are particularly sensitive to the ideologies and identities held by their viewers. *Arn* and *King Arthur* are national-foundation-myth epics in the same vein as *El Cid*, or *Braveheart*. As Jeffrey Richards and Kevin J. Harty both argue in this volume, their politics clearly relate to the time and place in which they were made, and the audience for whom they are intended. *King Arthur* is a revision of the Matter of Britain in which a half-civilised, half-native nation is facing an invasion of barbarian proto-Nazis. *Arn* crafts a myth of Sweden's formation from whole cloth, but laced with the ideologies of contemporary Swedes. *Kingdom of Heaven*, while still a Crusader-epic, takes a fundamentally different interpretation of that history from Cecil B. De Mille's 1935 epic *The Crusades*: the latter presents unimpeachably noble Christians fighting barbaric Muslims in a way that would be entirely inappropriate for a contemporary audience. As a result, epic films date themselves easily, not because their fundamental form changes, but because their audience does.

NOTES

1. There has been some debate among literary scholars over whether *Beowulf* should be considered an epic. Tolkien stated his opinion plainly: 'Beowulf is not an "epic".' This was in response to previous *Beowulf* scholars (e.g. Charles W. Kennedy and others) who sought to attribute the poem's epic qualities to influences from Classical epics like *The Aeneid*. Tolkien, instead, felt that *Beowulf* (and by proxy, Anglo-Saxon culture) did not require Classical influences in order to be respectable. That said, most modern scholars agree that *Beowulf* is an epic, though not one drawn from classical sources. J. R. R. Tolkien, 'Beowulf: The Monsters and the Critics', in Robert Dennis Fulk (ed.), *Interpretations of Beowulf: A Critical Anthology* (London: Indiana University Press, 1991), p. 41.
2. Constantine Santas, *The Epic in Film: From Myth to Blockbuster* (Lanham, MD: Rowman & Littlefield, 2008), p. 1.
3. Ibid., p. 2.
4. Ibid., p. 2.

5. Gary A. Smith, *Epic Films: Casts, Credits and Commentary on over 350 Historical Spectacle Movies* (Jefferson, NC: McFarland, 2004), p. 1.
6. Santas, *The Epic in Film*, p. 2.
7. Robert Burgoyne, *The Epic Film in World Culture* (New York: Routledge, 2011), p. 1.
8. Santas, *The Epic in Film*, p. 2.
9. John Aberth, *A Knight at the Movies: Medieval History on Film* (London: Routledge, 2003), pp. 135–47. Tom Shippey, in *Hollywood in the Holy Land*, argues that Aberth overestimates the film's concessions to 'Franco's fascist medievalism', while agreeing that the film production received extensive support from the Spanish government, and that the film is, in many ways, not a 'Hollywood film'. Tom Shippey, 'El Cid: Defeat of the Crescentade', in Nickolas Haydock and Edward L. Risden (eds), *Hollywood in the Holy Land: Essays on Film Depictions of the Crusades and Christian–Muslim Clashes* (Jefferson, NC: McFarland, 2009), p. 183.
10. Michael Martin, *Verstehen: The Uses of Understanding in Social Science* (New Brunswick, NJ: Transaction Publishers, 2000), p. 1. *Verstehen* (and other empathetic approaches to history or social sciences) has had many critics (e.g. Carl Hempel, Theodore Abel and Keith Jenkins) who debate its methodological rigour or ability to produce truthful analyses. Michael Martin, in the volume quoted here, goes on to argue that *Verstehen* is only useful with a 'flexible pluralistic approach' (p. 239) when used in conjunction with other methods. This having been stated, I believe that empathetic approaches are one of the most commonly used, and indeed the most powerful, ways in which people approach the past – whether that be presented to them on a page or in a film such as the ones examined in this book.
11. Simon Baron-Cohen, *The Science of Evil: On Empathy and the Origins of Cruelty* (New York: Basic Books, 2012), p. vii.
12. Ibid., p. vii.
13. Alex Neill, 'Empathy and (Film) Fiction', in David Bordwell (ed.), *Post-Theory: Reconstructing Film Studies* (Madison, WI: University of Wisconsin Press, 1996), pp. 175–6.
14. Ibid., p. 181. Neill uses the example of Nicolas Roeg's 1973 psychological thriller *Don't Look Now* to illustrate his point; however, his assessment can be broadened to a range of other films.
15. *Arn* has been through a handful of versions. It was originally released as two films, *Arn: The Knight Templar* (2007) and *Arn: The Kingdom at Road's End* (2008). It was then re-cut into a single film for the international DVD market, under the name *Arn: The Knight Templar*. It has subsequently been re-released in 2010 as a six-episode TV mini-series entitled *Arn*. To avoid confusion, I will refer to the two films as one under the collective title *Arn* (though it is highly recommended to see either the two-film version or the mini-series version).
16. Sweden maintained an official policy of neutrality in armed conflicts from the early nineteenth century until it joined the European Union in 1995 (though it retains its stance of non-alignment). Christine Agius also argues that neutrality and internationalism continue to be central parts of Swedish national identity, particularly as promoted by the Social Democratic Party. Christine Agius, *The Social Construction of Swedish Neutrality: Challenges to Swedish Identity and Sovereignty* (Manchester: Manchester University Press, 2006), pp. 90–2.
17. The two narrative strands of *The Lord of the Rings* – the 'Ring' and 'King' strands – are more clearly separated in Tolkien's novels than in the films.
18. Stephanie Barczewski, 'King Arthur, Robin Hood, and British National Identity', in *Myth*

and National Identity in Nineteenth-Century Britain: The Legends of King Arthur and Robin Hood (Oxford University Press, 2000), pp. 1–10.
19. Umberto Eco, 'Dreaming of the Middle Ages', in *Travels in Hyperreality: Essays*, trans. William Weaver (London: Picador, 1987), p. 68. Fuqua's *King Arthur* has been highly criticised not only for a catalogue of historical inaccuracies, but also for its reality claims – such as the first title card which proclaims that 'Historians agree' that King Arthur was a real person whose biography played out in the manner seen in the film.
20. Joseph Sandler and Meir Perlow, 'Internalization and Externalization', in Joseph Sandler (ed.), *Projection, Identification, Projective Identification* (Madison, CT: Karnac Books, 2012), p. 2.
21. Stephen Knight argues that Walter Scott's use of the 'Norman Yoke' in *Ivanhoe* differed from how it had been used by radicals in the eighteenth century as a rejection of aristocracy. For Scott, the problem was not that they were lords, but that they were Normans (since Ivanhoe himself is a virtuous Saxon lord). This racial/national division remains in Ridley Scott's version, though refigured as an English/French division and without a sense that the English aristocracy were different from common people. Stephen Knight, *Robin Hood: A Mythic Biography* (Ithaca, NY: Cornell University Press, 2003), p. 111.
22. Santas, *The Epic in Film*, p. 2.

CHAPTER 8

Special Effects, Reality and the New Epic Film

Andrew B. R. Elliott

The centrality of special, visual and digital effects to the epic film is – even at first glance – undeniable. The return of ancient subjects to the big screen, the focus of this book, has gone hand in hand with technological developments which allow for ever greater renditions of architecture, crowds, forums, panoramas and battle sequences, creating a new cinematic vocabulary which in part uses stylistic embellishments which were unavailable to earlier epics – high-definition, digital surround sound, post-production effects, etc. – and in part resurrects showy set pieces which have always been a standard ingredient for the epic film, but which are here enhanced by new technologies – battle scenes with armies of thousands, explosions, lifelike prosthetics to create bloody battles, blood spatters, and dizzying re-creations of classical architecture. These spectacular images, perhaps even more than earlier cycles of big-budget epics, have come to suggest that the surge and splendour which Vivian Sobchack once identified as characteristic of the 1950s and '60s epics are equally at home in the new epic film.[1] As Monica Cyrino comments, 'with the recent advent of computer generated imagery (CGI), blue-screen and other modern technological advances, extravagant digital special effects have become, and continue to be, an intrinsic part of the production of contemporary epic cinema'.[2] Likewise Kirsten Thompson makes a convincing case that, just as once 'the historical epic became indelibly linked to widescreen spectacle', now once again 'digital innovations in special effects have enabled the intensification of the historical epic's distinctive attributes of spectacularity, monumentality, and immersiveness'.[3]

However, arguments which connect these special effects to technological capabilities risk leading us into potentially dangerous territory, specifically that of technological determinism, which sees the return of the epic film as contingent upon, and indeed driven by, developments in the technical processes of film.[4] In a *Financial Times* article discussing the return of the epic film, for example, Sam Leith suggests that just as 'the last great surge of sword 'n' sandals filmmaking was associated with the emergence of a new technology' (in this case anamorphic widescreen processes like Cinemascope), so too are the new epics a result of technology. As a result of CGI:

> the mythological monsters in *Clash of the Titans* no longer needed to be fashioned from Plasticine and painstakingly animated by hand; sets on a DeMillean scale can be built in a computer; unthinkable legions of extras set in motion for crowd scenes with a few strokes on a keyboard.[5]

Though at base he is right to suggest a link between the two (as I shall explain later), arguments like this not only overlook the immense difficulty of using CGI technologies (which are in themselves labour-intensive, require painstaking attention to detail, and which are hardly the result of 'a few strokes on a keyboard'), but they also tie the emergence of genres or cycles to technological leaps, implying a degree of inevitability which, when examined further, is ultimately unsustainable. 'Holding a technological determinist view' is, according to Winston, 'like believing that it is the movement of the leaves on the trees which creates the wind'.[6]

Such a technological determinist view also overlooks that these CGI technologies had, for several decades, already been put to use in other genres – science-fiction, fantasy, or the action film – before they were harnessed by the historical epic, which somewhat undermines the argument that their emergence would lead ineluctably to the return of the historical epic. Indeed, Geoff King suggests that the use of expensive special effects sequences has been part of an industrial strategy since the 1950s which has little to do with individual genres and everything to do with maintaining large audiences.[7] The suggestion that these films emerged precisely because of technological innovations ignores the individual creativity of filmmakers; as James Russell observes, 'rather than viewing the epic film as a means to showcase technological advances, as many scholars have implicitly suggested . . . the epics of the 1950s and 1960s must be understood as serious films made by impassioned filmmakers'.[8]

Consequently, this chapter will argue that the relationship between the new epic film and special effects techniques like CGI is not one of technological inevitability, but one which is instead defined by their co-dependency and mutual convenience. This is a model according to which the return of the epic is not preconditioned by technological advances, but one in which the aesthetic is nevertheless augmented and improved by those same technologies, as the epic films under discussion can use new technologies such as set design in *Gladiator* (Scott 2000), crowd-building software in *Troy* (Petersen 2004), action sequences in *300* (Snyder 2006) and 3D in *Clash of the Titans* (Leterrier 2010) to fulfil audience expectations of an epic. As I demonstrate below, this is largely because, throughout their history, epics have always relied on special effects not for their own sake, but for two contradictory purposes; the first is their ability to showcase spectacular sequences (a *sine qua non* of the epic film), but the second is for its opposite function, to enhance verisimilitude by masking the artifice involved in creating such sequences.

One example of this dual use of effects can be seen at work in the approach and landing of the ships in *Troy*, in a scene anachronistically recalling the D-Day landings as depicted in *Saving Private Ryan* (Spielberg 1998) and later, equally anachronistically, in *Robin Hood* (Scott 2010). Beginning with an overhead shot of Achilles' ship crewed by his Myrmidons, the camera zooms out further to reveal two more Greek ships, then five, then a further dozen until, as it continually zooms and tilts upwards, in a shot lasting a little under thirty seconds the Greek fleet has risen from fifty men to thousands aboard a huge fleet, stretching away to the horizon. We are, then, firmly in the realm of spectacle, according to which the sheer numbers of the ships vie with those of earlier versions for supremacy in bringing to the screen ever greater numbers of conquering Greeks, thereby reflecting not only the epic scale of Book II of *The Iliad*, which is itself wholly given over to describing the armies arriving in their ships, but also tying the individual to the wider national and cross-cultural interests of groups of people, as we saw in Chapter 7. Likewise, the scene comes in part as Petersen's attempt to make good on an earlier line delivered by Odysseus, in which he tells Achilles that 'they're sending the largest fleet that ever sailed'. As a scene of pure spectacle, it patently wins hands down against earlier, pre-CGI, renditions of the Greek fleet; these are no mere models, but individually animated, moving ships which are characterised as much by their individuality as by their scale and number.

However, the spectacular zoom – reminiscent of the famous 'genesis' sequence of *Star Trek II: The Wrath of Khan* (Meyer 1982), or the zoom in *Agora* (Amenábar 2009) from space to the Serapeum, only in reverse – ensures a constantly moving camera. This simple trope of zooming out to show the spectacular scale of the operation acts as a double effect, since it fulfils the need for epic surge and splendour but at the same time it prevents us from seeing other ships in specific detail. It is, then, our distance from the objects which both creates spectacle by the size and scale of the shot, and also ensures credibility by forbidding us from lingering too long on the sequence or seeing any of the other ships too closely. This is, as Stephen Prince notes, a relic of earlier visual effects which required 'withholding [a creature's] appearance until the last moment or restricting it to a quick and fleeting appearance'.[9] A similar approach can be seen in the crowd-building software which creates the armies of thousands which beat at the gates of Troy later in the film – they are both spectacular but also ensure credibility, since the distance required from the individual simultaneously prevents us from studying him too closely. As

Figure 8.1 The digital creation of 'the largest fleet that ever sailed' in *Troy* (2004).

King wryly suggests, '"convincing" special effects sometimes serve a negative purpose, ensuring that our attention is not drawn to the fact that any trickery is involved'.[10]

Accordingly, epic films rely on visual effects both to *create the spectacular images* which audiences come to expect from the epic film and to *obscure their origins* in an effort to enhance credibility. This is what McClean terms their 'seamless' function, in which they pass unnoticed, but are detectable (perhaps because of the impossibility of filming them, like the Colosseum of *Gladiator*).[11] In order to demonstrate this dual use, then, this chapter begins by demonstrating the association of special effects with spectacle in the epic film, before moving on to look at their use in heightening visual authenticity. The final section turns to look at the ways in which these special effects have been harnessed in the service of the new epic film. Touching on examples from *Gladiator*, *Troy* and *300*, I argue that when we examine the uses of these effects, we can see that they are not *driven* by new processes as technological determinism would have it, but instead they have been readily adopted to create a seamless yet spectacular aesthetic which both confirms their pedigree as epic films and pushes the boundaries of heightened realism.

THE EPIC AS SPECTACLE

Visual effects have, in fact, had an association with the epic film long before the epics of the 1950s and '60s. 'The Roman Empire has featured in films from Hollywood's earliest days', and from the very beginnings of the film industry, filmmakers have often been drawn to depict the 'surge and splendour' of the ancient world, a quest which has in many cases pushed the boundaries of technical ability in the pursuit of an epic mise-en-scène, with 'some of the most well-known of these films calling upon all manner of special and optical effects to realistically convey the majesty of a time long past'.[12] Such an association is dependent on three specific functions which these effects serve: first, visual effects are often used to create larger-than-life sets, architecture and historical worlds, and thus are spectacular means of creating *believable* environments; second, these effects allow for huge crowds, battle scenes and entire city-states to be formed on-screen, which allows the films to depict the struggles, movements and origins of entire nations and peoples (which Burgoyne argues is symptomatic of the epic film); finally, the epic film becomes a way to showcase new technologies in and of themselves.[13]

Taking this last point first, James Russell rather provocatively suggests that these films become metaphors for Hollywood itself. Thus, instead of the struggle of the Hebrews being depicted:

> The hero of *The Ten Commandments* is not Moses, but De Mille himself, who set up the whole show, the voice of God and the burning bush and the miracles of Egypt included. And the hero of *Ben-Hur* is not Ben-Hur, who only won the chariot race, but William Wyler, the director, the man responsible for providing the chariot race for us.[14]

In a pedestrian sense, then, the spectacular images on offer in the epic film can be seen as part of a recurrent industrial strategy to foreground the capabilities of the cinematic medium, from its emergence through to competition from television, VHS and home viewing technologies. Much of the appeal, in fact, of some of the earliest historical epics such as *Gli Ultimi Giorni di Pompeii* (Caserini/Rodolfi 1913), *Cabiria* (Pastrone 1914), or *Quo Vadis?* (D'Annunzio/Jacoby 1925), lay in their use of spectacular and dazzling special effects to re-create suitably epic themes, and to beguile audiences into the bargain by showing off the technical capacity of the then new medium. Such showcasing continued into the post-war period, during which 'the historical epic certainly provided excellent opportunities for fifties cinema to show off its technical prowess, and Hollywood may take the major credit for the development of the spectacular side'.[15] Monica Cyrino suggests that, in fact, 'the film industry has always used the epic film as a showcase for the display of new cinematic techniques, as they sought to lure bigger audiences to the movie theatres by promising "the pleasures of the look" in all their widescreen CinemaScope and Technicolor glory'.[16] Likewise, Steve Neale argues that part of the definition of the term 'epic' is used in an industrial sense:

> epic is used to identify . . . large scale films of all kinds which used new technologies, high production values and special modes of distribution and exhibition to differentiate themselves from both routine productions and from alternative forms of contemporary entertainment.[17]

More cynically, for others, the widespread adoption of expensive effects as a hallmark of the Hollywood film served as a means of preserving Hollywood's hegemony over the film industry in the post-war period, since 'expensive productions maintain or raise "barriers to entry" that help to ensure continued oligopoly control by the major studios'.[18] In an argument which it is worth quoting at length, Geoff King observes:

> Keeping up with the latest technologies is generally expensive . . . and can be seen as part of Hollywood's traditional strategy of maintaining or raising 'barriers to entry'. Despite periodic calls for cost-cutting and savings, it has generally suited the majors for the costs of production, distribution and marketing to remain high because this prevents anyone else from getting a foot in the door. Once a certain level of special-effects technology has been deployed it creates a demand that other films match the same expensive standard. Issues of 'quality' and 'standards' such as this have long acted as a cover for the enshrining of just one – expensive, Hollywood – way of operating, when others, which do not have access to the same promotional resources, might be equally valid.[19]

However, at the same time, the sustained use of epic effects and costly set pieces was not wholly down to purely industrial concerns, but equally played an important role in the narrative of the epic films themselves. As Martin Barker asserts, 'special effects have to be both narratively integrated and convincing representations of a realistic fictional world for the audience to believe in them sufficiently, and so to engage with the resulting dilemmas posed for the film's characters'.[20] Geoff King writes:

> In line with more general principles of 'classical' Hollywood filmmaking, the act of creation, of artifice, is concealed in order to carry the spectator into the world of the story. This is a dominant strain in the history of Hollywood cinema: the attempt to establish an 'invisible' style that does not draw attention to its own process.[21]

The growing expertise of filmmakers in visual effects would further fuel this appetite for bigger and grander scenes, since 'the glory that was Greece, And the grandeur that was Rome' (to quote Edgar Allen Poe) seems to demand from filmmakers an equally glorious depiction in cinema. Epic subjects, argues Russell,

> must be treated 'epically', that is with the resources of cinematic style approximating the effects of the epic in literature, great events given the large scale of treatment; *great* as in *massive*, but also connoting grandeur and overwhelming cultural significance.[22]

In this sense, then, it is tempting to suggest that the history of Hollywood's historical epics could be summed up as ever grander shots of ever more grandiose spectacle, to the extent that, 'from its earliest representations in cinema, the ideal of ancient Rome is synonymous with spectacle'.[23] From Griffiths' super-sized physical sets in the Babylon sequence of *Intolerance* (1916) and Pastroni's huge *Cabiria* (1914), there would emerge a steadily increasing reliance on special effects to extend the pro-filmic world of Graeco-Roman epics, yet all the while those imagined historical worlds were constructed according to the same logic, which accorded visual authenticity to spectacle. 'While *Ben-Hur* (1959, Wyler), drew on optical techniques, Stanley Kubrick's *Spartacus* (1960), limited itself to a few matte paintings and thousands of extras. In some respects, although *Gladiator* is a triumph of digital-visual-effects usage, Ridley Scott's approach was quite in keeping with that of Kubrick.'[24]

However, even if the logic was the same, the techniques employed to achieve these effects were to become very different as the twentieth century wore on. The frenetic, fast-paced chariot races of *Ben-Hur* (Wyler, 1959) and the enormous sets built for *The Fall of the Roman Empire* and *King of*

Figure 8.2 CGI aerial shots in *Agora* (2009) transform the city of Alexandria into a site of spectacle wherein the personal and the political are interwoven.

Kings would eventually come to be replaced by huge, virtual re-creations of the Colosseum in *Gladiator*, the 'copy-and-paste', Massive crowd-building software creating armies of thousands in Petersen's *Troy* (2004), or Alexandria in *Agora* seen from vertiginous CGI aerial shots, replete with individually constructed crowd members and even flocks of birds swooping in and out of its arches. Such commonly-used tropes

> consolidated another spectacular image in the cultural imagination: that of the serried ranks of computer-generated combatants charging into battles stretching from the foreground to the horizon. The CGI battle sequence has become one of the most prevalent visual clichés of the twenty-first-century Hollywood blockbuster.[25]

In this way, the evolution of the epic film over the past century has been marked not only by rapid advances in cinematic and exhibition technologies, but by a concomitant association between these technologies and the scale of the historical epic, so that 'viewing an epic became an exceptional experience, where historical subjects and cinematic spectacle connected in a unique fashion'.[26] Neale suggests that 'in the epic, these [spectacular] moments are part of an overall process in which cinema displays itself and its powers through the recreation of a past so distant that much of its impact derives simply from the evidence of the scale of recreation involved'.[27]

SPECIAL EFFECTS AND CREDIBILITY IN THE HISTORICAL EPIC

Looking more closely at the use of special effects in the cinema, it seems that such an emphasis on technological capacities might also be seen to inhere in some of the very earliest films. As some film histories suggest, in its earliest incarnation, some aspects of cinema itself can be seen as a kind of special effect, in its capacity of using technological devices to re-create a 'false' sense of reality which passes for reality itself. Histories of the cinema frequently focus on a conceptual difference between its two pioneers, Lumière and Méliès, dividing early cinema into two opposing impulses.[28] According to this dialectic, Lumière comes to represent a form of cinema whose primary function is the documentation of reality, a genre which foregrounds immediacy and realism; to Méliès is ascribed the domain of fantasy, which abandons realism in favour of experimentation with cinema's technical aspects, forsaking credibility for imagination. Mary Ann Doane, recognising the oversimplification of such a position, observes that 'in this account, Méliès represents fantasy and the fantastic, the Ur-text of all genres that celebrate the "magic" effects of fictional cinema, while Lumière is said to anticipate the insistence upon realism'.[29]

Indeed, looking at the functions of special – and particularly digital – effects as they are used to depict reality, it is clear that such a simplification cannot survive close scrutiny. Several aspects of the special effects industry are not only designed to facilitate scenes which are impossible for live-action sequences (the fantasy of Méliès), but they aim to integrate the fantastic 'seamlessly' into a plausible, credible depiction of the world.[30]

Consequently, underpinning the use of special effects in the creation of epic films are two particular – though seemingly contradictory – impulses. The first is what McLean terms 'fantastical' effects, which 'use DVFx to create images of astonishing qualities and realize the impossible to the highest standards of perceptual realism'.[31] These are the spectacular effects which, according to Albert La Valley, 'show us things to be untrue, but show them to us with such conviction that we believe them to be real'.[32] The second reason is precisely its inverse – to render impossible worlds as real simulacra of an impossible fantasy. This second purpose makes of them what McClean terms 'seamless' effects, effects which are characterised by their ability to hide their origins in order to heighten verisimilitude (in fact, in trying to explain such seamless effects McClean uses the example of *Gladiator*'s Colosseum).[33] Geoff King puts it as follows:

> Hollywood special effects offer spectacular creations or re-creations that make claims to our attention on the grounds of their 'incredible-seeming reality'. *They can appear both 'incredible' and 'real'*, their appeal based

on their ability to 'convince' – to appear real in terms such as detail and texture – and on their status as fabricated spectacle, to be admired as such.[34]

Such a self-contradictory approach gives the new epic film a 'double audience, one that succumbs to the spectacle and one that appreciates it'.[35] Audiences of epic films are poised simultaneously to be *pushed away* from the film by impossible spectacle which they are aware is not real, but at the same time *drawn in* to the narrative by that same spectacle's realistic portrayal of those fantastic worlds.

As a consequence, several of the special effects sequences in the modern epic can be seen to fulfil these two opposing functions. On the one hand, like *Troy*'s huge fleet and anachronistic D-Day landing, they create spectacle which draws attention to itself, but on the other hand they are sometimes also working furiously to convince audiences of the veracity of those images (hence the careful crafting of individually animated crowds). During the sacking of the library in *Agora*, for example, the camera zooms out to an overhead shot of impossible proportions and speeds up the frame rate to make its human protagonists jerk around as if in fast-forward, which draws attention to itself as artifice, yet at the same time its meticulously created crowds are designed to reinforce credibility, declaring that it is no mere matte painting or scale model but an ostensibly real, populated city. Thus the visual effects which spectacularly re-create Rome in *Gladiator* are designed to demonstrate the city's importance as one which, as the pre-credit titles suggest, controlled one quarter of the world's population and which thus functioned as a spectacle of Roman supremacy, an extension of its martial dominance. Yet at the same time, the scene is not pure spectacle – narratively speaking, it is designed to allow us to reflect the wonder of Rome and situate its characters in a believable Roman world.

This combination of functions is, admittedly, not restricted to recent epics. The parting of the Red Sea, for example, in *The Ten Commandments* (De Mille, 1956) can be seen in part as a factor of De Mille's inherent showmanship in foregrounding cinema's spectacular capabilities (as King describes it, 'to exhibit and celebrate the sheer spectacle'),[36] but it also serves a narrative purpose, to link together a cinematic moment with the fates of an entire people in the formulation of a widely applicable nation-founding myth, and one with particular resonance after the creation of the state of Israel in 1948. As such, De Mille's film not only responds to the 'preconceptions and values of the period in which it was made', but also fulfils 'its traditional role as a vehicle of national ideology and aspirations'.[37] In the same way, the taking of Jerusalem in *Kingdom of Heaven* works not merely as an impressive action piece, but as one whose scale underlines the futility of armed incursions into the Middle East as a whole. As such, '"epic" may designate size, expense, specific types of historical setting', but it can also designate the struggles of 'protagonists caught up in large-scale events[,] those who sway the course of history or the fate of nations',[38] which feeds into Burgoyne's persuasive arguments that epics are simultaneously nation-centric myths as well as emblematic myths which hold enormous global sway.[39] As Santas summarises it, 'the enduring popularity of the epic film can be explained largely by its ability to preserve and re-create mythical patterns and thus remain in touch with the deeper wishes of national identity'.[40] In this way, by serving both the narrative and the spectacle, the special effects of the epic film are designed to prioritise credibility.

Admittedly, such an argument does seem counter-intuitive in films which make few claims to historical veracity, such as *300* and *Clash of the Titans*, both of which are set in the epic's often vague 'Egypto-Biblo-Classical era',[41] and which deliberately work against verisimilitude on the historical level. However, these aberrations can be explained by the frequent conflation of Hellenic culture with pseudo-mythical and fantasy worlds. Robert Niemi argues that

> typically a 'history film' is defined, in very broad and loose terms, as either a 'true story' or simply a period piece that conjures a bygone era . . . The theory goes that, even if the narrative and the characters are largely fictional, the setting is real and evocative enough to qualify the film as 'historical'.[42]

Though it is most definitely a discussion for another time, Gideon Nisbet playfully suggests that ancient Greece suffers from a lack of recognisable visual identifiers and thus occupies a liminal space in terms of popular culture's historical imagination:

> Unlike Rome, cinema audiences lack a distinct *visual* idea of Greece to which a director can appeal . . . What are Greeks to *do* in a film, except talk the plot to death? In the popular imagination, Romans win and lose empires, fight fur-clad barbarians and bring on the dancing girls. Greeks discuss the nature of Good or flirt with underage boys.[43]

It is in this sense that, where history remains unclear (see Chapter 5, for example) the special effects can be seen to enhance narrative *plausibility*, and not historical veracity. The CGI-enhanced spectacle of male bodies on offer in *300*'s Spartans is designed not only for show, but visually to distance them from the frailty of the male bodies of both the covered-up Persian warriors and the toga-clad (and therefore effete) Greeks who advocate against war. This is not to excuse the near-fascist glorification of brutal violence and the male body (and its corollary, the vilification of the non-white body), but rather to suggest that these CGI elements are part of the film's narrative logic. Even while dismissing the film itself, then, we can see that the visual effects are designed to suggest narrative plausibility as much as spectacle: such hyper-masculine specimens as Leonidas and his men can only be expected to hold their own against such odds if they are crafted to be near superhuman in strength and martial prowess. While we as audience members know that what is on screen is historically impossible, it becomes, at least narratively plausible.

Seen in this way, then, cinema no longer needs to be reduced to a dichotomy between Lumière's realism and Méliès' fantasy, but can combine the two, readily making use of fantastic elements created through visual effects precisely in order to depict a given reality more convincingly. As Joel Black describes it, the emergence of a special effects industry was designed, at least in part, to produce images which help to depict a distant, remote or even imaginary world as a credible but simultaneously 'not present' reality, an industry which relies on its ability 'to *produce a heightened illusion of reality itself*'.[44]

CONCLUSION

To return, then, to the question framed above, about the relationship between special effects and the return of the epic, we can see that it was by no means a case of technological determinism, according to which the epic returned *because* the technologies available to do so demanded it, but instead the relationship between those same technologies and the epic's sense of spectacle and verisimilitude made for ideal conditions for its cross-fertilisation. Thus the return of the epic was a logical extension of the availability of special effects, on the one hand, and the rise of the blockbuster on the other. Looking from an industrial perspective, the success of high-concept, and high-budget, films like *Titanic* (Cameron 1997), as well as the increasing importance of the summer blockbuster, meant that the conditions were ripe for Scott to pitch an expensive and risky historical epic to the studios. Scott's *Gladiator*, like any other film made in the commercial cinema, was conceived and formulated as a possibility first and later approved by a studio willing to fund it (for a whole host of reasons, most likely), after which it made use of whichever effects were available to it and were within budget. After the success of Scott's *Gladiator*, as the introduction suggests, other films followed in its wake to capitalise on the success of ancient and medieval worlds, and logically these would make use of recent developments in CGI and visual effects. From a technical perspective, in the wake of *Jurassic Park* (1993), *Toy Story* (1995), *A Bug's Life* (1998) and *Antz* (1998), the increasing prevalence of digital effects came to assume similar roles to those of the optical effects which, reaching maturity under Hollywood's studio system in the 1930s, had been so instrumental in the earlier wave of epic films.[45]

Writing of the increasing centrality of special effects departments over the course of the 1990s, Rickett describes how

> [c]rowds could be replicated, removing the need for hundreds of extras in expensive costumes. Physical effects were made practical and safe because safety wires used to protect actors during filming could easily be digitally removed. Futuristic or historical locations could be conjured up with the minimal use of sets and locations . . .[46]

In this climate, then, rather than having the effects dictate the film, it makes much more sense for us to explain it as being the other way round: the stories come first, and whichever special effects are available come later. As McClean neatly describes it, 'stories continue to seek exotic circumstances against which to pit their heroes. This challenge is being met through the rediscovery and reinvention of our past . . . Executing these large-scope projects without DVFx has become, from a film production perspective, unimaginable.'[47]

Accordingly, the return of the epic is in some ways contingent upon recent developments in digital visual effects, which allow for our historical, or pseudo-historical, worlds to be rendered according to changing tastes in visual authenticity. However, this contingency is no different from that of earlier cycles of epics in terms of its logic; epic has always been a spectacular mode of filmmaking, and one which uses all of the technologies, tricks and processes at its disposal to create as monumental, spectacular and immersive a viewing experience as possible. Rather than a gratuitous use of such technologies, the demands of the studios – at their most basic, that the film appeals to as wide an audience as possible in order to recoup the massive costs – as well as the narrative demands of the epic film mean that these visual effects are also designed to heighten credibility and verisimilitude, both in terms of narrative (the last stand at Thermopylae is less plausible if those left to fight it are visible weaklings; Rome can scarcely build an empire if it cannot build a city) and in terms of their usual function as spectacle. As such, the extensive reliance on special effects visible in the epic film's return in the twenty-first century is designed both to support the narrative by its seamless integration within the logic of the film, and to shake the audience into a state in which they simultaneously accept the world on offer while admiring the craft on offer. In this sense, *Gladiator*'s Juba could speak for all of us when he, and we, first catch sight of the Colosseum and he exclaims in awe: 'I did not know men could build such things.'

NOTES

1. Vivian Sobchack, 'Surge and Splendor: A Phenomenology of the Hollywood Historical Epic', in Barry Keith Grant (ed.), *The Film Genre Reader III* (Austin, TX: University of Texas Press, 2003), pp. 296–323.
2. Monica Cyrino, 'This is Sparta!', in Robert Burgoyne (ed.), *The Epic Film in World Culture* (London: Routledge, 2011), pp. 19–38, p. 34.
3. Kirsten Moana Thompson, '360° vision and the historical epic in the digital era', in Burgoyne (ed.), *The Epic Film in World Culture*, pp. 39–62, p. 45.
4. For an in-depth account, and powerful critique, of technological determinism, see Brian Winston, *Technologies of Seeing* (London: BFI, 1996), especially Introduction and Chapter 1, pp. 1–38. See also Raymond Williams, *Television: Technology and Cultural Form* (London: Fontana, 1974).
5. Sam Leith, 'The Return of Swords 'n' Sandals Movies', *Financial Times*, 14 May 2010.
6. Winston, *Technologies of Seeing*, p. 2.
7. Geoff King, *Spectacular Narratives: Hollywood in the Age of the Blockbuster* (London: I. B.Tauris, 2000), p. 5. See also Dan North, *Performing Illusions: Cinema, Special Effects and the Virtual Actor* (London: Wallflower Press, 2008); Geoff King (ed.), *The Spectacle of the Real: From Hollywood to Reality TV and Beyond* (Bristol: Intellect, 2005).
8. James Russell, *The Historical Epic and Contemporary Hollywood: From* Dances with Wolves *to* Gladiator (New York: Continuum, 2007), p. 23.
9. Stephen Prince, *Digital Visual Effects in Cinema: The Seduction of Reality* (Piscataway, NJ: Rutgers University Press, 2012), p. 36. See also pp. 31–7.
10. King, *Spectacular Narratives*, p. 50.
11. Shilo T. McClean, *Digital Storytelling: The Narrative Power of Visual Effects in Film* (Cambridge MA: MIT Press, 2007), p. 78.
12. Ibid., p. 116.
13. Since there is scarcely space to discuss the entire history of special effects here, for more information on this see McClean, *Digital Storytelling*; King, Spectacular Narratives and Prince, *Digital Visual Effects*. However, to my mind the single best study of the implications of special effects remains Dan North's excellent *Performing Illusions*, especially Chapter 1.
14. Russell, *The Historical Epic*, p. 144.
15. Derek Elley, *The Epic Film: Myth and History* (Routledge & Kegan Paul, 1984), p. 20.
16. Cyrino, 'This is Sparta!', p. 34 (my emphasis).
17. Sobchack, 'Surge and Splendor'. Steve Neale, *Genre and Hollywood* (London: Routledge, 2000), p. 85.
18. King, *Spectacular Narratives*, p. 5.
19. Ibid., pp. 67–8.
20. Martin Barker, *From Antz to Titanic: Reinventing Film Analysis* (London: Pluto Press, 2000), p. 83.
21. King, *Spectacular Narratives*, pp. 50–1.
22. Russell, *The Historical Epic*, p. 9.
23. Holly Haynes, '*Rome*'s Opening Titles: Triumph, Spectacle and Desire', in Monica Cyrino (ed.), *Rome, Season One: History Makes Television* (Oxford: Blackwell, 2008), pp. 49–60 (p. 49).
24. McClean, *Digital Storytelling*, p. 116.
25. North, *Performing Illusions*, pp. 175–6.
26. Russell, *The Historical Epic*, pp. 10–11.

27. Stephen Neale, *Genre* (London: British Film Institute, 1980), p. 35.
28. Paul Grainge, Mark Jancovich and Sharon Monteith, *Film Histories: An Introduction and Reader* (Edinburgh: Edinburgh University Press, 2009), pp. 7–9.
29. Mary Ann Doane, *The Emergence of Cinematic Time: Modernity, Contingency, the Archive* (Cambridge, MA: Harvard University Press, 2002), p. 136.
30. McClean, *Digital Storytelling*, p. 72 (my emphasis).
31. Ibid., p. 89.
32. Quoted in Ibid., p. 89.
33. Ibid., p. 78.
34. King, *The Spectacle of the Real*, p. 13 (my emphasis).
35. Sean Cubitt, *The Cinema Effect* (Cambridge, MA: MIT Press, 2005), p. 277.
36. King, *Spectacular Narratives*, p. 51.
37. Richards, *Hollywood's Ancient Worlds*, foreword; Burgoyne, 'Bare Life and Sovereignty in Gladiator', in Burgoyne (ed.), *The Epic Film in World Culture*, pp. 82–97, p. 82.
38. Sheldon Hall and Steve Neale, *Epics, Spectacles, and Blockbusters: A Hollywood History* (Detroit, MI: Wayne State University Press, 2010), p. 5.
39. Burgoyne, *The Epic Film in World Culture*, p. 2.
40. Constantine Santas, *The Epic in Film: From Myth to Blockbuster* (Lanham, MD: Rowman & Littlefield, 2007), p. 4.
41. George MacDonald Fraser, *The Hollywood History of the World: From One Million Years BC to Apocalypse Now* (New York: Columbine Trade, 1989), p. 7.
42. Robert Niemi, *History in the Media, Film and Television* (Santa Barbara, CA: ABC-CLIO, 2006), pp. xxi–xxii.
43. Gideon Nisbet, *Ancient Greece in Film and Popular Culture* (Exeter: Bristol Phoenix Press, 2006), pp. 17–18.
44. Joel Black, *The Reality Effect: Film Culture and the Graphic Imperative* (London: Routledge, 2002), p. 8 (my emphasis).
45. For more on this see David Bordwell and Kristen Thompson, *Film History: An Introduction* (New York: McGraw-Hill, 2003), 2nd edn, Chapter 10, 'The Hollywood Studio System, 1930–45', especially pp. 221–2. Here Bordwell and Thompson observe that where 'most trick photography in the silent era was done by the cinematographer during shooting', the increasing complexity of special effects in multi-camera setups led to the emergence of dedicated special effects departments (p. 221).
46. Richard Rickett, *Special Effects: The History and Technique* (London: Virgin Books, 2000), p. 37.
47. McClean, *Digital Storytelling*, p. 209.

PART III

Epic Films and Challenging the Canon

CHAPTER 9

Pass the Ammunition: A Short Etymology of 'Blockbuster'

Sheldon Hall

This chapter stems from my long-standing interest in the etymology, or linguistic history, of film-industry and showbusiness terminology or slang. In particular, my interest is in the origins and use of the now-ubiquitous word 'blockbuster'. Its use today – indeed, overuse – tends to be in connection with what I and Steve Neale, in our book *Epics, Spectacles, and Blockbusters: A Hollywood History*, refer to as 'unusually expensive productions designed to earn unusually large amounts of money'[1] – that is to say, films which are not just exceptionally successful box-office hits but those which are *specifically intended to be so*, and are budgeted, made and marketed accordingly. However, while scholars and critics may attempt a certain precision in its use, popular usage is far less circumspect. In my experience as a university film studies tutor, 'blockbuster' is often assumed to be synonymous with the contemporary action film, the genre in which the largest sums are typically invested today and which often heads the box-office charts. Furthermore, it is not unusual to find 'civilians' (those moviegoers who are not members of the academic film community or elite film culture) describing virtually any and every Hollywood movie as a blockbuster, regarding the word as a synonym for the kind of mainstream picture the American film industry typically produces irrespective of genre. (In much the same way, 'Hollywood' itself is sometimes taken to stand for the whole of the film industry rather than the major American corporations in particular.)

In researching my share of *Epics, Spectacles, and Blockbusters* I attempted to locate the first uses of 'blockbuster' in the American trade press – in particular, the major showbusiness newspaper *Variety* – as a way of tracing its adoption into film-industry vernacular. Additional research clarified the word's extra-cinematic origins (of which more later). My extensive searches of *Variety* – which were initially confined to its weekly editions, more readily available on microfilm in UK libraries than the daily version – suggested that the 'original' use of the term in its modern sense occurred in the journal's review of *Quo Vadis* (LeRoy 1951) in the weekly issue of 14 November 1951, which described the film as 'a b.o. blockbuster . . . right up there with *Birth of a Nation* [Griffiths 1915] and *Gone With the Wind* [Fleming 1939] for boxoffice performance . . . a super-spectacle in all its meaning'.[2] But I was subsequently alerted to an earlier use by Jeffrey Richards' book *Hollywood's Ancient Worlds*, which quotes a review from the British newspaper the *Daily Mirror*, dated 22 December 1950, of Cecil B. De Mille's *Samson and Delilah* (De Mille 1949), predicting it, too, to be 'a box office block buster'.[3] The strikingly similar vocabulary suggested a longer history for the film-specific use of the term than I had anticipated, and the recent digitisation of the *Variety* archive made viable a more detailed word search than could be achieved with microfilm.[4]

With the aid of this research tool it has been possible to construct a reasonably accurate history of 'blockbuster' before the mid-1950s, by which time it had become recognised and accepted by both the trade press and the film industry at large as betokening the kinds of film identified above: one which would 'gross $2,000,000 or more in domestic (U.S. and Canada) rentals' as well as 'a relatively expensive picture that can head the program in all situations'.[5] Both these definitions are taken from *Variety*'s reports of United Artists' own categorisation of its product, in 1954 and 1957 respectively. In its annual surveys the journal identified 1953 as 'a year of boxoffice blockbusters', with 135 releases grossing $1,000,000 or over as against 119 in 1952, and 1958 similarly as 'the year of the blockbusters for the picture business'.[6] Heading the revenue chart in 1953 was *The Robe* (Koster 1953) and, in 1958, *The Bridge on the River Kwai* (Lean 1957), which, along with *The Ten Commandments* (De Mille 1956) and *Around the World in Eighty Days* (Anderson 1956), that year joined *Gone with the Wind* and *The Robe* to top the annually updated 'All-Time B.O. Champs' list. All these secured the common understanding of the blockbuster as a 'kingsize' picture, large in scale, spectacle, cost and income, as well as wide in scope (or 'Scope) and long in running time (all five films ran for between two-and-a-quarter and three-and-three-quarter hours).

ORIGINS

In teaching about the blockbuster, I often pose students the questions of how the word originated and what it first referred to. Their answers often echo those that I suggested to myself before beginning sustained research into the matter. They typically hinge on the understanding, in the context of cinema history, of the 'block' prefix.

One sense of this is in relation to the common practice, prior to 1948 (and especially up to 1940), of block booking: that system of distribution, on which

Figure 9.1 Trade advertisements in the 1930s and 1940s frequently showed long queues of patrons in lines extending around the block.

the dominance of the eight major Hollywood corporations depended, in which the exhibitor client was obliged to book an entire year's output from a major studio rather than being free to choose only the particular picture or pictures desired.[7] Within a block package, it was common for the distributor to nominate a small number of films as 'specials' or, less frequently, 'superspecials': big-budget or prestige productions which would carry a higher-than-average price tag in terms of the proportion of box-office income demanded by way of rental. In some cases, a particular attraction might not be offered as part of a block at all, but instead be sold singly and only to those select clientele in whose theatres the film could best be presented, possibly on a 'roadshow' or high-priced, exclusive pre-release basis. Such films – which included, for example, *Gone with the Wind* – correspond closely to our modern understanding of what a blockbuster film is. But by the time the term entered common parlance, the era of block booking was over. After the 1940 Consent Decree, block booking was limited to groups of five, and in the 1948 Paramount et al. decrees the practice was outlawed altogether and every film had to be sold singly, without the sale being conditional on the booking of another picture. So however much we might now want to describe pre-1948 superproductions as blockbusters, that is not how they would have been known at the time.

A second, more directly relevant, sense of 'block' is that of a city block. Trade advertisements for films in the 1930s and 1940s frequently included illustrations showing long queues of patrons waiting outside theatres for the chance of admission, with such lines often extending around the block of buildings on which the theatre was located.[8] 'Blockbuster' might therefore refer to a film so popular as to attract round-the-block queues; but, again, the term was never used in this way. In fact, the word does not owe its origins to the film or entertainment industries at all, so does not derive from any habitual trade practices. Its first use by the film trade press, in 1943, was purely opportunistic, on the basis of its topicality and current newsworthiness.

In that year, the Allied air forces began to employ a type of heavy explosive shell in the bombing of military and industrial targets in Nazi-occupied Europe. Newspaper reports of its being tested had appeared the year before and subsequent press coverage described the extensive damage it inflicted on cities and factories. The nickname given to these large bombs, typically weighing 4,000 pounds or 8,000 pounds, was 'blockbuster', indicating their capacity for large-scale destruction: a bomb powerful enough to demolish an entire city block. Until early 1944, the 8,000-pounder (over five tons) was the largest aerial bomb ever deployed; it was superseded when the RAF introduced the 12,000-pound 'factory buster' and again when in August 1945 American air crews dropped the first atomic bombs on Hiroshima and Nagasaki – the former of which was reportedly described by *Chicago Sun-Times* as a 'city-buster'.[9]

The earliest use I have been able to locate of 'blockbuster' to describe a motion picture occurs in trade advertisements placed in *Variety* and *Motion Picture Herald*, and presumably also in other contemporaneous trade publications, in May 1943 for RKO's war film *Bombardier* (Wallace 1943); the tagline reads: 'The block-buster of all action-thrill-service shows!'.[10] (Blockbuster was often hyphenated or written as two separate words in this period.) As the film's title indicates, the choice of metaphor was a deliberate play on the story's dramatic content, which concerns a squadron of trainee bombardiers and climaxes with an aerial assault on Japanese munitions factories. Another trade advertisement for a war-themed film, the documentary *With the Marines at Tarawa* (1944), describes its emotional impact by way of analogy: 'It hits the heart like a two ton blockbuster!'[11] An appeal for industry support for a fundraising campaign similarly invoked the image of a large bomb, and was accompanied by a graphic illustration showing a shell landing on the flag of Japan: 'Let's make the 6th War Loan a six-ton block-buster!'[12] In all these instances, the publicists were drawing upon industry readers' presumed awareness of the blockbuster bomb, its current prominence in the public mind and its connotations of massive impact.

Not surprisingly, reporters, reviewers and editorial copywriters for the trade press also began to exploit the word for its shorthand descriptive vividness, albeit as a way of indicating commercial potential rather than a role in the war effort. Thus MGM's combat film *Bataan* (Garnett 1943) was trumpeted

A SHORT ETYMOLOGY OF 'BLOCKBUSTER' 151

Figure 9.2 *Bombardier* (1943) was advertised as 'the blockbuster of all action-thrill-service shows'.

in the company's house organ *The Lion's Roar* as 'a block-buster to scatter those wise guys in the industry and the press who are always telling us that the public won't support war films'.[13] Paramount's *No Time for Love* (Leisen 1944) was described by *Boxoffice* magazine as a 'comedy block-buster. Theatre grosses should be blown to ceiling heights.'[14] *Variety*'s review predicted that the musical *Brazil* (Santley 1944) would 'prove a block-buster at the wickets, a musical investment for Republic that promises to out-gross any previous top-bracket film from this company'.[15] In all these instances, 'blockbuster' has been added to the already extensive trade vocabulary for describing hits (a word whose own associations with the effect of military ordnance hardly need to be stressed) in martial terms. A further example can be adduced from an article in *The Lion's Roar*: 'Behind the big guns that fire the loudest box-office salvoes in the industry must be men who know how to load them with the industry's most potent ammunition.'[16]

The potency of the blockbuster bomb as a metaphor or simile for the film trade seems, however, to have been limited by its immediate topicality. After 1944, once its novelty value had passed and even before its wartime currency had expired, the word ceased to appear in advertising or editorial copy.[17] The reason for its obsolescence is suggested by a line quoted in a

Figure 9.3 An appeal for industry support for a fund-raising campaign drawing upon readers' presumed awareness of the blockbuster bomb and its connotations of massive impact.

trade advertisement for CBS's experimental colour television service in 1946: 'I think it obsoletes [sic] black-and-white as the ATOM Bomb made Block busters obsolete.'[18] The much more powerful image of nuclear destruction, as well as the cessation of hostilities, had seemingly rendered the blockbuster outdated as a descriptive analogy as well as an actual weapon. One quaint reference in 1946 would have been most appreciated by readers with long memories, when an MGM publicist reassured *Variety*'s gossip columnist that Elizabeth Taylor's first screen kiss, in *Rich Full Life* (Leonard 1946), would be only a 'peck, not a blockbuster'.[19]

POST-WAR CONFLICT AND COMPETITION

After a hiatus of several years, 'blockbuster' reappeared in *Variety* in 1948, in two articles announcing programmes of forthcoming releases from all the major studios. In April, *Daily Variety* led its survey of the year's upcoming releases with several MGM pictures 'packed with stars', including *Words and Music* (Taurog 1948), *Homecoming* (LeRoy 1948), *State of the Union* (Capra 1948) and *The Three Musketeers* (Sidney 1948), and a further group of 'Leo's Blockbusters' headed by *Command Decision* (Wood 1948).[20] In December, in an article listing sixty-five big-budget films in the pipeline, the daily noted that 20th Century-Fox's 'blockbusters' are '*The Black Rose* (Hathaway 1950), $3,500,000; *Lydia Bailey* (Negulesco 1952), $3,000,000; *The Snake Pit* (Litvak 1948), $2,700,000; and *Prince of Foxes* (King 1949), *Twelve O'Clock High* (King 1949), *Down to the Sea in Ships* (Hathaway 1949) and *The Beautiful Blonde from Bashful Bend* (Sturges 1949), $2,000,000 apiece'.[21] Here we have at work the twin definitions of blockbuster which still hold sway: potentially successful releases and high-cost productions. Though *Command Decision*, adapted from a successful Broadway play about wartime bombing missions, is (like *Bombardier* five years before) thematically suited to the description of blockbuster – it was one of the first post-war films to return to a Second World War setting after it had been deemed box-office poison owing to the public's satiation with war pictures during the conflict – it was not the only film mentioned in that category; others listed alongside it included comedies, musicals and crime thrillers.[22] Instead, the term had begun to acquire a more general significance unrelated either to a time of literal conflict (intensive bombing campaigns held no relevance to America's subsequent involvement in the Korean War) or to specific story material. Subsequent iterations in trade discourse over the next three years confirmed this.

Curiously, the version of the April article which appeared in the weekly, rather than the daily, edition of *Variety* (it is common for the weekly paper to reprint, revise or expand articles that first appeared in the daily) did not use the word 'blockbuster'. It did, however, likewise pursue a wartime analogy. The opening paragraph reads as follows:

> Paced by Metro, studios are rushing to aid the sagging b.o. with the biggest array of star-studded pix in Hollywood history. The next 12 months will see the industry's big guns fired in a simultaneous barrage designed to crumble stiffening buyer opposition, and to hasten return of healthy business.[23]

The tone of this passage, which is taken up by other contemporaneous articles and many more in the next few years to come, gives an indication of the state of mind which was increasingly taking over the industry and its press at this time. It suggests the onset of a siege mentality and a related commitment to an aggressive form of defence. To understand the reasons for this, it is necessary to offer a brief contextualisation of the post-war era as it was experienced by the entertainment industry.

As is well-known, Hollywood faced a number of crises in the late 1940s and early 1950s. The most pressing of these in commercial terms (setting to one side the investigations of supposed Communist influence in the film industry undertaken by the House UnAmerican Activities Committee) were (1) the results of the Supreme Court decision (handed down in May 1948) in the long-running antitrust case, which enforced the divorcement and divestiture of the theatre chains owned by the 'Big Five' major corporations; and (2) the initially gradual but increasingly precipitous decline in domestic theatre admissions as the greater availability of both disposable income and affordable consumer durables, the greater variety of post-war leisure options and the population shift to an increasingly middle-class, suburban base all combined to draw potential audiences away from the cinema. In five years, according to one report, attendance declined by one-third, from a peak of 80 million admissions per week in 1946 to 53 million in 1951.[24]

The antitrust action was the most visible manifestation of a long-standing hostility to the major producer-distributors of sections of the independent exhibitors (those not owned by or affiliated to the majors), who depended on them for a regular supply of product. It was the resentment against certain entrenched trade practices (such as block booking) on the part of some of these exhibitors which led them to urge the Department of Justice to investigate illegal collusion and unfair competition within the industry, and ultimately to the Consent Decrees signed by RKO in 1948, Paramount in 1949 and Fox, Warner Bros. and Loew's (the parent company of MGM) in 1950. The ultimate result of the court action that drew a line under the vertically integrated studio system was not, however, to the universal benefit of independent exhibitors. While they had hoped to gain greater freedom of choice in film bookings and consequent economic benefits from the ruling, they found instead to their cost that the majors had other ways of retaining control over the market than outright ownership of theatres. One of these was the practice of competitive bidding, or auction selling, for top product, which had actually been introduced at the behest of the New York district court in its own ruling on the antitrust case on 11 June 1946.[25] Under this system, rival exhibitors in each area were forced to bid against one another for the right to show the most desirable new pictures in first run. By law, the picture had to go to the highest bidder, but offers were made 'blind' (that is, bidders were not permitted to know what their rivals had bid), so in order to be sure of securing a picture exhibitors were obliged to offer terms highly favourable to the distributors.

In March 1949, *Variety* noted that a deliberate drive by 20th Century-Fox 'to hoist film rentals another 25% shows signs of developing into an offensive by all the majors for bigger returns in distribution ... indications this week point to a determination by the other companies to stay abreast the growing battle. The entire industry is gearing for what may be the bitterest exhib-distrib fracas in many years.' The paper stated that

> the campaign is expected to touch off an unprecedented string of attacks from exhib organizations. With the growing tension, every theatre group, ranging from Allied to Theatre Owners of America, will line up in an effort to stave off distrib assault on rentals. Already the opening gun has been fired in the form of a challenge by Harry Brandt's Independent Theatre Owners of America to 20th's Spyros Skouras, Al Lichtman, and Andy W. Smith, Jr., for a full-dress debate.[26]

Variety had reported in late 1948 that, rather than being liberated by divorcement, exhibitors were afraid that it would make distribution the dominant sector of the industry, with the majors able to demand higher rentals for fewer films now that they were no longer obliged to keep their own theatres supplied. This threatened to leave exhibitors with a product shortage, higher operating costs and increased competition from other forms of recreation, including television.[27]

As an alternative form of audio-visual entertainment and the newest arrival on the leisure-time scene, broadcast network television was of course the most conspicuous rival for audience loyalty. In 1948 *Variety* reported general agreement among exhibitors that TV was not yet a significant threat to the film box office, and that any such future threat would be temporary until the novelty of the new medium wore off, as had happened previously with radio. But in the same year a survey of 270 families in Long Island, New York, found that 20 per cent of those owning television sets visited cinemas less often than those without, and that 58 per cent attended less often than they had before purchasing the TV. The survey suggested a national annual loss of rental income of $3,400,000 if the same was true for the whole country.[28] This was of course if the present proportion of TV ownership remained constant; but in the next few years it grew exponentially, as did the television broadcasting industry itself.

Writing in the *Variety* anniversary issue of 2 January 1952, looking back like other contributors on the trends and patterns of the year just gone, Frieda Hennock noted:

> There were many outstanding events in TV during 1951. Perhaps the most fundamental and far-reaching change was found in the balance sheets of the 108 TV stations now on the air. Telecasting finally climbed out of the pit of unprofitable operation; black ink came widely into use and the red was happily stored away, let us hope forever, by the majority of broadcasters. Choice nighttime was already SRO [standing room

only], with this condition spreading to other time segments. Television had become, in *Variety* lingo, 'a B.O. Blockbuster.'[29]

The reference here to 'blockbuster' as being part of the journal's characteristically idiosyncratic, idiomatic vocabulary offers confirmation that *Variety* itself was most likely responsible for the term's renewed currency, and that it was applied by the journal as much to television and to other areas of showbusiness, including popular music and radio, as it was to the cinema. Thus in 1949, Dean Martin and Jerry Lewis's new show on the NBC radio network was said to face 'the rugged competition of the front end of Columbia's blockbusters'. Another report identified this competitor as 'CBS's new Sunday comedy blockbuster' fronted by Red Skelton.[30] In reporting on the competition for viewers among the television networks in the start of the new 1951–2 season, *Variety* ran the headline 'NBC-TV's Blockbustin' Lineup; Net's Torpedoes Trained on CBS'. For CBS's response to its rival, an article on the same page adopted a pugilistic rather than a militaristic metaphor: 'CBS Prepping Big Sunday Punches to Right-Cross NBC's "Big Show".'[31]

The important point to note here is the repeated emphasis on rivalry, competition and conflict, terms in which 'blockbuster' seems to play a regular and representative role. Similarly aggressive terminology abounds in trade journalism and advertising throughout the late 1940s and early 1950s. *Variety*'s 1948 previews of upcoming product, cited above, are early instances. Another is this similar report from two years later:

> Hollywood will unleash its biggest guns in the 1950 fall season with a record list of completed top product calculated to revive a lagging boxoffice . . . Spectacle, adventure, music, comedy and romance have been molded into mass appeal yarns and united with boxoffice stars, color and the top production know-how to give one of the greatest mass attacks on TV yet provided.[32]

The intensified pressure on the film industry to fight the inroads of television provides one explanation for this hostile tone. It is noticeable also in ad campaigns run by several of the majors. In a four-page preview of its new releases for the first quarter of the year, Paramount used language identical to that of *Variety*'s copywriter. As well as the slogan 'The Big Gun: Paramount in '51' the ad included a banner headline, 'First Hits in a Year-Long Boxoffice Barrage' and the sub-headline 'Manpowered by the strongest army of talent ever recruited at one studio'.

A logo depicting a cannon appearing to fire an exclamation mark appeared on the first page and in miniature alongside the title of each film to be released from January to April (nine in all, including the wide general release of

Figure 9.4 Paramount's 'Big Guns'.

Samson and Delilah, identified as being already 'the Greatest Grosser of Our Time' from its roadshow engagements).[33] In June and July of the same year 20th Century-Fox ran a series of advertisements in *Variety* on the theme of 'The Industry's New Rallying Cry: Let's Attack Together!'. The first ad in this series continued: 'A new fighting spirit's in the air! A new smile's on Showmen's faces! 20th passes the ammo . . . and the big offensive is on!'[34] The series culminated in an eight-page splash in the 4 July issue, including the text:

> we've got the *ammunition*! Powered by the leadership that set off the industry's showmanship crusade . . . and told the world the movies are the greatest of all entertainment! Once again 20th comes through with a tremendous barrage of hits – supported by the know-how that made a showmanship [*sic*] famous! The industry's biggest offensive is on! Let's attack together!!![35]

This ad series, aside from trailing the studio's new releases for the remainder of the year (including 'special engagements' of the biblical epic *David and Bathsheba* (King 1951)), was dedicated to a show of unity with exhibitors, who had only recently been widely regarded by the vertically integrated studios as their virtual enemies (thanks to the antitrust proceedings) rather than as allies. The copy for the 4 July ad also included the line 'We are determined to back up our exhibitor friends with every resource at our command'.[36] This emphasis on friendship rather than enmity, on mutual support rather than rivalry, was undoubtedly an attempt to ameliorate the situation which, according to the March 1949 article cited above, threatened a potential 'exhib-distrib fracas'. It diverted attention from the conflict of interest which saw exhibitors hoping for greater freedom of choice in which films they booked and, crucially, when and on what terms they were able to book them, and producer-distributors seeking to secure not only a sufficient number of bookings for their product but also favourable rental terms to guarantee a profit on their investment and to compensate for the decline in theatre admissions. The hostility which resulted from the renters' introduction in 1946 of competitive bidding or auction selling was one sign of this conflict, in which movies could be seen not so much as ammunition in a common cause as weapons with which one sector of the industry could do battle with another.

In order to justify auction selling as a way of driving up rentals, the majors needed to make available films for which exhibitors would be willing to compete with one another to pay prices favourable to the producer-distributors. In an increasingly uncertain marketplace, with audience tastes no longer as predictable nor their attendance as reliable as in the recent past, the most attractive commodities for exhibitors were those containing proven box-office ingredients, including major stars, 'pre-sold' stories (such as those with a basis in established literary or stage properties, or indeed previously successful films) and high production values (the kind of spectacle afforded by a big budget). Such films could then be offered to audiences at selectively increased admission prices, a practice actively encouraged by the majors even though, legally, they could no longer either set admission prices themselves (unless hiring a theatre outright on a 'four-wall' basis, for which they would need to secure court permission) or dictate prices to exhibitor clients, as they had done in the recent past. Nevertheless, in their bids interested exhibitors were advised to 'suggest' the admission prices they intended to charge for particular pictures, as a way of allowing the distributor to assess the potential value of the competing offers. Not all films were sold to exhibitors in this way; indeed, besides the inconvenience of the time consumed by receiving and processing bids, only a relatively small proportion of any major's annual output was suited to it and it therefore tended to be reserved for specials and superspecials. One such, though far from the first, was MGM's release of *Quo Vadis*.[37]

Costing $7,623,000, *Quo Vadis* was the most expensive production made up to that time. Following the opening of its premiere engagements in eight key cities including New York and Los Angeles, used by MGM to test the market for exhibition policy, the film was made available for first-run bookings after 1 January 1952 under strictly specified conditions. Exhibitors were required to stipulate minimum guarantees for: the total sum they would remit to MGM

Figure 9.5 Weapons of Mass Distribution.

as rental; the length of the run they would give the picture; control figures for 'holdovers' (that is, the minimum weekly take that would justify the booking being retained for the following week); the amount the exhibitor was prepared to spend on local advertising following the first week, which MGM would pay for; and the admission price before taxes at which tickets would be sold. MGM's trade advertisement announcing the sales plan carefully set out the argument for its policy on ticket prices:

> We cannot and will not have anything to do with the fixing or determination of admission prices; they will be decided by the theatre operators and no-one else ... The sole purpose in asking for admission prices which the exhibitors intend to charge is to enable us to evaluate the offers received and thus award the picture on the basis of the best bid. Any offer which contains a participation in the gross requires an estimate of such receipts for proper appraisal. This estimate, of course, necessitates a knowledge of the admission prices prevailing during the engagement.

The failure to include proposed admission prices in an offer will not disqualify the bid, but their inclusion will enable us better to evaluate the bids.[38]

Distribution agents were not permitted to suggest admission prices to theatre bookers, but could indicate prices charged by other theatres showing the film as a guide.

Initially, only theatres situated in communities of over 100,000 in population were permitted to bid for *Quo Vadis*, and even exhibitors not in competitive situations were required to submit a satisfactory offer in order to be able to play the picture. As the release progressed the film was to be made available for first run to theatres in successively smaller communities that would be invited to bid for it on the same basis, and then for second and subsequent runs in localities where the film had already played. Under no circumstances was it allowed to be shown as part of a double bill, but as *Quo Vadis* ran for nearly three hours there was not likely to be any dispute in this particular matter. Although MGM's sales plan drew protests and even questions as to its legality from some exhibitor organisations there was little actual resistance from theatre owners themselves. Instead, MGM reported being 'deluged' by offers, many of them from exhibitors outside the largest cities or in other ways contrary to the stipulations of the plan.[39] As rental, theatres were effectively required to pay around 70 per cent from the first dollar (the top rate paid for the most in-demand pictures in the past, including *Gone with the Wind*, *Samson and Delilah* and *David and Bathsheba*). Such high terms in effect obliged them to increase their prices for the length of the engagement in order to ensure a profit on their operating costs (standard booking deals stipulated a rental figure after deduction of costs) and the average admission price charged in most first-run theatres was reported as $1.25.[40] Nevertheless, by the end of 1957 domestic rentals totalled $11,143,000 with overseas earnings of $9,894,000 for a total gross of $21,037,000 and a profit of $5,440,000 (thus distribution, marketing and other expenses over the six years of first release amounted to $7,974,000).[41]

The success of *Quo Vadis* and other 'big pictures' in the early 1950s set the pattern for others still to come, in ever greater numbers and on ever larger budgets. If *Variety*'s designation of the film as a blockbuster in its review of 14 November 1951 was not the first instance of the word being used to mean a purpose-built box-office giant, it undoubtedly marked the point at which it had been definitively accepted into the industry's vocabulary, and not only in the trade press. The week before the journal ran its review, it had reported MGM production head Dore Schary's disdain for going into partnership with television because of the far greater rewards available from the theatrical market:

> forgetting those $5,500,000 blockbusters, or even the $3,000,000 and $4,000,000 top grossers we've been turning out, it's obvious that . . . the millions in potentials from orthodox theatre boxoffice exhibition makes TV a peanuts operation for the majors anyway . . . That's why Metro is maintaining its 40-picture schedule. We're upping the ratio of the so-called 'blockbusters' to 20, that is in color and more costly, and naturally hope the other 20, despite the more modest budgets, will likewise measure up.[42]

Thus in the space of a single interview Schary used the term to refer to high-grossing movies and to high-cost films designed for high earnings, confirming that its dual modern sense had already been accepted into the Hollywood lexicon.

In February 1952 Schary was again reported, this time according to an interview with RCA's David Sarnoff, as stating that MGM was opposed to dealing with television or 'to further building up "the monster", which is inimical to the film boxoffice; and that the main objective is to produce box-office blockbusters or any other type of film which will lure them out of the home'.[43] This is now the commonsensical view of the role of the blockbuster in 1950s film economics, but it was not regarded without some scepticism or ambivalence at the time. In *Variety*'s anniversary issue (its annual forum for retrospective and topical overviews of entertainment affairs) of 2 January 1952, no fewer than four articles addressed this topic. James R. Grainger, executive vice-president of Republic Pictures, argued that 'theatres must have a steady flow of product to keep their screens occupied, and every picture can't be a "blockbuster". All the producing companies together barely make 52 pictures in that category.' Understandably, given his company's long-standing commitment to B movies and other low-budget entertainment, he felt that it was not 'only "big" pictures [that] do business. In my opinion, the picture that does business, whether it is a so-called blockbuster or not, is the one which has the entertainment value to which the public responds.'[44]

This point was echoed by veteran producer Hal B. Wallis, then an independent based on the Paramount lot, whose current productions included the Dean Martin and Jerry Lewis series of musical comedies:

> Undoubtedly, the so-called 'blockbusters,' colossi like *Quo Vadis, Samson and Delilah, David and Bathsheba* and *Greatest Show on Earth* [De Mille 1952] are great for the business. They attract customers who haven't been around for years and their very exploitation is a stimulant for our industry, which thrives on excitement.
>
> However, I do not subscribe to a full program of multi-million-dollar negative costs. For one, too frequent repetition of this type of picture

would very quickly sate the public. Then consider the grosses rolled up by any Martin and Lewis picture . . . and you see why there is still profit possible in films that are brought in for a million or less.[45]

Wallis articulated a widespread concern in the industry over rising production costs – the result, variously, of the increasing cost of materials, increasing union demands for minimum wages and minimum crewing levels, and increasing demands of talent for participation in film revenues – at a time when income and profit were under threat. He questioned also the value of big budgets as far as the audience was concerned: 'In more than 20 years in this business I have never heard a passing patron at a theatre ask, "How much did this picture cost to make?"'[46]

Another highly regarded producer, Stanley Kramer, similarly resisted the imminent prospect of industry-wide commitment to the production of films designated by the term 'blockbuster', to the possible exclusion of other kinds of product aimed at other kinds of audience such as the more discriminating over-25s:

> Obviously the film industry as it has been constituted couldn't long survive just producing blockbusters, which I assume mean pictures that are replete with thousands of plunging horses and necklines, plus gigantic, spectacular, lavish situations and expenditures of millions of dollars. In the final analysis, we are a story-telling medium, and our success depends directly on our ability to select and tell stories well. If we must substitute size for all of the other well-tested elements that comprise expert storytelling, we belong to the circus business instead of motion pictures. It is possible that a wave of the super-colossal will engulf the industry.[47]

The terms 'colossal' or 'super-colossal' – long associated with the scale, spectacle and lavish expenditure now identified with 'blockbuster' – were used in the trade press to describe *Quo Vadis*, *David and Bathsheba*, *The Greatest Show on Earth* and others, and this was indeed just the kind of production on which Hollywood was poised to embark in unprecedented numbers and expense over the next two decades.

CODA: THE NUCLEAR ALTERNATIVE

I have tried to show that the adoption of 'blockbuster' into film-industry discourse was occasioned by the context of industry conflict and aggressive competition between media for both economic dominance and audience loyalty at a time of great instability in the field of entertainment. However, it could reasonably be asked why, given the usual ephemerality of slang terms, it has survived to remain in common use for more than sixty years. Why have alternative, more up-to-date terms not emerged to replace it, at least in common parlance? One reason, I would suggest, is precisely that the original meaning of the term, its etymological root, has been forgotten, making its appropriation by colloquial, industrial and even academic discourse all the easier. Even by the 1950s awareness of its original sense was fading, and this was seemingly a condition for its subsequent ubiquity. The point is made clearer if we briefly compare it to another post-war expression that has not survived.

Intermittently throughout the late 1940s and early 1950s, 'atomic' is used as a descriptive term to describe the power of particular performers or films. For example, the earnings of *The Outlaw* (Hughes 1943) on its long-delayed 1946 release in Los Angeles were said by *Variety* to be an 'Atomic 70G'; Broadway columnist Radie Harris referred to the imminent return to the 'Gay White Way' of tempestuous star 'atomic Tallulah' Bankhead; Martin and Lewis were said to be 'readying an atomic sock' for an upcoming nightclub appearance; and a *Variety* headline reported 'Broadway Biz in Atomic Boom' over the New Year holiday of 1949–50.[48] But these were atypical uses of a word that was more commonly, and extensively, used in its literal sense to refer to developments in the use and abuse of nuclear fission. The call by Robert M. Weitman, vice-president of United Paramount Theatres, 'for the film industry to "set off its own atomic bomb" in the entertainment world in order to rekindle public interest in theatre-going'[49] must have seemed tasteless even in 1950. Although there is an abundance of explosive imagery in trade advertising around this time – such as references to United Artists' *The Sound of Fury* (Endfield 1950) making a 'Boom at the Boxoffice' and *He Ran All the Way* (Berry 1951) as 'Boxoffice Dynamite'; or MGM's *Lone Star* (Sherman 1952) being 'Box-office Combustion' and *Somebody Up There Likes Me* (Wise 1956) 'Bursting on the Industry like a Bomb-Shell!'[50] – references to the more topical nuclear bomb are scarce except where the subject demands it. This was the case with Republic's serial *The Purple Monster Strikes* (Bennet and Brannon 1945), concerning a secret weapon: 'See ... the "Electro-Annihilator" at work ... disintegrating all before it ... as it harnesses the tremendous energy of the sun ... just like the ATOMIC BOMB!' The serial itself is further said to possess 'the power of an Atomic Bomb'.[51]

When the film industry launched its own 'secret weapons' in the form of the various new screen technologies of the 1950s, their description in the trade press sometimes invoked nuclear analogies: Todd-AO, the 70mm widescreen process developed by the American Optical Co. for showman Mike Todd, was said to have been called 'the T-bomb of the picture business' by interested exhibitors.[52] In the field of popular music, a trade advertisement placed by

RCA Victor Records for singer Tony Martin proclaimed: 'New "M" Bomb Explodes! Tony Gets Direct Hit . . .'[53] Yet again, however, these are not at all typical. I would suggest that the very immediacy of the threat posed by the atom bomb in the age of nuclear anxiety prevented such vocabulary and its associated imagery catching on except as an occasional gimmick, and that protocols of taste and tact militated against their continued use. 'Blockbuster', however, though its literal namesake undoubtedly produced a greater loss of life than the A-bomb during the years of its active use in the Second World War, was ultimately rendered safe not only by the fact of its obsolescence as a military weapon or by the collective amnesia of the general public, but by its very pervasiveness as an expression during the post-war period, which detached the word from its linguistic roots and ensured that it came to be associated exclusively with popular entertainment in general and with the big-budget, high-impact Hollywood hit in particular.

POSTSCRIPT

Since this chapter was written, another article has appeared on the history and use of the term 'blockbuster': Charles R. Acland, 'Senses of Success and the Rise of the Blockbuster', *Film History*, 25.1–2 (2013), pp. 11–18. Acland draws on similar trade-paper material and makes some similar points while reaching his own conclusions. The two pieces might usefully be read in conjunction with one another.

NOTES

1. Sheldon Hall and Steve Neale, *Epics, Spectacles, and Blockbusters: A Hollywood History* (Detroit, MI: Wayne State University Press, 2010), p. 1.
2. *Variety*, 14 November 1951, p. 6. See also Hall and Neale, *Epics, Spectacles, and Blockbusters*, p. 139. This and subsequent references to *Variety* are for the weekly edition unless otherwise noted.
3. Jeffrey Richards, *Hollywood's Ancient Worlds* (London: Continuum, 2008), p. 99.
4. Archival editions of *Variety* are available on microfilm at the British Film Institute Library and in some university libraries, including my own at Sheffield Hallam University. The journal's digital archive is available online for individual (but not institutional) subscription. It includes both weekly and daily editions and is fully searchable. See http://www.varietyultimate.com, last accessed 14 October 2013.
5. *Variety*, 4 August 1954, p. 15; 20 February 1957, p. 7.
6. *Variety*, 6 January 1954, p. 5; 7 January 1959, p. 59.
7. See, for example, the article 'Hays Must Not "Railroad"' in *Variety*, 5 October 1927, p. 5, which actually includes the subheading 'Block or Bust'.

8. See, for example, the advertisement for *Her Jungle Love* (1938) headlined 'Block Sock!' in *Variety*, 20 April 1938, p. 14.
9. For reports of the Allies' use of blockbuster and factory-buster bombs, see *The Times*, 22 December 1943, p. 4; 31 December 1943, p. 4; 4 March 1944, p. 4; 16 October 1945, p. 7; and *Variety*, 10 November 1943, p. 88. I am indebted to Matthew Wilhem Kapell for the information about the *Chicago Sun Times*. John Huston's documentary *Report from the Aleutians* (1943) includes shots of 1,000-pound bombs being loaded onto US aircraft, while Huston's voiceover narration explains the strategic use of such 'blockbusters' for carpet-bombing large or scattered targets.
10. See, for example, *Variety*, 12 May 1943, pp. 14–15, and 26 May 1943, p. 24.
11. *Variety*, 1 March 1944, p. 19.
12. *Variety*, 8 November 1944, p. 22.
13. *The Lion's Roar*, 18.34 (20 August 1943), p. 3. The item is headlined '*Bataan* Block-busts All Records since Easter'.
14. *Boxoffice*, quoted in trade advertisement, *Daily Variety*, 18 January 1944, pp. 8–9.
15. *Variety*, 25 October 1944, p. 12.
16. *The Lion's Roar*, 19.2 (21 January 1944), p. 1.
17. It should also be pointed out that *Block Busters* (1944) was the title of an episode in the Bowery Boys series of B pictures released by Monogram; that advertisements for 'Blockbuster Popcorn', distributed by the Mellos Peanut Co., appeared in *Variety* throughout 1947–8; and that a song entitled 'Blockbuster', by songwriter and composer Frank DeVol, was published by his company Derby Songs in 1950.
18. E. J. Rosenwald, Account Executive, Blow Company, quoted in trade advertisement, *Daily Variety*, 29 May 1946, pp. 12–13 (capitalisation as per original).
19. *Daily Variety*, 16 October 1946, p. 4.
20. *Daily Variety*, 27 April 1948, p. 3.
21. *Daily Variety*, 2 December 1948, p. 14.
22. Among the other films labelled blockbusters in the next few years was Sam Katzman's Columbia production *Bomber Command*, 'a Technicolor blockbuster' (*Daily Variety*, 19 December 1950, p. 4).
23. *Variety*, 28 April 1948, p. 5.
24. *Variety*, 1 August 1951, p. 5. As this brief report points out, there were no official figures available for cinema attendance and estimates of 90 million or even 100 million for weekly admissions in 1946 were unsupported by evidence. The figures reported had been agreed upon by the Audience Research Institute (the Gallup poll) and Paramount executive and industry economist Paul Raibourn, on the basis of audience polls and 'studies of theatre and distribution takes' respectively.
25. *Variety*, 12 June 1946, pp. 1, 4.
26. *Variety*, 30 March 1949, p. 5. The report continues in similar militaristic vein: 'In a string of explosions, five groups riddled the campaign in bulletins', and so on.
27. *Variety*, 15 December 1948, pp. 5, 6.
28. *Variety*, 26 May 1948, pp. 1, 2.
29. *Variety*, 2 January 1952, p. 112.
30. *Daily Variety*, 4 April 1949, p. 4; 3 October 1949, p. 6.
31. *Variety*, 22 August 1951, p. 31.
32. *Variety*, 9 August 1950, p. 7.
33. *Variety*, 3 January 1951, pp. 25–8.
34. *Variety*, 20 June 1951, p. 8.

35. *Variety*, 4 July 1951, p. 10. The preceding page showed a photograph of a 'showman' passing cans of film as a graphic illustration of the ammunition in question.
36. Ibid., pp. 14–15.
37. See the discussion in Hall and Neale, *Epics, Spectacles, and Blockbusters*, pp. 128, 137–9. The first film to be sold on a competitive-bidding basis was MGM's musical *Holiday in Mexico* (1946). Although the Supreme Court antitrust ruling in 1948 discouraged the use of competitive bidding because of its complexity, it remained legal and the Department of Justice was unable to prevent its continued use by the major distributors, who saw its financial advantages.
38. *Variety*, 21 November 1951, pp. 16–17 (advertisement). On the distribution of *Quo Vadis*, see *Variety*, 10 October 1951, pp. 5, 13; 7 November 1951, pp. 7, 53; 14 November 1951, pp. 5, 13; 21 November 1951, pp. 5, 23; 28 November 1951, pp. 5, 12; 26 December 1951, pp. 14–15 (advertisement).
39. *Variety*, 23 January 1952, pp. 5, 24.
40. *Variety*, 2 October 1952, p. 7.
41. Cost, revenue and profit figures for *Quo Vadis* are from the Eddie Mannix Ledger, Howard Strickling Collection, Margaret Herrick Library, Los Angeles. Earnings from reissues brought the film's domestic rental to an eventual total of $11,901,662 by 1991 (*Variety*, 6 May 1991, p. 96).
42. *Variety*, 7 November 1951, p. 22.
43. *Variety*, 6 February 1952, p. 18.
44. *Variety*, 2 January 1952, p. 28. Republic ceased producing theatrical films in 1956.
45. Ibid., p. 7.
46. Ibid.
47. Ibid., p. 53. Kramer's article is headlined 'Pix Can't Live by Bigness Alone'.
48. *Variety*, 10 April 1946, p. 20; *Daily Variety*, 8 October 1948, p. 6; *Daily Variety*, 5 August 1949, p. 4; *Variety*, 4 January 1950, p. 3.
49. *Variety*, 8 March 1950, p. 3.
50. *Variety*, 3 January 1951, p. 55; 4 July 1951, p. 26; 20 February 1952, p. 16; 30 May 1957, p. 10.
51. *Variety*, 15 August 1945, p. 15. A firework sold in Britain in 1952 was named 'The Atomic Block-buster' (*The Times*, 5 November 1952, p. 9).
52. *Variety*, 24 June 1953, p. 5.
53. *Variety*, 20 June 1951, p. 45.

CHAPTER 10

Epic Stumbling Blocks

Saër Maty Bâ

INTRODUCTION: RACE, INSUBORDINATION, METHOD

Truth is the proof of itself. There is no external guarantee.[1]

Space, entity or knowledge is (a) nowhere or now/here – as Fischlin and Heble claim, it is 'the here and now of conventional knowing' – for it embodies an 'elsewhere that is the "other side" to that "nowhere"'.[2] The 'epic' film/cinema[3] is such a space/entity/knowledge, embodied with humanist potential of planetary proportions. Yet two interconnected stumbling blocks, which constitute this chapter's main focus, prevent this humanism from reaching the other side of the epic's nowhere: (1) how that planetary possibility has been constructed, and (2) opaque whiteness.[4] Opacity signifies: the other side of transparency; an obscurity through which whites represented on screen become potentially or actually unknowable; and, from a not-white perspective, whiteness as an obstacle to full knowledge of whiteness's world, though that obstacle (or whiteness or opacity) does not need transparency or cultural destruction, despite being potentially perceived as 'other' by not-whites.

Reaching the other side of nowhere is crucial to fully realising the epic's humanist potential, which, in turn, is central to evaluations of the return of the epic in twenty-first-century cinema. Beyond or despite aesthetic differences, the return of the epic film is a changing same, shot through with race and white opacity; following philosopher Édouard Glissant, opacity thus becomes a useful critical and theoretical tool against hyper-visibility or exaggerated transparency, a cultural and corporeal state or process which tends to obliterate difference(s) within and/or between those rendered hyper-visible. We shall see that white opacity is routinely ignored even though whiteness is an aggregate of familiar devices, that is, 'mythification' and 'marking', two of the 'most frequent [ways] whereby blacks have been consigned to minor significance on screen'.⁵ These devices or spotlights have been so effectively beamed onto not-white bodies in epic films that scholars have tended to focus on not-whites and/or treat whiteness as un-mythified and un-marked – hence their assumed transparency. I therefore argue for a focus shift towards whiteness, and race as the place where examinations of whiteness should begin.

Race

From the turn of the nineteenth through to the twentieth century, race belonged to an 'enterprise of knowledge' located inside power relations which were dominated by the West.⁶ Accordingly, in this chapter race is understood as an interconnection of complexities: a 'floating signifier' and discourse irreducible to biology; a constant filtered through variables like gender, age, sexuality; a sociological-historical-ideological construct always-already entangled with class issues.⁷ Therefore, race is invented while its invention itself speaks to a host of issues, including cultural, legal, labour and class separations, and matters of access determined by skin colour; and to freedom, citizenship and/or privilege.

To routinely overlook such complexities and stubbornly foreground race as a biological factor pushes whiteness into recesses of unacknowledged opacity – and must call for the recognition of new, real forms of racism which may emerge as a result.⁸ Moreover, critical whiteness is a field of study into which, as far as I am aware, film and cinema studies in general, and studies of epics in particular, have still not delved – unlike literary studies.⁹ This is due perhaps to whiteness studies having been conceived as 'a distracting premise . . . fixated to the possibility of a sense of white selfhood without white supremacy'.¹⁰ Either way, whiteness as discourse and practice permeates film, cinema and epics but does not need reclaiming or recuperating. Whiteness must be taken seriously and studied more in its social context so as to 'prioritise [how] white actions, definitions and understanding are implicated within cultures of racism'.¹¹

Insubordination and method

I focus on whiteness not as a symptom which reveals its hidden matters, but to address the epic film's surface, which, like the concept of surface cinema, 'can yield only cinematic truth, cinematic depth, cinematic reality'.¹² This explains my interrogation of 'the already-said at the level of its existence' in a chapter standing as both an enunciation and a discourse that pertains to a particular general archive system and a Foucauldian statement whose objects of study (films) come with substance, support, place and date attached. ¹³ Simultaneously, I question the past and present of epic films and cinema in order to address and challenge received views of whiteness both on the screen-surface of epic cinema and within writings about epic films. As such, I embrace interdisciplinary approaches; transcend assumptions of knowledge about, and groupings of, epic films; interrogate history and historiography in relation to epic films and whiteness; and offer groundwork for future research. Therefore, cinema as body or apparatus becomes crucial both to this chapter and to the epic film per se.

The cinematic apparatus controls (white) bodies but also affirms them through their image. It thus makes sense to investigate white opacity by taking a cue from Steven Shaviro's postmodern theoretical rebellion (against Lacanian and psychoanalytic film theory), in two ways: first, in terms of how cinema is positioned at the borders of phenomenology and fantasy while undoing both; and second, by grasping that the cinematic body/apparatus enables and hinders cinematic processes, something which should alter film theory into 'a theory of affects and transformations of bodies'.[14] These transformations are tied up with, and result in, the unsubordinated (white) flesh's opacity.

Opacity and insubordination stimulate thought while constituting its essential condition. This chapter is therefore unsubordinated to received views on whiteness in the epic film. It also makes whiteness insubordinate to non-mythification and non-marking and the epic film a challenge to (film) historicism. Put otherwise, whiteness is un-concealed and its un-concealment is connected to the cinematic apparatus through selected bodies and film-texts. The chapter's method is indeed 'a monstrous hybrid of empirical description and simulacral fabulation' while it rethinks the epic film through theoretical anarchism.[15] This is because '[t]o be without method is deplorable. But to depend on method is entirely worse';[16] theoretical anarchism is both 'more likely to encourage progress than its law-and-order alternatives' and proof that any idea, 'however ancient and absurd', is able to improve knowledge.

Therefore, summoning Kant against epic stumbling blocks via Žižek, this chapter aims to counter the motto 'Don't think, obey' with 'Obey, but think!'.[17] Epic stumbling blocks are forms of chantage – a synonym for the potentially racist word 'blackmail' – against which acting out one's annoyance cannot help. Anger should be transformed into 'an icy determination ... to think things through in a really radical way, and ask what kind of society [and cinema/film: genre, industry, culture and so on] it is that renders such [chantage] possible'.[18] Accordingly, each epic film is discussed through selected film moments 'within which an operation is legible'; legibility signifies simultaneous understanding of 'the subjacent material' which ensures the film's contemporaneity, 'the protocol of purification' or artistic index, and 'the passage of the idea (or encounter with the real)' which results from the protocol.[19] In this chapter, the index generating the passage of the idea is non-purified; it also tracks opacity while seizing (epic) cinema as the latter gathers around 'identifiably non-artistic materials, which are ideological indicators of the[ir] epoch'.[20] 'Epic' films discussed thus include *300* (Snyder 2006), *Vénus noire* (Khechiche 2010), *Planet of the Apes* (Schaffner 1968), *Amazing Grace* (Apted 2006), *Amistad* (Spielberg 1997), *Zulu Dawn* (Hickox 1979), *Zulu* (Endfield 1964), and *Men in Black 3* (Sonenfeld 2012).[21]

PARTIAL RECALL: PLANETARY HUMANISM REPERCEIVED

This chapter continues my earlier work on epic films, focused on black masculinities and planetary humanism respectively.[22] The second project (2011) attempted to generate new debates on planetary humanism as post-race by adopting a doubly panoptic framework able to reposition raced bodies as postmodern and deceptive. I argued that the so-called post-race moment had to critique prophecies, extra-terrestrial contact zones and/or black-and-white alliances inspired by science-fiction cinema. I also acknowledged the epic stumbling blocks unpacked here as indicative of problems with/in post-racial strategies, before concluding that planetary humanism was nowhere, that its other side had to be found, and that race is not dead. If a decade ago the challenge had been to 'bring even more powerful visions of planetary humanity from the future and to reconnect them with democratic and cosmopolitan traditions',[23] in 2013 the tools and methods used to meet it must be rethought. I would provisionally argue that, because planetary humanism is nowhere, it objects to futurisms and prophecies while demanding a comprehensive toolkit able to give access to its nowhere: this chapter seeks to reach and plumb the here and now of conventional knowing, something which cannot be achieved without examining whiteness/the white body. This is because, as shown next, whiteness is both an invention and 'the provisional space of the "now/where" that always remains to be made'.[24]

INVENTING WHITENESS

we are captive audiences unless we make agency our aim.[25]

Inventing whiteness is a perceptual notion and process with a history; it is at least as old as seventeenth- and eighteenth-century (biological) concepts of race and was thus already in place when the cinematic apparatus was invented and developed. Furthermore, to discuss race on screen must always-already include the history of film colour, for 'the cultural assumptions of those concerned with the development and applications of colour film are those of the society at large'.²⁶ Certainly, be it in 1935 when Hollywood technicians were told that colour brought better realism to the cinema or during our current digital-/post-digital-technology moment, film colour's connection to race remains crucial, not least because to say that '[w]hite uplifts and ennobles . . . any colour'²⁷ is as problematic as the whiteness shown in epic films discussed below. Mythified and marked but also unacknowledged as such, whiteness 'erupts and continues to be reinvented . . . and it would be up to all forms of popular culture, including . . . motion pictures, to maintain and further [its] construction'.²⁸ Whiteness is also a white-Western cultural creation achieved by virtue of 'white people hav[ing] had so very much more control over the definition of themselves and indeed of others than have those others'.²⁹

Dyer understands how the perceptually non-raced is implicitly empowered to speak for humanity – to just be human – while the raced one is confined within her/his own race. Hence Dyer's resolve to '[see] the racing of whites' and thereby dislodge whiteness 'from the position of power . . . by undercutting the authority with which they/we speak and act in and on the world'.³⁰ I contend, however, that Dyer's approach to race is problematic because it is grudgingly fixated on the phrase 'non-white' which 'marks and measures all the peoples who are not white with or against whiteness [while maintaining] whiteness into a coloniser's position of hegemony'.³¹ I take a different position: whiteness's position of power was always-already dislodged (not concealed) and, that being so, attempts must be made to understand (1) mechanisms and strategies used for centuries to achieve white opacity and (2) the problematic nature of gender depictions within those devices and tactics.

Gorgo (Lena Headey), queen of Spartans in *300*, is a potent example. Set in 480 BCE, *300* tells the story of the battle of Thermopylae, opposing the 'Persian' army of king Xerxes (Rodrigo Santoro) – over 100,000 soldiers – to a Greek alliance of 301 Spartans and around 700 Thespians. Gorgo is always-already dislodged from a position of power through gender, yet kept opaque within unconcealed whiteness as a sexual body available to Spartan men defending their nation against hyper-visible black so-called 'Persians'. Put differently:

> Gorgo, [whiteness] invented from outside *300*'s historical sources, is presented as the epitome of a physically-perfect female figure . . . with a sexualised, fetishised and barely clothed body . . . Yet, in the grand scheme of *300*'s body politics and gender hierarchy, Gorgo's diegetic elevation only serves two purposes: to fulfil male sexual needs and have babies. . . . she willingly offer[s] herself to corrupt Spartan politician Theron (Dominic West) for brutal rape in order to save Sparta.³²

Figure 10.1 *300*'s (2006) Queen Gorgo (Lena Headey) serves two purposes: to fulfil male sexual needs and have babies.

'Insistent presence': towards opacity-in-action

Foster argues that 'whites need to begin to challenge the validity of whiteness, question white privilege and norming, and study the images and performances that seek to define them'.[33] Although such challenges had begun before the twenty-first century, Foster's argument remains valid and will be returned to after opacity is unpicked further:

> transparency no longer seems like the bottom of the mirror in which Western humanity reflected the world in its own image. There is opacity now at the bottom of the mirror, a whole alluvium deposited by populations, silt that is fertile but, in actual fact, indistinct and unexplored even today, denied ... more often than not, and with an insistent presence that we are incapable of not experiencing.[34]

I would add that opacity is as old as the European imperial colonisation of not-white worlds. Consequently, instead of denouncing how whiteness victimises its Others, I seek to move into and stay within its opaque sphere where opacity-seeking strategies can be seen at play. Examples would include the act of performing 'white otherness', and the meanings of 'white other': that is, 'victim', 'disabled', 'white trash', 'ethnic type'.[35]

It follows that, as an old trope, opacity helps one ask and answer questions such as how we might have gone from white-knight hyper-visibility in *The Birth of a Nation* (Griffith 1915) to white-knight opacity in *A Knight's Tale* (Helgeland 2001). Granted, knighthood is 'apparently, mediated by being white, even in 2001'.[36] However, one must add Eurocentric myths, heroism and so-called medieval magnificence, mediated through cinema as apparatus/ body, that transform white-knight abominations into 'a fairy tale of white heterotopia or a comfortable white man's (or boy's) tale'.[37] Thus, there is not much difference between the Klansmen of *Birth* and the young William Thatcher (Heath Ledger) of *A Knight's Tale*, except for how white opacity may operate differently from within one (Hollywood) film and diegetic setting to the next.

Imbalances of power dictate that we proceed 'with extreme caution' when contemplating Hollywood, or Bollywood and Nollywood, 'as merely one cinema among others':[38] Hollywood is 'the garment center of white fabrication'.[39] So pervasive is Hollywood's power, and European cinema's before its conscious decision to 'utilis[e] the exotic appeal of the other to rebrand itself',[40] that cinema per se has been extremely successful in imposing whiteness as a norm while holding up fabricated binaries like white/black, heterosexual/homosexual and so on. Consequently, whiteness is allowed to retreat safely into unconcealed opacity while, unsurprisingly, cinema – that is, Hollywood and European – insists on defining the white body through constructed repetitive performance. Such performance makes the unconcealed powers of whiteness appear so natural that they are unseen, unacknowledged and/or unraced.

Therefore Dyer, Foster, Snead and others interested in dislodging whiteness from its simulacral status or comfort zone are, in fact, questioning and marking whiteness with indelible impurity. When combined, these processes can penetrate the cracks of performative whiteness where processes of dismantling whiteness as norm can begin, and linkages between whiteness and affective power become inevitable again. Affective power affects others while being affected by them; affective power is also 'practiced before it is possessed'.[41] Whiteness as practice-possession thus appears to be one's only hope of reaching 'postracial and postanthropological' or 'radically non-racial humanism'.[42] Put otherwise, white opacity's affective power must be sought because opacity-as-on-screen-strategy empowers whiteness to safely absolve itself of historical accountability (namely, in relation to slavery, imperialism, racial discrimination, ethnic absolutism, and so on), and sections of white spectatorship to turn responsibility-skipping into heteronormative visual pleasure[43] – in the USA, the white West and white (neo-)colonised places generally. White opacity in action includes how whiteness relates to both 'the Negro-ape metaphor'[44] and de-narration, as illustrated in legible operations from *Vénus noire* and *Planet of the Apes*.

Vénus noire tells the story of Saartjie Baartman (Yahima Torres), a domestic who followed her Dutch-settler boss Hendrick Caezar (Andre Jacobs) to Europe (London, then Paris) from Southern Africa in 1808. Against her will, Baartman exhibited her body as freakish and savage, ending up a prostitute before dying of sexually transmitted diseases and pneumonia in France. Emphases on Baartman's black body as animalistic in *Vénus* are compounded by whiteness being in the background, as spectator or unquestioned and

Figures 10.2 and 10.3 *Planet of the Apes*: (1968) Opaque entities and complex reversals.

unaccountable. This whiteness is accessible only by transcending superficial diegetic and non-diegetic white-on-white quarrels and debates about Baartman's body, from her nineteenth-century European ordeal to the twentieth century when her remains were finally returned to South Africa.[45]

Planet of the Apes is about George Taylor (Charlton Heston) and two other astronauts whose ship has crashed on a planet where apes speak and live as civilised beings while savage humans do not communicate via speech. The enslaved astronauts are subjected to scientific scrutiny. Adilifu Nama argues that *Planet of the Apes* criticises institutional racism and debunks celebratory individualism by locating a white man 'in the crosshairs of institutional discrimination'.[46] I contend that *Planet of the Apes* should be dislodged from end-of-1960s-American race relations to which, Nama argues, it is an allegorical answer, and its white-man-as-victim trope debunked. Hence the need to invoke and nuance Nama's reading of the film as an aggressive decentring of whiteness which allows whites to (1) 'symbolically trade places with blacks' and (2) sensationally experience the oppressive consequence of American racism.⁴⁷ It follows that the slave Taylor kissing a female ape, anthropologist Dr Zira (Kim Hunter) who helps him escape, makes whiteness less victim than opaque. That kiss is a complex reversal of a widely held eighteenth-century racist fallacy, circulated in Europe, according to which male apes had mated with black African women. Thus, *Planet of the Apes* does not simplistically picture whiteness as imperfect, human, subject to enslavement, able to love enemies and so on. Additionally, therein whiteness is so opaque that white bodies like Taylor supersede African women within ape-metaphor fallacies, while white opacity projects apes – its diegetic others – into hyper-visibility: white equals African, and ape equals white. Therefore discussions of *Planet of the Apes*' legibility (that is, its subjacent material, artistic index, and encounter with the real) should transcend apes or racist associations of apes with African-Americans and the US Civil Rights Movement to include the making of white opacity. This is not least because *Planet of the Apes* affects *Vénus noire* at the same time as, and in the same way that, Taylor and Zira affect Baartman.

In summary, *Planet of the Apes* makes whiteness opaque while its context transcends America in order to create links with films and topics mentioned or analysed in this chapter. Put otherwise, race and gender variables are transcended – Taylor as Baartman, for example – and, as a result, white opacity cannot but problematise the indexical connection Nama makes between *Planet of the Apes*' 'temporal disavowal' (its distant future time frame) and its release in the context of black riots, protests, demonstrations and 'growing black militancy'.⁴⁸ Furthermore, *Planet of the Apes*' sequels (1972, 1973) signify white opacity in action since they 'mark a dramatic shift away from the white protagonist as a symbol of black racial struggle' while presenting 'a racial apocalypse ushered in by an enslaved ape population, oppressed primarily by whites who liberated themselves and . . . overthrew the dominant political order'.⁴⁹

It follows that two questions must be asked: after *Planet of the Apes*, how do whites become white again and blacks once more black? What about *Planet of the Apes*' symbolism/allegory that Nama argues for? Indeed, white retreat into opacity informs, contextualises and gives voice to *Vénus*, and scores of ape-themed epics made between 1933 and 2001 which display Negro-ape metaphors and/or 'the supposed close connection between Africans and apes'.⁵⁰ This pervasive opacity in action deeply infiltrated the Abolitionist Movement, for it was (most) white abolitionists' overwhelming belief in so-called race science – William Wilberforce (1759–1863), the Evangelical Christian and British human rights activist included – which ushered in their fight to abolish the slave trade, not their belief in Christianity or equality between so-called races.⁵¹ *Amazing Grace* (2006) and *Amistad* (1997) are potent examples.

'Amazing Grace' is a hymn by former slave-ship captain John Newton (Albert Finney). Haunted by slaves' ghosts, Newton found Christianity and wrote an account of his shipboard experiences for Wilberforce to publish. Newton

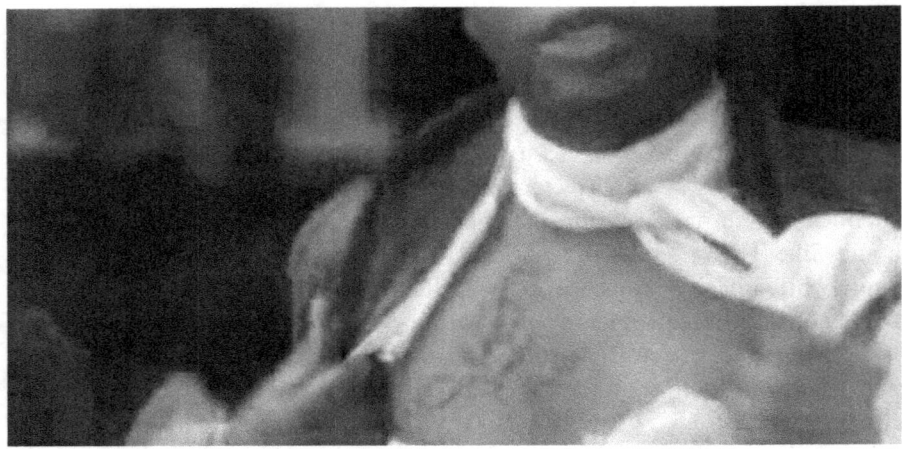

Figure 10.4 *Amazing Grace*: (2006) Equiano shows a scar on his chest, in tears.

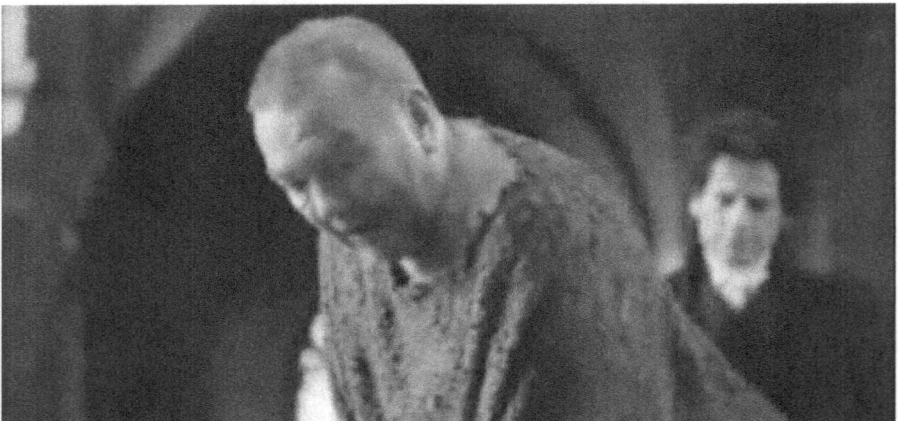

Figure 10.5 White opacity rules: 'we were apes; they were humans'.

dresses voluntarily in sackcloth and rags, and personifies a literal opacity in action whose words speak to Negro-ape metaphors: 'we were apes; they [black captives] were human. I couldn't breathe until I wrote ['Amazing Grace'].'

Wilberforce became an MP in 1782 and took up the Abolitionist cause in 1787. *Amazing Grace* centres on his fight to abolish the English slave trade[52] to recount how his cause was helped or inspired by, for instance, members of his 'Committee for the Abolition of the Slave Trade': William Pitt (Benedict Cumberbatch) persuaded him to introduce an anti-slavery bill, Thomas Clarkson (Rufus Sewell) was a zealous Christian and believer in freedom, and Olaudah Equiano (Youssou N'Dour) an author and Nigerian-born ex-slave.

Amazing Grace reveals key facets of Wilberforce's person: faith, friendships, family life, ill health (colitis), political shrewdness, intelligence and passion.

And yet opacity in action diverts our gaze away from his flaws, class position, or struggles to remain a Christian when faced with persistent economic and pseudo-scientific racism in England. That opacity directs us instead towards the anti-slave-trade legislation or act, at the same time as it paints Wilberforce's bourgeois gradualism as radical or revolutionary.[53] Conversely, black slaves are in the foreground, to be lifted up from slavery but, crucially, without proclaiming black and white racial equality. In summary, then, while blackness/slavery is in the foreground, Equiano's performance being a case in point, whiteness/race science is in the background.

Amistad tells the story of Cinqué, leader of forty-nine rebelling black African men and women aboard a slave ship in 1839. Captured and tried in the USA for murder and piracy, the Africans were ultimately acquitted and allowed to return home after a successful Supreme Court hearing. Instrumental to that hearing was ex-US President John Quincy Adams (Anthony Hopkins), a non-Abolitionist relied upon to endorse the Africans and to help solve their case, a compelling example of white opacity in action. Adams's late endorsement makes him opaque, but he is even more so because only concerned with 'the state of the American nation' in 1839.[54] He says to Cinqué about the case: 'we're about to do battle with a lion that is threatening to rip our country in two': slave trading and Africans become tools with which to fix America, a 'dysfunctional family ripped apart by bitter disputes about slavery'.[55]

THE MACHINE DISMANTLED: DE-NARRATION, TRANSPARENCY, MYTHIFICATION AND MARKING

Ultimately, *Amazing Grace* and Wilberforce, and *Amistad* and Adams, enforce white opacity-in-action. This white opaque motion does not reveal race and ethnicity but resists a breakdown/breakup and cracking open of whiteness. Such reticence bleeds into films like *Tomb Raider* (2001), precisely regarding whiteness's attempt to '[embody] cyberfantasies as non-racially marked cyberspieces'.[56] Therefore, the issue of transparency may emerge, but makes sense only when one emphasises ways in which its function has shifted from providing illusory insights into the workings of the machine (a modernist approach) to the interface screen (postmodernist). This shift, or postmodern transparency-as-process, echoes Glissant's opacity while de-narrating whiteness and class. Put differently, assumption – not narration – is what takes place in the epic film-text, de-narrated whiteness being an intrinsic part of white opacity in motion.[57] Simultaneously, since Dyer's *White* and perhaps Forster's *Performing Whiteness*, scholarly explorations of subtleties of white un-concealment and its connection to the cinematic body seem all but inexistent. This is because this scholarship's concern should be to enable a process of touching and cracking open the foundations of 'the inhumanity inspired by and associated with the idea of "race"'[58] or the workings of 'race and ethnic absolutism in securing... modes of inclusive exclusion'.[59] It follows that un-concealment becomes synonymous with working out the mechanisms and then dismantling 'the machine of whiteness' on (the interface) screen,[60] a process that entails mythifying and marking a category never once omitted in the white Western cinematic imaginary: whiteness.[61]

Mythification is 'the replacement of history with a surrogate ideology of elevation or demotion along a scale of human value [which] engages audiences on the level of their racial allegiance, social background and self-image'.[62] Marking 'makes it visually clear that [white] skin is a "natural" condition turned into a "man-made" sign ... Marking is necessary because the *reality* of [whiteness] or of being [white] cannot always, either in films or in real life, be determined.'[63] How do mythification and marking work with whiteness on the epic-film screen?

Mythification asks what elements of race remain un-dead and how those undying components are preserved; mythification is also a political interrogation of history because on-screen representations of whiteness accent its inherent psychological difference. Thus, the epic film mirrors 1930s debates on race science, for in epic cinema, as in race-focused conceptions of nation, 'every race is prescribed with its own mentality which, like physical difference, could pollute or undermine the body politic if allowed to enter the [white] racial stream of the nation'.[64] Moreover, the racial-cultural power of whiteness to pass as its Other (or vice versa) is obliterated or denied, while the epic film mutates into a xeno-racist text, yet another strategy of opaque whiteness. One cannot colour-code xeno-racism, 'directed as it is at poor whites as well and ... therefore passed off as xenophobia ... It is racism in substance, but "xeno" in form.'[65] *Zulu Dawn* (1979) and *Zulu* (1964) are helpful examples of mythification filtered through xeno-racism.

Set in 1879 South Africa, *Zulu Dawn* recounts how a British colonial administration in the Cape Colony attempts to expand the British economy by massacring the Zulu. They provoke a war with King Cetshwayo (Simon Sabela) counting on Commander Lord Chelmsford (Peter O'Toole)'s seemingly mightier army to win it. However, Cetshwayo defeats the British at the battle of Isandlwana. *Zulu*'s diegesis gives an account of the ensuing battle of Rorke's Drift during which the British Army's 24th Welsh Regiment, though outnumbered by the Zulu, repels their assaults until they withdraw.

English xeno-racism is at play in *Zulu Dawn* when the constantly haughty, and patronising, Chelmsford says to Lt Harford (Ronald Pickup), who follows his commanding officer's refusal to have lunch at Chelmsford's table while his men go hungry: 'Learn nothing from that Irishman, Harford, except

Figure 10.6 *Zulu Dawn* (1979): mythified and xeno-racist: Lord Chelmsford.

how not to behave.' Similarly, in *Zulu* a tense camaraderie is at play between soldiers of the 'Welsh' regiment: 'Private 593 Jones' (Richard Davies) says to a Swiss-born Natal Mounted Guard soldier, 'This is a Welsh Regiment, man. Though there are some foreigners from England in it, mind. I am Jones from Bwlchgwyn'; and English sergeant Windridge (Joe Powell) tells two low-ranking soldiers, 'take your bandook, you dozy Welshmen!'

Marking encodes biology culturally, or determines genetically our 'understanding of bodily practices and attributes'[66] – while overlooking class. When combined with mythification, and at once related to whiteness and the epic film, marking manufactures perfect, pure bodies, such as Chelmsford in *Zulu Dawn*, the upper-class, haughty, borderline-xeno-racist Lt Bromhead (Michael Caine) of the 24th Welsh Regiment in *Zulu*,[67] and Leonidas and Gorgo in *300*. For example, Gorgo is marked in order to satisfy her own (husband's) sexual needs and birth Sparta's 'real' men.[68] Hers and other Spartans' crafted screen purity is legible through a love-making sequence where '[c]amera angles and shot types emphasize Gorgo and Leonidas' bodily perfection while slow motion, slow music and black-and-white cinematography accent their sensuality and gentleness'.[69] It follows that unless the couple's whiteness is marked, one cannot see their love-making as the result of a specific protocol of un-purification, encounter with the real, or how the epic screen and opacity enable the couple to transcend their earlier sharp-tongued brutal incitement to kill – and bloody execution of – 'Persian' messengers.

Ultimately, against the inventions of whiteness discussed above one should posit a recalibrated planetary humanism aimed at reaching the epic film's other side of nowhere.

TOTAL RECALL: RECALIBRATING PLANETARY HUMANISM

Science is the theory of the real.[70]

Whiteness shows us that the now/here of planetary humanism is linked to race as un-dead entity. This is partly because Hollywood and other rigidly-raced cinemas persist in combining with 'Euro-American – the better Eurowestern – centeredness and arrogance' to redivide 'knowledge, praxis, "races", bodies, images, cultures, etc., into camps'.[71] As I write in late 2013, systematic multi-levelled and -disciplinary processes are still needed 'to tackle Eurowesternness as an idea and defect', as *Men in Black 3* (*MiB3*) usefully demonstrates.[72]

'Boris the Animal' (Jermaine Clement), a Boglodite alien, escapes from the moon-based prison Lunar Max and descends upon Earth to go back to 16 July 1969, when his arrest and the cutting off of his arm occurred, in order to eliminate the MiB agent responsible (Agent K/Tommy Lee Jones). However, Agent J (Will Smith) travels back to 15 July 1969 to stop Boris. Griffin the Archanan (Michael Stuhlbarg), an optimist alien, helps K and J: he is able to compute multiple time fractures and save Earth from Boglodite destruction with a shield. *MiB3* does embody planetary humanism, for example the legible operation where J saves K and Earth: J time jumps; Griffin helps; J and K kill Boris; K places Griffin's shield on a rocket bound for the moon and Earth is saved. Temporal fracture – or break in time line, time travel – is a useful trope in *MiB3*, though the film represents a type of alliance which is unhelpful and detrimental to planetary humanism: before dying Boris kills J's father, 'Colonel' (Michael Colter), without whom the shield would not be on the rocket, and K neuralyses an eleven-year-old child he would later recruit as Agent J. Colonel's death is a familiar and tired trope of black screen-sacrifice for America's survival – and Earth's in *MiB3*.[73]

Conversely, white bodies in *MiB3* function similarly to other bodies – namely, as MiB agents, crooks, and/or disguises for bad/good aliens. Simultaneously, however, whiteness is mostly opaque, and survives: J is orphaned while saving K – but K pays no price for/in this process. Therefore, one must ask again if anything of race has actually died. Epic cinema – particularly of Hollywood – is shot through and plagued with the complex constructs of race discussed above, as well as with how epic cinema seems actively to overpower its others – whoever they may be. Accordingly, the epic film's real should be sought primarily in how 'historiography' and 'history' relate. This is because, regarding planetary humanism and the epic film, contrasts between these word-concepts can solve the opacity-related problems already identified above.

TOWARDS PERMANENT 'PRESENCING': 'HISTORY' THROUGH/VERSUS 'HISTORIOGRAPHY'?

Historiography means 'to explore and make visible, and therefore names a kind of representing', whereas history is 'set in order and sent forth, destined'.[74] Historiography is thus the investigation of history, but (1) 'historiographical observation does not first create history itself' – even if everything historiographical is historical – while (2) 'history is never necessarily historiographical'.[75] The point of this distinction is to suggest that epic films and their historians should perhaps avoid arguing for the 'modern renaissance of the ancients' or advocate 'historiographical curiosity', with historiography being that which is clearly in the past but could elucidate chronologically the origins of some trends 'in the modern world'.[76] Put otherwise: to experience *Gegenwart*, a form of ancient-world-history presence in modern technology, one 'must' escape 'the historiographical representation of history[,] an object wherein a happening transpires that is, in its changeability, simultaneously passing away'.[77] That makers of epics embrace this type of history may explain why white opacity and the race-ing of white bodies have been so elusive. Indeed, if historiographical representations of history dominate (in) rethinking epic processes or grasping white opacity is attempted through historiography, white opacity always-already slips away/remains hard to pin down. Similarly, to study film history and un-concealed bodies via automatic adherence to chronology may prove epistemologically limiting; hence the need to return to Heidegger's apposite statement on science and the 'real' below.

Words and concepts name matter in motion; substance moves within realms. Heidegger's real 'brings to fulfillment' the realm of 'that which works.'[78] In turn, to work is (1) 'to do', (2) the moment when 'physis' (nature) becomes 'thesis' (setting, place, position) or (3) 'from out of itself to lay something before ... to bring it ... into presencing'. What 'does' is then what 'works' and 'that which presences, in its presencing'.[79] With this line of argument, I would contend that in order to grasp how the opaque white machine works, un-concealed bodies and whiteness per se must (be made to) operate in line with the Heideggerian 'real'. This is because the real signifies 'the working, the worked; that which brings hither and brings forth into presencing', and the result of this work-process – 'reality' or 'presencing' – succeeds when it is, fundamentally, 'something [that] comes to stand and to lie in unconcealment'.[80] Once reality/presencing/whiteness arrives in un-concealment, it remains there and persists in remaining there.[81]

CONCLUSION: TOWARDS NEW SENSES IN CINEMATIC PLANETARY HUMANISM

contemplate what the 'arrival lounge' of humanity might be like.[82]

This chapter has shown that 'body' can mean, at once, real, presencing, un-concealment and theory. 'Theory is the viewing, the observation of the real' and, crucially, 'never passes that which presences by, but rather remains directed toward it'.[83] This is why this chapter has addressed bodies both on screen and in epic cinema-as-body, the real and epic cinema need 'race', and mythification and marking show how epic cinema embraces race. Ultimately, to reiterate a key point, whiteness has always been a presencing or reality persistently un-concealed.

If un-concealment is about working out the mechanisms of and dismantling the machine of whiteness, then rethinking the epic should draw and learn from Heidegger's radical critique of Western thought,[84] especially dialogic encounters he generates between contemporary technology on the one hand, and ancient thinking, poetry and knowledge on the other. Indeed, the shift from *Birth of a Nation* to *A Knight's Tale*, or bodies and issues discussed in *300*, *Vénus*, *Amazing Grace*, *Amistad*, *Zulu Dawn*, *Zulu*, *Planet of the Apes*, *MiB3* and so on, problematise any insistence on grasping history through historiography.

One must be freed from history filtered through historiography so that a happening – for example, 'film' – can transpire, be changeable, and remain alive: a film which engages 'directly or obliquely, the issues, ideas, data, and arguments of the ongoing discourse of history'[85] is historical, a statement which echoes Heidegger's ideas about science, theory and the real, while bringing us back full circle to Badiou's basic unit of film investigation. This is why epic films have been analysed through moments and non-artistic materials. The same legibility can be mobilised to suggest openings for cinematic planetary humanism, not least because today, I would suggest, whiteness in epic cinema is in a transitional phase where 'the weight of non-art is crushing [and] it is necessary to engage in the work of [identifying] operations including those occurring within films which are globally deficient'.[86] Furthermore, as Badiou incisively points out, (film) material changes and prevents anybody from maintaining a mastered and constant connection to it.[87]

Thus, the openings suggested below could be developed further by investigating 'the details' of epic films, directed by 'our instinct [and] the decoding of current [and future] criticism'.[88] In turn, one would avoid 'profound ellipses and omissions and glosses' which Godard's *Histoire(s) du cinéma* (1998) epitomises in the sense that watching it cannot make one realise that 'black people have been in the cinema'.[89] Yet, Akomfrah's 'analogic stack [where] histories are privileged on the basis of what is available'[90] is more of a problem than a possibility. The digital may indeed allow instant and direct retrievals conducive to constructing manifold histories, but with caveats attached, for, unless (hegemonic) whiteness comes to the epic screen always-already mythified and marked by opacity – not merely demonised like Boris in *MiB3* – and race is acknowledged as undying, this side of conventional knowing about the epic/cinema will continue to rule. Conversely, addressing the stumbling blocks identified in this chapter as I suggest may open new lines of enquiry into the epic film, through possibilities offered by a definition of cinema

> which would start with how cinema from the 1890s was somehow implicated in a kind of biopolitics ... you could look at its Eugenic moment by [exploring] all the cinematic travelogues in which the black body was not simply the object of fascination but also a certain squeamish disquiet; *The Birth of a Nation* [and films discussed above] would thus make complete sense in this genealogy.[91]

Cinema's planetary humanism is reachable, and rethinking the epic film outside conventional knowing can lead to that space. Certainly, to enter planetary humanist space must mean (1) acknowledging that whiteness is complex, raced and opaque, mythified and marked; and (2) conceding the existence of necessary vertigos of dis-placement and re-placement to which the epic film can be subjected.

Therefore, for the sake of humanity one should seek to conceptualise 'a becoming that is also a refusal, that is, becoming "not white"'.[92] Becoming not white acknowledges 'but cuts its root[s], like a pianist lifting her finger from the major third to make a minor chord'.[93] The major third is a metaphor for a race logic which fixes one inside 'the visual lens of racial classification' and colonises the culture–subjectivity connection.[94] Accordingly, 'becoming otherwise necessitates a shift to the minor, a negation comparable to the flattening of a third', a process which must forestall, with equal measure, slippage into a doubly destructive melancholia: licence for hatred, and compensation for becoming otherwise.[95] Ultimately perhaps, to rid the epic cinema discussed above of its stumbling blocks means asking 'who wants to be white when there is the hope ... of being human?'.[96]

NOTES

1. Alain Badiou, *Infinite Thought: Truth and the Return to Philosophy*, trans. O. Feltham and J. Clemens (London: Continuum, 2005), p. 130.
2. Daniel Fischlin and Ajay Heble (eds), *The Other Side of Nowhere: Jazz, Improvisation and Communities in Dialogue* (Middletown, CT: Wesleyan University Press, 2004), p. 17.

3. 'Epic' may designate size, expense, specific types of historical setting, 'protagonists caught up in large-scale events[,] those who sway the course of history or the fate of nations [and/or] the presence of spectacular settings, actions, and scenes'. Sheldon Hall and Steve Neale, *Epics, Spectacles, and Blockbusters: A Hollywood History* (Detroit, MI: Wayne State University Press, 2010), p. 5.
4. As shown below, I have discussed Planetary Humanism elsewhere. Here I will revisit key points so as to shift focus from blackness to whiteness, a complex entity not always reducible to race.
5. James Snead, *White Screens/Black Images: Hollywood from the Dark Side* (New York: Routledge, 1994), p. 5.
6. Peter Wade, *Race and Sex in Latin America* (London: Pluto Press, 2010), p. 5.
7. See Wade, *Race and Ethnicity*, pp. 21, 22. See also Sut Jhally, *Stuart Hall – Race, the Floating Signifier* (film) (USA: Media Education Foundation, 1997); and Ira Berlin, *Many Thousands Gone: The First Two Centuries of Slavery in North America* (Cambridge, MA: Harvard University Press, 1998).
8. Some forms of racism are lethal, the recent (1982) Ku Klux Klan lynching of blacks being potent examples. See Jhally, *Stuart Hall*.
9. See for example Jay Watson (ed.), *Faulkner and Whiteness* (Jackson, MS: University Press of Mississippi, 2011). Books with titles like *Whiteness as Cinema* are perhaps called for.
10. Les Back, 'Whiteness in the Dramaturgy of Racism', in P. H. Collins and J. Solomos (eds), *The Sage Handbook of Race and Ethnic Studies* (Los Angeles, CA: Sage, 2010), pp. 444–68 (p. 445).
11. Ibid., p. 445.
12. Kenneth W. Harrow, *Postcolonial African Cinema: From Political Engagement to Postmodernism* (Bloomington, IN: Indiana University Press, 2010), p. 30.
13. Michel Foucault, *The Archaeology of Knowledge* (London: Routledge, 2011), 3rd edn, p. 148.
14. Steven Shaviro, *The Cinematic Body* (Minneapolis, MN: University of Minnesota Press, 1993), p. 256.
15. On theory as monstrous hybrid, see Shaviro, *The Cinematic Body*, p. 266. On theoretical anarchism and its implications, see Paul Feyerabend, *Against Method* (London: Verso, 2010), p. xxix.
16. Charlene Nagy Hesse-Biber and Patricia Leavey (eds), *Handbook of Emergent Methods* (New York: Guilford Press, 2010), p. 2, quoting Chinese painter Lu Ch'ai, who spoke in 1701.
17. Slavoj Žižek, *First as Tragedy, Then as Farce* (London: Verso, 2009), p. 17.
18. Ibid., p. 17.
19. Badiou, *Infinite Thought*, p. 87. I have no interest in the binary art/non-art upon which Badiou's protocol of artistic purification resides: my focus is on the other two meanings of legibility.
20. Ibid., p. 86.
21. Other films mentioned include *The Birth of a Nation* (Griffiths, 1915), *A Knight's Tale* (Helgeland, 2001) and *Rise of the Planet of the Apes* (Wyatt, 2011).
22. S. M. Bâ, 'Diegetic Masculinities: Reading the Black Body in Epic Cinema', in R. Burgoyne (ed.), *The Epic Film in World Culture* (New York: Routledge, 2010), pp. 346–74. S. M. Bâ, '"Planetary Humanism" Calling: New Sightings of "Black Bodies" in Epic Cinema', *Film International Online*, 2 March 2011, http://filmint.nu/?p=911, last accessed 14 October 2013.
23. Paul Gilroy, *Between Camps: Nations, Cultures and the Allure of Race* (London: Routledge, 2000), p. 355.

24. Fischlin and Heble, *The Other Side*, p. 30.
25. Gwendolyn Audrey Foster, *Performing Whiteness: Postmodern Re/Constructions in the Cinema* (Albany, NY: State of New York Press, 2003), p. 137.
26. Brian Winston, *Technologies of Seeing: Photography, Cinematography and Television* (London: BFI Publishing, 1996), p. 43.
27. Natalie Kalmus, quoted in Winston, *Technologies of Seeing*, p. 43: she was Herbert Kalmus's wife. Herbert Kalmus was credited with inventing Technicolor.
28. Foster, *Performing Whiteness*, p. 26.
29. Richard Dyer, *White* (London: Routledge, 1997), p. xiii.
30. Ibid., p. xiv.
31. Saër Maty Bâ, 'Malcolm X and Documentary Film Representation: Text and Intertext', unpublished PhD thesis, University of Exeter, 2006, pp. 16, 17.
32. Bâ, 'Planetary Humanism'.
33. Foster, *Performing Whiteness*, p. 7.
34. Édouard Glissant, *The Poetics of Relation*, trans. Betsy Wing (Ann Arbor, MI: University of Michigan Press, 1997), p. 111.
35. Foster, *Performing Whiteness*, p. 137. The Jewish actor Jeff Chandler, or Cochise in *Broken Arrow* (Daves 1950), never played a Jew on screen, while Jack Palance played only Native Americans or stereotypical roles.
36. Ibid., p. 23.
37. Ibid., p. 23.
38. Saër Maty Bâ and Will Higbee (eds), *De-Westernizing Film Studies* (London: Routledge, 2012), p. 6.
39. Foster, *Performing Whiteness*, p. 2.
40. Daniela Berghahn and Claudia Sternberg (eds), *European Cinema in Motion: Migrant and Diasporic Film in Contemporary Europe* (Basingstoke and New York: Palgrave Macmillan, 2010), p. 40.
41. Gilles Deleuze, *Foucault* (London: Continuum, 1999), p 60.
42. Gilroy, *Between Camps*, p. 15.
43. See for example Sara Ahmed et al. (eds), *Transformations: Thinking through Feminism* (London: Routledge, 2000).
44. Tommy L. Lott, *The Invention of Race: Black Culture and the Politics of Representation* (Boston, MA: Wiley-Blackwell, 1999).
45. About this return, see http://www.southafrica.info/about/history/saartjie.htm, last accessed 26 January 2013.
46. Adilifu Nama, *Black Space: Imagining Race in Science Fiction Film* (Austin, TX: University of Texas Press, 2008), p. 127.
47. Ibid., p. 127.
48. Ibid., p. 129.
49. Ibid., p. 131.
50. Foster, *Performing Whiteness*, p. 13. *Rise of the Planet of the Apes* (Wyatt, 2011) and its forthcoming sequel (2014) open new Badiouan legible operations beyond the limits of this chapter. The last scene and credits of *Rise* seem to suggest that the experimental drug given to the ape Cesar (Andy Serkis) contaminates an airline pilot, who spreads it in his travels around the world. Thus, humans will either be progressively wiped out or on a collision course with stronger apes.
51. See Lott, *Invention of Race*.
52. Wilberforce had already challenged child labour laws and penal conditions for female prisoners, and founded the 'Society for the Relief of the Manufacturing Poor'.

53. In fact, Wilberforce did not publicly raise the issue of abolishing slavery in the British territories.
54. Bâ, 'Diegetic Masculinities', p. 363.
55. Lester D. Friedman, *Citizen Spielberg* (Chicago, IL: University of Illinois Press, 2006), p. 276.
56. Foster, *Performing Whiteness*, p. 18.
57. On de-narration see also Foster, *Performing Whiteness*, p. 19.
58. Gilroy, *Between Camps*, p. 18.
59. Paul Gilroy, *Darker than Blue: On the Moral Economies of Black Atlantic Culture* (Cambridge MA: Harvard University Press, 2010), p. 87.
60. Foster, *Performing Whiteness*, p. 8.
61. Omission is 'exclusion by reversal, distortion, or some other form of censorship. Omission and exclusion are perhaps the most widespread tactics of racial stereotyping but are also the most difficult to prove because their manifestation is precisely absence itself' (Snead, *White Screens*, p. 6).
62. Snead, *White Screens*, p. 4.
63. Ibid., p. 5.
64. Gavin Schaffer, *Racial Science and British Society, 1930–42* (Basingstoke: Palgrave Macmillan: 2008), p. 7.
65. Liz Fekete, *A Suitable Enemy: Racism, Migration and Islamophobia in Europe* (London: Pluto Press, 2009), pp. 19–20.
66. Gilroy, *Between Camps*, p. 127.
67. Note Bromhead's accent, body language, and attitude towards/words about the Zulu/Blacks: 'Damn the levies, man. More cowardly blacks!'
68. Bâ, 'Planetary Humanism'.
69. Ibid.
70. Martin Heidegger, *The Question Concerning Technology and Other Essays*, trans. William Lovitt (New York: Garland, 1977), p. 158 (emphasis in original).
71. Bâ, 'Planetary Humanism'.
72. Ibid. It still seems useless to mobilise 'Sun Ra, George Clinton, Will Smith (present and past), the films *Independence Day* (1996) and *Men in Black* (1997), good aliens in alliance with humankind, and the like'. Ibid.
73. On black screen sacrifice, see *Classified X* (Mark Daniels, 1998), a documentary written and narrated by Melvin Van Peebles.
74. Heidegger, *Question*, p. 175.
75. Ibid., p. 175.
76. Ibid., p. 158.
77. Ibid., p. 158.
78. Ibid., p. 159.
79. Ibid., p. 159.
80. Ibid., p. 160.
81. Cf. with Deleuze's more recent statement in *Cinema 2: The Time-Image*, trans. Hugh Tomlinson and Robert Galeta (Minneapolis, MN: University of Minnesota Press, 1989), p. 189: 'the body . . . forces us to think, and forces us to think what is concealed from thought, life'.
82. Les Back, 'Whiteness', p. 465.
83. Heidegger, *Question*, pp. 166, 174.
84. I am aware of Heidegger's link with Nazism in 1934–7.
85. Robert A. Rosenstone, *Visions of the Past: The Challenge of Film to Our Idea of History* (Cambridge, MA: Harvard University Press, 1995), p. 72.

86. Badiou, *Infinite Thought*, p. 87.
87. Ibid., p. 88.
88. Ibid.
89. John Akomfrah, 'Digitopia and the spectres of diaspora', *Journal of Media Practice*, 11.1 (2010), p. 28.
90. Ibid., p. 28.
91. Ibid., p. 28.
92. Back, 'Whiteness', p. 464.
93. Ibid.
94. Ibid.
95. Ibid.
96. Ibid., p. 466.

CHAPTER 11

The Greatest Epic of the Twenty-first Century?

Deborah Bridge

Between the first and last instalments of this series, an entire generation grew up. Totalling some twenty hours, it is unprecedented in length; it features a protagonist who embodies all the characteristics of an epic hero; it includes many special effects, some of which are filmic firsts; and it tells a mythic story that narrates one of the most common epic themes – the struggle between good and evil. However, there is hardly a breath of a mention of these films in all the critical material on modern epic currently available.

The series? Harry Potter, of course.

Although there is an increasing body of scholarly work in a wide-ranging number of disciplines on the books and their influence, there is virtually nothing discussing the films as an epic. As Diana Patterson eloquently assesses it:

> There are many who are dismissive of these books: they are too popular to be of any value; they are long and repetitive; they are childish; they are derivative; they are insufficiently 'literary' to be worthy of attention, much less of study. Each of these claims might as easily be made against Dickens. Some still persist against J. R. R. Tolkien.[1]

Admitting Harry Potter to the epic cinematic canon will enable us to examine how the series is unique in being the first epic made for, featuring, and largely made popular by children. Before considering this, however, I want to address the scarcity of academic discussion of the films and speculate about why they have never previously been examined as epic. Next, I identify some classic characteristics of epic and discuss how the Harry Potter films embody these. Finally, I show how the series addresses children's fears and aspirations, appeals to 'cross-cultural structures of belonging and identification',[2] and speaks to an unspecified or 'inchoate sense of collective desire'[3] in ways that only an epic can.

As mentioned above, the critical writing on epic scarcely mentions Harry Potter. Understandably, Robert Burgoyne does not include the series in his book *The Hollywood Historical Film*, though he does allude to it in a simile acknowledging that his taxonomy of historical film, which subsumes other genres, 'is a little like subjecting films to Hogwarts' sorting hat: sometimes the designation seems odd, and the films seem to resist'.[4] I would argue that regarding the Harry Potter series, it is the scholars who are resistant, not the films.

More inclusively, Constantine Santas, in his book *The Epic in Film*, mentions Harry Potter three times. He refers to the series as a fantasy epic,[5] and twice he puts Harry in admirable company, first in saying that 'epic film has re-created, reshaped, and expanded the heroic images and archetypes of the past, connecting them to the present . . . from Odysseus . . . to Harry Potter',[6] and again when he includes Harry with such epic heroes as Gilgamesh, Hercules and King Arthur before observing that 'Audiences delight to see heroes win in the end'.[7]

Still, Santas does not discuss the films themselves, and I continue to think it very odd that no one else does either. On the other hand, *Lord of the Rings* dominated the litany I found everywhere I looked. To be sure, the filmic interpretation of Tolkien's classic is laudable, but why, I wondered yet again, had no one commented on the cinematic significance of Harry Potter, even though he has been described as one of the 'most important non-religious global cultural icons in history'?[8] There are a number of possible answers.

One explanation is 'the popular conception that adaptations of books are always inferior'.[9] While it is true that cinematic retellings of many epic tales are condensed from – and thus likely to be much less effective than – their print counterparts, not all adaptations are inferior. How many people who have seen *Troy* (Petersen 2004) have read *The Iliad*? How many who have seen *King Arthur* (Fuqua 2004) have read the *Mabinogion* or Geoffrey of Monmouth or Chrétien de Troyes or Malory? Are the films better or worse than these text sources? And again, the discussion returns to *Lord of the Rings, Lord of the Rings, Lord of the Rings*.

A related explanation is that since book- (and comic book-) to-film adaptations were commonplace by 2001 when the first film, *Harry Potter and the Philosopher's Stone* (Columbus 2001), was released, perhaps people had grown weary of yet another adaptation hitting the big screen. Although 'popularity [does not] guarantee quality',[10] it is not necessarily true that something which has become popular in modern culture cannot be worthy of serious academic attention. Once again, *Lord of the Rings* demonstrates an example of a series of books and films which enjoyed significant popularity as popular cultural products, but which have nevertheless attracted serious scholarly attention not only in terms of their status as global products, but also as genuine engagements with serious themes in their own right.[11]

A third reason may be that because Warner Bros initially bought the rights only to the first two films, no one knew whether they would adapt all seven books or not. Though Rowling claims to have understood, from her first inspiration for the character, that 'she would need to write a series of seven books to tell the boy wizard's complete story – one for each year he attended wizarding school', it is by no means clear that the studio shared her faith in the longevity of the series.[12] Much has been made in the surrounding literature of the inherently cinematic quality of Rowling's series, with Gupta claiming that 'very seldom have films been so preordained to be blockbusters'.[13] However, as other book-to-film franchises dictate, such qualities do not necessarily translate into box-office success. It is possible, had the first films not been the tremendous box-office successes they were, that Warner may not have made the rest of the series. For example, film versions of the remaining two books in Philip Pullman's *His Dark Materials* trilogy are not in the works, nor are films planned for the second, third and fourth books of Christopher Paolini's *Inheritance Cycle*, the first of which was *Eragon* (Fangmeier 2006).[14] Despite Spielberg's belief that the films were guaranteed to be bankable (in an interview with Hollywood.com, he passed on the project as it posed no challenge and would be 'like shooting ducks in a barrel. It's a slam dunk'),[15] the potential for box-office failure lay in the difficulty of translating a beloved book faithfully to the screen. Gupta continues: the adaptation to screen was going to be 'a test of the skill of film-making', since 'spectators were going to receive the *Harry Potter* films to an extraordinary degree not straightforwardly as simply a story of simply entertainment . . . but as films'.[16] Related to this explanation is yet another: perhaps scholars have been waiting for the series to be complete before discussing it as an epic; regarding this latter issue, time will tell.

While some of these reasons for not recognising and studying the series are plausible, perhaps the main reason is more subtle and has to do with our paradoxical attitude towards and treatment of children, in particular preadolescent children. On one hand, there has never been a time when adults have regarded children as highly and treated them as well as they have since the late twentieth century. Viviana Zelizer observes that the 'The twentieth-century . . . emotionally priceless child . . . occup[ies] a special and separate world, regulated by affection and education'.[17] We begin doting on and nurturing children before they are even born, and after, we provide them with the best clothing, toys, entertainment and education we can afford, all the while worrying about whether we are doing too much or not enough to help them grow into mature, responsible, well-adjusted adults. One researcher describes this behaviour as 'the almost obsessive preoccupation of parents and specialists with the child's every movement, whim, and . . . indulgence'.[18]

On the other hand, as another writer asserts, we have a 'tendency . . . to view children as inept, shallow beings'[19] and 'our current understanding of the moral and cognitive capacities of children still seem[s] to be laden with condescension and disdain'.[20] Indeed:

> Even our language reflects and reinforces negative child stereotypes. Children are often referred to as incompetent and immature. *Per contra*, adults are developed, competent and mature – unless of course, they are 'acting like kids'. Also, pre-adolescents are frequently excused for immoral behaviour on the grounds that they are '*just* children'.[21]

Seeing children as 'inept, shallow . . . incompetent and immature'[22] enables us to be dismissive when they see merit in anything we, as adults, regard as being 'just for kids'. However, the growth of the Harry Potter phenomenon – much of which can be attributed to children – eventually forced adults to pay closer attention, and now, people in fields from international relations to law to psychology and beyond are finding plenty to say about the story and its relevance to an increasingly wider variety of situations and disciplines.[23] Nevertheless, despite its wide applicability to scholarly debates, the films have not yet received as much serious attention from film studies as the books have from literature, again, I believe, because of our tendency to dismiss 'childish' things; no one thought a film series made for children, featuring children, addressing the fears and hopes of children, could be an epic. But since 'children grapple with the same problems confronting the rest of us – along with their own, which are no less serious to them',[24] why not a children's epic?

Epic works for children have long been recognised in the field of children's literature, though they do not take the traditional poetic form. Examples of literary epics for children include C. S. Lewis's *Chronicles of Narnia* and, of course, Tolkien's *Lord of the Rings*. Maria Nikolajeva asserts that 'Traditional children's literature is . . . epic; that is, based on typical epic narrative structures, telling a story with a clear beginning, middle, and end, with a clear-cut plot, a permanent setting, a set of characters with pre-determined roles, an unambivalent message and moral'.[25] Furthermore, Nikolajeva argues that 'the history of children's literature presents mainly the evolution of epic structures'.[26] It is interesting to note that the exclusion of films aimed at child audiences from the epic canon runs counter to the perspective in literature.

Though also enjoyed by adults, there is no question that the Harry Potter series is aimed at children – specifically at pre-adolescent 8- to 12-year-old children.[27] Both J. K. Rowling, who exercised considerable control over the films' content, and Warner Bros have identified this group as the primary target audience, though this fact was not widely publicised, probably so as not to influence the films' appeal to both older children and adults, which naturally translates to more profits.

But what, exactly, makes Harry Potter a 'work we might easily dub an epic'?[28] Most characteristics of epic film derive from Aristotle's *Poetics*; these are the 'generic qualities that a modern epic film shares with the classical epic'[29] – length, unified action, multiple plots, a story that arouses pity and fear, an epic hero, spectacle, and a happy resolution. Constantine Santas says action, length, and spectacle are 'the most essential ingredients of the epic'.[30] He also asserts, regarding action and plot, that 'the battle between good and evil is the topic more explored by epics than any other'.[31] While there is plenty of action related to the numerous sub-plots, the main action in Harry Potter always revolves around the central plot – vanquishing the evil Lord Voldemort and his followers, which usually also necessitates Harry's dealing with some shortcoming in his own character. As for length, among epics made for theatre release it is the longest to date; all together, the eight films run for almost twenty hours. What about spectacle, usually defined in film as special effects?

Although Aristotle wrote that spectacle is the 'least artistic' of epic elements, Santas argues that spectacle 'has defined the epic' in modern film (see also Chapter 8).[32] Some of the many special effects in Harry Potter include 'things that there was no other filmic reference for', such as 'a ceiling that [magically] reflects the night sky . . . Quidditch', and mythical and magical beasts not previously depicted in any other visual medium.[33] Each film in the series, in addition to the usual displays of ghosts, moving portraits, and magical wand-waving, unveils a new array of spectacular images created using computer generated imagery (CGI) and other tools. Some scenes evoke the 'monumental' kind of spectacle Vivian Sobchack attributes to 1950s and '60s epics,[34] such as the Quidditch World Cup Final in *Harry Potter and the Goblet of Fire* (Newell 2005) and the Battle of Hogwarts in *Harry Potter and the Deathly Hallows Part 2* (Yates 2011).[35] The opening scene of the Quidditch World Cup Final shows a digitally-created crowd of thousands as the camera zooms in on the gigantic open-roofed stadium from above, while the Battle of Hogwarts depicts two 'armies' – the evil Death Eaters and the good wizards – engaged in a battle that is evocative of those in adult epics like *Spartacus* (Kubrick 1960) and *The Fall of the Roman Empire* (Mann 1964). Many other scenes, including the chess game in *Harry Potter and the Philosopher's Stone*, Aragog the giant spider in *Harry Potter and the Chamber of Secrets* (Columbus 2002), and the arrival of the Beauxbatons carriage and the Durmstrang ship in *Harry Potter and the Goblet of Fire*, are spectacular because of their depiction of magical/fantastic/powerful creatures and objects in the wizarding world.[36] Indeed, there are so many scenes throughout the films in which spectacular effects abound that it is difficult to isolate only a few to exemplify their epic nature.

Among the remaining classic epic characteristics – multiple plots, an epic hero, pity and fear, and a happy resolution – again, we find them all in Harry Potter. There are several sub-plots woven throughout the films, ranging from minor threads like the difficulty of navigating the minefield of young romance to more significant, ongoing threads connected to the main plot, such as where Snape's true loyalties lie. Brown and Patterson, in fact, partly attribute the series' global success precisely to the prevalence and complexity of these subplots, and to the marketing power of its 'story-dominant logic' and 'narrative superabundance'.[37]

Though he is a scrawny, bespectacled child when the series begins, Harry is nonetheless an archetypal epic hero: he comes from humble beginnings to achieve greatness on several levels, and he experiences a number of reversals and recognitions. Although Harry has been famous in the wizarding world since his infancy, he is less than ordinary in the Muggle or non-magical world, reflecting Christopher Booker's 'rags-to-riches' plot in which 'an ordinary, insignificant person, dismissed by everyone as of little account ... suddenly steps to the centre of the stage, revealed to be someone quite exceptional'.[38] It is worth noting here, however, that he is only 'dismissed by everyone' in the Muggle world (in the wizarding world he is already 'someone quite exceptional'), which does not quite fit Booker's mould so neatly. Continuing Booker's archetype, the rags-to-riches story

> first introduces us to its hero in childhood, or at least at a very young age before he has ventured out on the stage of the world. As yet he is not fully formed, and we are aware that in some essential way the story is concerned with the process of growing up.[39]

Accordingly, Harry is an infant when he (inadvertently) first overcomes Voldemort, and then faces and overcomes him again ... and again ... and again. Viewers' pity is initially aroused in *Harry Potter and the Philosopher's Stone* when they see how small Harry's 'room' in the cupboard under the stairs really is and how unkindly the Dursleys, the Muggle aunt and uncle who reluctantly raise Harry after he is orphaned, treat him; that sympathy is frequently supplanted by empathy, as the audience identifies increasingly with Harry by dint not only of extended screentime in which we share his perspective, but by the elision of antipathetic reactions from the Muggle community which increasingly isolate him both within the screen space and within the developing narrative. Similarly, viewers fear for Harry in varying degrees as the films progress, from sharing his apprehension about starting at a new school to being terrified that he may fail in the battle to save both the magical and Muggle worlds from evil. Finally, the story has a happy resolution; Harry and the forces for good defeat Voldemort and the Death Eaters once and for all, save both the magical and Muggle worlds (something the majority of Muggles are completely unaware of, just as they are unaware of the existence of a parallel magical world), and essentially establish a new community. Thus, even more than Booker's 'rags-to-riches' archetype, Harry epitomises the epic hero as described by Joseph Campbell, who 'ventures forth from the world of common day into a region of supernatural wonder: fabulous forces are there encountered and a decisive victory is won'.[40]

The series, besides exemplifying these classic aspects of epic, also fits definitions applicable specifically to film, one of which says that an epic is 'characterized by sweeping visual images'.[41] In addition to the previously-mentioned scene in *Harry Potter and the Goblet of Fire* wherein the camera sweeps over and then into the crowd and stadium at the Quidditch World Cup Final, others that include 'sweeping visual images' occur in *Harry Potter and the Prisoner of Azkaban* (Cuarón 2004) when Harry rides Buckbeak, the Hippogriff,[42] and in *Harry Potter and the Goblet of Fire* when Harry battles the Hungarian Horntail dragon during one task in the Triwizard Tournament. In the latter two scenes, Harry (and the camera) soar over the grounds of Hogwarts castle, giving the audience not only an exhilarating panoramic view, but also enabling them to see things from the hero's perspective, which, in turn, further enables them to see themselves in Harry.

Another film dictionary classifies epics as 'films dealing with major historical . . . themes'.[43] In Harry Potter, we learn some of the wizarding world's history, and although the events depicted in this world take place in the recent past – from 1991 to 1998[44] – and although the world itself is familiar in many ways, it seems older and much further removed from ours because it exists in a magical, but non-technological, realm and because many of its settings and costumes are evocative of ancient times. The simultaneous familiarity and 'foreign-ness' of this fantasy world makes it easier for viewers to reconcile what Burgoyne refers to as 'the central paradox of the epic genre[:] the contradiction between the traditional messages embedded within epic form – the birth of a nation, the emergence of a people, the fulfilment of a heroic destiny – and . . . the epic film as an international, global narrative not bound by nation or ethnicity'.[45] As Diana Patterson observes, the 'closeness [of the magical world] to our modern life . . . is around an invisible corner of our own',[46] so Hogwarts and its environs are familiar enough to us, on the one hand, to enable us to relate to them, but foreign enough on the other that we can appreciate both the epic's traditional messages and its appeal as 'an international, global narrative'.[47] Further, Roni Natov argues that 'the interpenetration of the two worlds suggests the way in which we live, not only in childhood, though especially so – on more than one plane, with the life of the imagination and daily life moving in and out of consciousness'.[48]

A secondary element of the epic qualities is revealed by the ways in which Harry Potter interacts with its cultural context. In this next section, then, I examine how Harry Potter as an epic series addresses children's fears and aspirations, in addition to appealing to 'cross-cultural structures of belonging and identification'[49] and children's 'inchoate sense of collective desire'.[50]

Children themselves say their main fears and aspirations revolve around issues of 'identity and belonging; feeling safe and being cared for; freedom; and having a say'[51] – the very concerns typically addressed in epics and the kind of concerns that transcend 'the bounds of nation, ethnicity, or religion'.[52] In fact, Levander and Singley argue that in the case of the USA, these two assertions about children's need for identity and the sense of national belonging are interwoven in cultural meanings of childhood, so that

> the American nation, since its inception, has been identified with and imagined as a child ... Narratives of U.S. national identity are persistently configured in the language of family: national identity is implicated in shifting notions of childhood, from the first colonial separation ... to the repeated figuring, in nineteenth-through late-twentieth-century American culture, of the child as a nostalgic symbol of lost innocence and youth.[53]

The Harry Potter films speak to these concerns of children on two levels: individually through Harry, and collectively through the community of which he is a member.

On an individual level, although Harry is a hero, children first encounter him as an ordinary boy of almost eleven who is like them, but is much less fortunate in many respects. Orphaned in infancy and reluctantly raised by his non-magical aunt and uncle, he is unloved and regarded as being of little worth.[54] His identity has necessarily developed intrinsically because he has had no extrinsic validation of who he is. When the story begins, there is much about himself of which he is unaware. He does not know how his parents really died, does not know he is a wizard, and nor does he know that he is already famous in the wizarding world. He senses that he does not belong in the Muggle world,[55] where he has not been made to feel either safe or cared for, where he has no freedom, and where he has no say or agency in the non-magical world – in short, he inhabits a domain in which he is completely powerless. Children relate to Harry and sympathise with his situation; they also empathise with him, because he is imperfect and makes mistakes, just like them, and because, also like them, he 'worries about who he *is*'.[56] Despite, or perhaps because of, Harry's imperfections, he is a role model that children not only relate to but want to emulate; as Harry's 'world becomes increasingly uncertain',[57] children recognise that the choices he makes in the face of difficult challenges have a strong moral dimension and are based on 'the right thing to do rather than the easiest'.[58] Throughout the series, although Harry is helped by peers and mentors, ultimately he must face and overcome problems on his own.

'Harry is a character through whom [children] can live vicariously [as they] learn to embrace [their] failures as well as [their] successes.'[59] By vicariously 'confronting fears, finding inner strength and doing what is right in the face of adversity',[60] children also learn the importance of self-reliance, 'endurance, perseverance, self-discipline, reason, solidarity, empathy, and sacrifice'.[61]

On the collective level, Harry is part of a community within the wizarding world – Hogwarts School of Witchcraft and Wizardry[62] – and the films 'chronicle the process of the child's movement from the initial consciousness of himself as the central character in his story . . . to a sense of his own power and responsibility to a larger community'.[63] Beginning the saga in a place that Harry and the other first-year students have never seen before and immediately subjecting them to a ritual whose outcome is unknown – the Sorting Ceremony – puts everyone on an equal footing. So students like Ron Weasley, who comes from a poor but pure-blooded wizarding family, and Hermione Granger, whose parents are Muggles, have as much opportunity to succeed as Draco Malfoy, the spoiled son of rich, powerful and bigoted magical parents. Also, the films depict children of both genders from a variety of racial and cultural backgrounds and exhibiting a variety of skill levels who ultimately unite to defend their community. Not only is Harry's world cross-cultural, so too is the audience to which the films appeal, as evidenced by their having been released in more than forty 'dubbed or subtitled versions';[64] furthermore, Harry's world combines 'both fantastic and familiar elements drawn from history, legend, and myth'.[65] The fantastic elements give the films their otherworldly, larger-than-life dimension, making them more appealing than stories set in the real world, while the familiar elements remind viewers that the magical realm is like ours in many ways.

As the epic progresses, the destructive forces of discrimination and intolerance – embodied in the extreme by Voldemort and the Death Eaters but also exhibited to a lesser extent by the Dursleys in the Muggle world and families like the Malfoys in the wizarding world – become the biggest threats to the magical and Muggle communities' identity and freedom. So when the primary institution upholding the dominant ideology – the Ministry of Magic – becomes corrupt, when Hogwarts is infiltrated by corrupt Ministry members, and when both worlds are on the brink of annihilation, Harry and the forces of good engage in the final battle. Ultimately, good triumphs, and the children, now young adults, having been instrumental in saving two worlds, will be integral in rebuilding them. The idea of accepting diversity, of being tolerant and non-discriminatory, appeals to children's sense of belonging and identification and, I believe, helps fulfil their 'inchoate sense of collective desire'[66] to contribute to and be part of a strong, positive community.

Children who immerse themselves in Harry Potter's world discover 'an epic fantasy conveying important moral lessons',[67] one of the most significant of which is that any community worth belonging to and fighting for must recognise and accept difference as an integral part of its identity. This is a powerful message.

Robert Burgoyne writes:

> The contemporary epic represents, in its production circumstances, narrative forms, and subject matter, a transnational orientation and an appeal to cross-cultural structures of belonging and identification. This theme . . . encourages us to look at epics . . . in terms of a postnational project focusing on broad stories of affiliation and community across ethnic, religious, and geographic boundaries.[68]

The Harry Potter series is precisely one of those 'broad stories of affiliation and community' that has something to say about how 'we think about childhood, adulthood and the family . . . and about questions of good and evil, personal and collective responsibility'.[69] The fact that the films are saying this to children, who are quite literally the future of the world, makes Harry Potter worthy of consideration as the greatest epic of the twenty-first century.

NOTES

1. Diana Patterson (ed.), *Harry Potter's World Wide Influence* (Newcastle upon Tyne: Cambridge Scholars Publishing, 2009), pp. vii–xi, p. vii.
2. Robert Burgoyne, 'Introduction', in Robert Burgoyne (ed.), *The Epic Film in World Culture* (New York: Routledge, 2011), pp. 1–16 (p. 3).
3. Ibid., p. 7.
4. Robert Burgoyne, *The Hollywood Historical Film* (Oxford: Blackwell, 2008), p. 4.
5. Constantine Santas, *The Epic in Film: From Myth to Blockbuster* (Lanham, MD: Rowman & Littlefield, 2008), p. 179.
6. Ibid., p. 4.
7. Ibid., p. 182.
8. Andrew Blake, *The Irresistible Rise of Harry Potter* (London: Verso, 2002), p. 91.
9. Kara Lynn Andersen. 'Harry Potter and the Susceptible Child Audience', *CLC Web: Comparative Literature and Culture*, 7.2 (June 2007), pp. 1–11 (p. 8). http://docs.lib.purdue.edu/clcweb/vol7/iss2/2, last accessed 14 October 3013.
10. Edmund M. Kern, *The Wisdom of Harry Potter: What Our Favorite Hero Teaches Us about Moral Choices* (Amherst, NY: Prometheus Books, 2003). p. 22.
11. See, for example, Martin Barker and Ernest Mathijs (eds), *Watching the Lord of the Rings: Tolkien's World Audiences* (New York: Peter Lang, 2008); Wayne G. Hammond and Christina Scull (eds), *The Lord of the Rings, 1954–2004 Scholarship in Honor of Richard E. Blackwelder* (Milwaukee, WI: Marquette University Press, 2006); Janice M. Bogstad and Philip E. Kaveny (eds), *Picturing Tolkien: Essays on Peter Jackson's The Lord of the Rings Film Trilogy* (Jefferson, NC: McFarland, 2011); I. Q. Hunter, 'Post-classical Fantasy Cinema: The Lord of the Rings,' in Deborah Cartmell and Imelda Whelehan (eds), *The*

Cambridge Companion to Literature on Screen (Cambridge: Cambridge University Press, 2007); Jane Chance, *Lord of the Rings: The Mythology of Power* (Lexington, KY: University Press of Kentucky, 2010); Hal Colebatch, *Return of the Heroes: The Lord of the Rings, Star Wars and Contemporary Culture* (Christchurch, NZ: Cybereditions, 2003); Robert Eaglestone, *Reading The Lord of the Rings: New Writings on Tolkien's Classic* (London: Continuum, 2006); Ernest Mathijs (ed.), *The Lord of the Rings: Popular Culture in Global Context* (London: Wallflower Press, 2006); John G. West, Jr (ed.), *Celebrating Middle-Earth: The Lord of the Rings as a Defense of Western Civilization* (Seattle, WA: Inkling Books, 2002).

12. Susan Gunelius, *Harry Potter: The Story of a Global Business Phenomenon* (New York: Palgrave Macmillan, 2008), p. 3.
13. Suman Gupta, *Re-Reading Harry Potter* (Basingstoke & New York: Palgrave Macmillan, 2009), p. 143.
14. See Gunelius, *Harry Potter*, Chapter 12.
15. 'Potter Movie No Challenge for Spielberg', *The Guardian*, 4 September 2001, http://www.guardian.co.uk/film/2001/sep/04/news.stevenspielberg, last accessed 3 March 2013.
16. Gupta, *Re-reading Harry Potter*, p. 143.
17. Viviana A. Zelizer, *Pricing the Priceless Child* (New York: Basic Books, 1985), p. 209.
18. Laura Oswald, 'Branding the American Family: A Strategic Study of the Culture, Composition, and Consumer Behavior of Families in the New Millennium', *Journal of Popular Culture*, 37.2 (2003), pp. 309–35 (p. 316).
19. Monique Wonderly, 'Children's Film as an Instrument of Moral Education', *Journal of Moral Education*, 38.1 (March 2009), pp. 1–15 (p. 1).
20. Ibid., p. 2.
21. Ibid., p. 2.
22. Ibid., pp. 1–2.
23. *Harry Potter* has been used as an allegory for a wide number of disciplines throughout disparate scholarly fields. To adduce only a random sample, the boy wizard crops up in debates about gender, addiction, religion, international relations, politics, ethics, disability, and even DNA fingerprinting. See Meredith Cherland, 'Harry's Girls: Harry Potter and the Discourse of Gender', *Journal of Adolescent & Adult Literacy*, 4 (2008), pp. 273–82; Stephen Deets, 'Wizarding in the Classroom: Teaching Harry Potter and Politics', *PS: Political Science and Politics*, 4 (2009), pp. 741–4; Paul V. M. Flesher, 'Being True to the Text: From Genesis to Harry Potter', *Journal of Religion and Film*, 12.2 (2008); Maria Carolina da Silva and Marlucy Alves Paraíso, 'The Harry Potter's Syllabus: Representations of School and Syllabus in Children's and Adolescent Literature', *Educação : Teoria e Prática*, 39 (2012), pp. 99–116; Alice Mills, 'Harry Potter: Agency or Addiction?,' *Children's Literature in Education*, 41.4 (October 2010), pp. 291–301; Laura K. Palmer, 'Using Harry Potter to Introduce Students to DNA Fingerprinting & Forensic Science', *The American Biology Teacher*, 4 (2010), pp. 241–4; Roslyn Weaver, 'Metaphors of Monstrosity: The Werewolf as Disability and Illness in "Harry Potter" and "Jatta"', *Papers: Explorations into Children's Literature*, 20.2 (2010), pp. 70–82; Shira Wolosky, 'Harry Potter's Ethical Paradigms: Augustine, Kant, and Feminist Moral Theory', *Children's Literature*, 40 (2012), pp. 191–217.
24. Kern, *The Wisdom of Harry Potter*, p. 39.
25. Maria Nikolajeva, 'Exit Children's Literature?', *The Lion and the Unicorn*, 22.2 (1998), pp. 221–36 (p. 225).
26. Maria Nikolajeva (ed.), *Aspects and Issues in the History Children's Literature* (Westport, CT: Greenwood, 1995), p. x.

27. Gupta, *Re-reading Harry Potter*, Chapter 2.
28. Patterson, *Harry Potter's World Wide Influence*, p. vii.
29. Santas, *The Epic in Film*, p. 29.
30. Ibid., p. 23.
31. Ibid., p. 197.
32. Quoted in Ibid., p. 28.
33. *Harry Potter and the Philosopher's Stone*, DVD (USA, Warner Bros, 2002), comments by the director, Chris Columbus, in the 'Interviews' section of the extra credits DVD.
34. Vivian Sobchack, '"Surge and Splendor": A Phenomenology of the Hollywood Historical Epic', *Representations*, 29 (Winter 1990), pp. 24–9 (pp. 24–5).
35. *Harry Potter and the Goblet of Fire*, DVD (USA, Warner Bros, 2005), and *Harry Potter and the Deathly Hallows, Part 2*, DVD (USA,Warner Bros, 2011). Interestingly, the last film in the series is described on the back cover of the DVD case as an 'epic finale'.
36. In traditional literary epic, spectacle – what Pope called supernatural 'machinery' – includes gods, goddesses and other mythical creatures, and the 'magic' they are capable of making. Interestingly, whereas, for example, the film version of *Troy* departs from the original tale by removing this machinery, thus securing its classification as a historical rather than a fantasy epic, the Harry Potter films retain all the epic machinery of the books.
37. Stephen Brown and Anthony Patterson, 'Selling Stories: Harry Potter and the Marketing Plot', *Psychology & Marketing*, 27.6 (June 2010), pp. 542–3.
38. See Christopher Booker, *The Seven Basic Plots: Why We Tell Stories* (London: Continuum, 2004), Chapter 3. The quotation here comes from p. 51.
39. Ibid., p. 54. In a footnote about Harry Potter, Booker says 'In a story combining elements of Voyage and Return, Rags to Riches, Overcoming the Monster and Quest, the young orphan hero . . . finds himself transported into a mysterious "other world" governed by magic and peopled by wizards, dragons, trolls, and other fabulous creatures', pp. 319–20.
40. Joseph Campbell, *The Hero with a Thousand Faces* (Princeton, NJ: Princeton University Press, 1968), 2nd edn, p. 30.
41. Steve Blandford, Barry Keith Grant and Jim Hillier, 'Epic film', in *The Film Studies Dictionary* (London: Arnold, 2001), p. 84.
42. Interestingly, at one point while Buckbeak is soaring over the lake at Hogwarts, Harry throws his arms out, raises his head, and whoops, which is evocative of Leonardo DiCaprio's 'I'm the king of the world' scene in *Titanic*, another disputed 'epic'.
43. Moya Luckett, 'Epic', in Roberta E. Pearson and Philip Simpson (eds), *Critical Dictionary of Film and Television Theory* (London: Routledge, 2001), p. 157.
44. 'Time lines', *The Harry Potter Lexicon*, 16 August 2007. www.hp-lexicon.org, last accessed 14 October 2013.
45. Burgoyne, 'Introduction', *The Epic Film in World Culture*, p. 2.
46. Patterson, *The World-Wide Influence of Harry Potter*, p. vii.
47. Burgoyne, 'Introduction', *The Epic Film in World Culture*, p. 2.
48. Roni Natov, 'Harry Potter and the Extraordinariness of the Ordinary', *The Lion and the Unicorn*, 25.2 (April 2001), pp. 310–27 (p. 314).
49. Burgoyne, 'Introduction', *The Epic Film in World Culture*, p. 3.
50. Ibid., p. 7.
51. Mary Grey, 'The disenchantment and re-enchantment of childhood in an age of globalization', *International Journal of Children's Spirituality*, 11.1 (April 2006), pp. 11–21 (p. 16).
52. Burgoyne, 'Introduction', *The Epic Film in World Culture*, p. 7.

53. Caroline Field Levander and Carol J. Singley (eds.), *The American Child: A Cultural Studies Reader* (New Brunswick, NJ: Rutgers University Press, 2003), p. 4.
54. See, for example, Scenes 2 and 3 of *Harry Potter and the Philosopher's Stone*. In these scenes, we see that Harry is locked into his 'room' in the cupboard under the stairs at night and that his uncle, aunt and cousin clearly have little regard for him.
55. Ibid.
56. Kern, *The Wisdom of Harry Potter*, p. 19.
57. Ibid., p. 20.
58. Linda DeNell, quoted in Kern, *The Wisdom of Harry Potter*, p. 41.
59. Hidingfromsomeone, 'The "Harry Potter" Generation', *Mugglenet.com*.
60. Stephen King, quoted in Hidingfromsomeone, 'The Harry Potter Generation'.
61. Kern, *The Wisdom of Harry Potter*, p. 19.
62. See also Gupta, *Re-reading Harry Potter*, Chapter 11.
63. Natov, 'Harry Potter and the Extraordinariness of the Ordinary', p. 311.
64. Daniel H. Nexon and Iver B. Neumann, *Harry Potter and International Relations* (Lanham, MD: Rowman & Littlefield, 2006), p. 3.
65. Kern, *The Wisdom of Harry Potter*, p. 180.
66. Burgoyne, *The Epic Film in World Culture*, p. 7.
67. Kern, *The Wisdom of Harry Potter*, p. 196.
68. Burgoyne, *The Epic Film in World Culture*, p. 3.
69. Blake, *The Irresistible Rise of Harry Potter*, p. 19.

CHAPTER 12

The *Ramayana* and Sita in Films and Popular Media: The Repositioning of a Globalised Version

Aarttee Kaul Dhar

All our mythology may vanish ever, our Vedas may depart and our Sanskrit language may vanish forever, even if speaking the most vulgar patois, there will be the story of Sita present . . . Sita has gone into the very vitals of our race. She is there in the blood of every Hindu man and woman.[1]

The Indian epic *Ramayana* has its place among the greatest epics of the world. It is omnipresent, found in language, art, culture, literature, ethics, festivals and ceremonies. It is not just an epic but a tradition. Sita–Ram is not just the epic couple; Ram is the ultimate male, and representations of Indian womanhood are grounded firmly in Sita, making Sita–Ram together integral to the Indian subconscious. It is impossible to conjecture its origin, as it existed in an oral form for an unknowable period of time and evolved as an environmental and socio-cultural process, as not just a homogenised work but one having many voices with a basic unity as well as amazing diversity. The poet Valmiki documented the *Ramayana* for the first time in Sanskrit, inspiring the next thousand years of the literary tradition of Ramkathas,[2] which were rewritten in all Indian languages, with each contributing local colour, and contemporary historical, regional, cultural and political dynamics; such a rich and varied tradition encouraged its perpetuation through texts and theatrical performances as well as pictorial and oral traditions. It also travelled outside India with labourers, immigrants and missionaries. With three hundred variants, the *Ramayana* can now be called a 'global text', since almost every country has its own version. Year after year, films inspired by or based on the *Ramayana* are made, awaited and consumed with a lot of interest and critiqued with equal gusto. With the *Ramayana* the issue is never what is shown, but always how: each film in this way becomes an epic film, as the *Ramayana* is a national tale with epic implications both in India and abroad.

The *Ramayana* is one of the greatest epics of India and one of the seven greatest epics of the world, along with *Mahabharata*. Documented for the first time by the Hindu sage Valmiki, it forms an important part of the Hindu canon and is considered to be a kind of history. Not only does it tell the tale of a prince in exile with his princess but it also tells of the duties of people in various relationships, portraying ideal characters like the ideal father, mother, brother, wife, and king. The name '*Ramayana*' literally means 'Ram's journey': it consists of 24,000 verses in seven books and 500 cantos and tells the story of Ram (an incarnation of the god Vishnu), whose wife Sita was abducted by Ravan, the king of Lanka. The *Ramayana* largely explores human values and the concept of *dharma* or righteousness. It has parallel versions in various countries, appearing as *Reamker* in Cambodia, *Ramakein* in Thailand, *Phra Lak Phra Lam* in Laos, *Hikayat Seri Ram* in Malaysia, *Kakawin Ramayana* in Indonesia, *Maharadia Lawana* in the Philippines, *Sidhi Ramayana* in Nepal and many more.[3]

Over the course of time it moved from being a literary text to being a visual one, with films, documentaries, television and also animations, where it is found in both traditional and contemporary forms. Continual experimentation marks these narratives, which are rooted in tradition; nevertheless, these experimentations also transform those same narratives by absorbing socio-environmental influences in subsequent iterations. These films mark the transition from a local to a larger national, and indeed international, audience and a shift from a particular perspective to a more generic one. *Ramayana* traditions are multiple, and hence there is scope for experimentation; these are, as Richman terms it, the 'two key characteristics at the heart of the *Ramayana* tradition in South Asia: its multiplicity and its ability to accommodate questioning within its boundaries'.[4] With that in view, we can observe that the *Ramayana*'s chief female figure Sita has travelled a long way in time. Found first in the *Rig-Veda* as Sita-Savitri, a goddess of agriculture, she next appears in the epics. However, her canonical depictions raise some questions. Are these epics read in the modern day? Do their characters inspire readers? Do twenty-first-century youth audiences still look up to Sita, or does the leading female icon of India risk fading out from public memories in its changed milieu and ethics? Furthermore, the *Ramayana*'s transition from text to film raises similar questions about its meaning. Does the medium contribute to the nature and efficacy of the message of *Ramayana*-based films? What is that message? Has the *Ramayana* been turned into a consumer product through new, experimental films?

This chapter studies two modern interpretations of the *Ramayana* in modern media, and examines the above-stated issues thematically as well as on basis of the narratives of two films: Madhureeta Anand's 2007 documentary *Laying Janaki to Rest* and Nina Paley's 2008 film *Sita Sings the Blues*. The objective is to explore whether Sita's character can be understood in a new, contemporary and hence more relevant perspective, and whether this is a national version of the favourite epic of India, or whether it forms part of a global epic tradition. The documentary is made by an Indian woman in India, whereas the film is made by a female Jewish director in the USA, with just one common denominator, which is the *Ramayana*. Though strictly speaking neither film can be categorised as 'epic' in the traditional sense of the term, both reinforce the 'cross-cultural structures of belonging and identification' which Robert Burgoyne argues are fundamental to the epic in world culture.[5] Both use the epic as a vehicle for telling personal experiences, and both suggest that the continual relevance of an important national and transnational myth further challenges our traditionally Western-oriented definitions of the epic film. Both films follow a somewhat similar pattern, showing personal journeys with the epic plot moving parallel to them, until gradually the epic plot takes a back seat and the journey of the modern women becomes more important. Both films encourage the audience to question tradition by employing experimental techniques and alternative forms, inextricably fusing together feminist, psychoanalytical and literary readings of the epic subject matter. The films project the role model of Sita and sustain her as the central character in the narrative, simultaneously analysing and interrogating it.

In the context of war films Robert Burgoyne talks of 'generational memory', foregrounding questions of memory, cinematic affect and the changing meaning of the past for the present, bringing out the fact that each generation finds its own objects of value in the past and reads the past differently, discovering narratives and events that had been ignored or repressed in earlier accounts.[6] The same can be said of a *Ramayana*-based film. Its potential to provide the subject matter of transnational cinema hence cannot be denied. It also reconsiders the *Ramayana*'s place as a purely national epic. Existing in its oral form in the early stages, the *Ramayana* has now appeared in the form of a transnational film, though it nevertheless retains similarities to its origins in terms of its function and themes. Oral renditions were traditional but never the same twice; subject to a continual process of innovation and renewal by the bards, the *Ramayana* was continually reshaped, showing sensitivity to the audience and its cultural needs. The same can be said of *Ramayana*-inspired movies; here we see that it is essentially the same story but never told the same way twice, because the problems of every age and time period are unique, meaning that new and unprecedented ways of dealing with them are considered. The films could be a step in the direction of finding imaginative solutions for modern-day issues and in the process may also guide perceptions that may assert new actions.

These retellings are actually serious attempts to address culture through media that could be seen as a potential tool capable of ushering in change.

Different films have a different impact on different audiences, each of which is often subjective and the result of cultural memory. A research student of film and media will look at the *Ramayana* differently from an expatriate Indian, and both of these interpretations will in turn differ from those of a young unmarried girl for whom the film may pose troubling questions about injustice to womenfolk being institutionalised in the name of marriage.

A LOCAL EPIC? *LAYING JANAKI TO REST*

Laying Janaki to Rest is a reflexive documentary of around twenty-six minutes which begins with an autobiographical note in which director Madhureeta Anand's reminiscence about her personal past moves from the personal to public space. The film is especially topical for India as Indian culture is marked by a predominance of familial bonds and traditions. It depicts a handful of women taken as representative sample for their gender and their struggle for survival. It is a personal narrative of selected women violated and transgressed, articulating their pain, in first discovering their self and then constructing it. Their new-found realisation and understanding of an independent and meaningful identity provides them with a form of redemption.

The film begins with the title of the production house, 'Open Frame', which brings to mind a picture of confinement, periphery or structure, suggesting that an enclosure is being challenged. The chief protagonist was still in her teens when her views and opinions were formed, excited about leading a romantic life with her Prince Charming. Her act of seeking approval from an astrologer arises from cultural specifics originating from and having roots in tradition: namely, the tradition of Sita Ram and of stereotyped ideas and beliefs. She is an archetypal character in her own story, now looking at Indian culture and traditions from outside the frame. The traditional Indian marriage is central to the narrative and the theme. The next scene has a middle-aged security guard with some education and awareness of contemporary issues speaking to the camera. When he is asked about young girls of today, his reference point is revealed to be highly revered and mythological female icons such as Sita and Savitri, suggesting that Sita is a deep-rooted icon in the collective Indian cultural memory.[7] The camera next shows a cleaning woman who believes that although Indian women are as hardworking, selfless and loyal as Sita was, nothing on the ground has actually changed for her as she remains as wronged. This character displays an undercurrent of conviction and self-assertion and ideas of purity and chastity find a spontaneous way into her conversation, which is important in the Indian context. Her demeanour suggests she may have the courage to push the frame to make it more inclusive.

The question that comes to mind is whether the frame is really open, or whether the term 'Open Frame' is a misnomer. Anand demonstrates, through her interviews, that Sita lives and breathes in Indian minds and aspirations. Her vox-pops with women demonstrate that what they think about themselves becomes important as the film is *by* a woman and constitutes the voices *of* women but is not necessarily only *for* women. The film then shows the male gaze objectifying women, with the soundtrack playing a popular Hindi movie song *Sita Bhi Yahan Badnam Huyi*, which suggests that, by seeking to challenge the boundaries, Sita becomes stereotyped through her negation. A group of girls debate the logic of being Sita as she was too good and idealistic. Even when the film ends, the debate most emphatically does not.

Present-day realities are different, and the viewers see that the three women interviewed broke away from a hostile environment and stood up to seek an identity when they found themselves boxed up in a corner. They sought refuge in an independent, meaningful existence of social and financial liberty and dignity. They work, provide for their children, look after them with love and care as Sita did. They were traditional women rooted deep in cultural values, wanting only a little recognition for their person within the domestic space which was denied to them, leading them to question all social constructs such as love, romance, marriage and even motherhood. In the process they realise that woman as a silent suffering stoic species is so deified that she is never seen as an individual or a person.

Despite the sensitive subject, the film avoids melodrama in favour of a deliberate style in which even the evocation of myth seems to be natural. Towards the end, the film shows Anand arriving at a point of self-realisation; the film employs the myth of Purush and Prakriti, suggesting that Sita's union with Ram is symbolised by the natural phenomena of Indian mythology. Her abandonment and transformation from a queen to an ordinary woman (which Namita Gokhale calls *sahaj*)[8] while living in neglect and hardship shows her to be a woman of substance, making her the first single mother known in Indian myth who could also handle much more than royal status. The popular gaze is nevertheless still fixed on Sita as Ram's consort, and, as Malashri Lal mentions in the film, 'this cardboard Sita is a convenient tool of control for society, as a device for perpetuating the myth of a useful but invisible wife'.

The film thus asserts that this tale is enacted everyday and everywhere. The patriarchal system at every step accuses, questions, doubts, interrogates and rejects young brides, and bride burning is still rampant in a country that claims to worship women as part of its deep-rooted ancient culture. It is a film about choices, and in re-rendering this tale the film sends out a potent message that a woman should have a right to choose a different and distinct path from what tradition expects from her. The film does not seem far from reality, and is an answer to Lalitha Lenin's poem *In The Shadow of Sita*.[9] It concludes with emergent young voices contributing to an ongoing debate about the fate of a stereotypical Sita, with the possibility of becoming a prototypal one. The visual text is problematic as it shows the male and female worlds as two dialectics and shows no conclusive end, meaning that ultimately the film – and therefore the debate itself – lacks finality.

SITA SINGS THE BLUES

Sita Sings the Blues (2009) is a film by Nina Paley made available as a free download from the internet under a CC-SA licence. It can be mixed, remixed and carried forward as long as the credits of the original are given to its maker. Its characteristic features are:

1. The *Ramayana* tale as the main plot and its contemporary parallel – the story of Nina and Dave, an American couple.
2. The chirpy trio of the Indonesian puppets, as an added tool of narration reminding one of the traditions of a *Sutradhar*[10] in ancient Indian classical drama, also hinting at the Ramayana puppet traditions existing outside India in Indonesia, Malaysia, Thailand and Cambodia.
3. Musical interludes as in a Bollywood film that take the narrative forward, with a two-minute, forty-five-second intermission also providing entertainment.[11]

The storyline closely follows the Valmiki *Ramayana*. The film received great critical acclaim with many awards, though it also generated its fair share of controversy. In its parallel contemporary, and autobiographical, episode, Nina and Dave live in a San Francisco apartment with a cat. Dave travels to Trivandrum and, after several months of little contact with him, Nina travels to India bewildered by his callous indifference. Dave's cold welcome, where he displays no emotional or sexual interest in her, flummoxes her. After she reaches New York for a meeting she receives a brief e-mail with the message 'Nina, don't come back'. Heartbroken and miserable, she eventually comes to terms with the situation, settling in a new apartment, in a new city, with a new cat, finding solace in reading the *Ramayana* as a self-therapeutic text. No logical explanation for the husband's insensitivity is given. Past, myth and present reality all get intertwined for Nina at this point. The question of who bears the responsibility for her suffering is a perplexing question, and one which receives no explicit answer in the film. At this point in the plot, the demarcation between fact and fiction melts, and the Sita myth travels from fiction to reality and stands firm and central in Nina's life.

The film begins by showing the primordial waters set against the titles. A beautiful glittering Laxmi, the Indian goddess of wealth and prosperity, with curly hair and classical features emerges from the waters. She has four

Figure 12.1 In *Sita Sings the Blues* (2009) the goddess Laxmi creates a forceful identification between the Earth itself and womanhood, recalling a range of ideas drawn from Indian mythology.

hands that bless, and hold a conch shell, a lotus and the *Sudarshan Chakra*.[12] A nineteenth-century gramophone plays the song 'He is the kind of man that needs a woman like me', while Laxmi gyrates her slim waist. The cosmic sounds are followed by a great explosion. The Earth comes into existence spinning madly; all cosmic powers and mythical figures including the Holy Trinity (Lord Brahma, Vishnu and Mahesh), Sheshnag, the five-headed serpent with Lord Vishnu reclining on it, and the Goddess Laxmi pressing his feet appear in animated form. These images inter-mix, rotate, spin and merge into the Earth. Laxmi's heart beats loudly and everything becomes a part of it including Earth, creating an identification between the Earth and the woman.

This is followed by a witty discourse between the three shadow puppets found in Andhra Pradesh and Kerala in India. They narrate the *Ramayana* tale, perpetually interrupting and correcting each other, putting it together piece by piece in an apparently unrehearsed and unscripted conversation, bringing modern perspectives to it by raising poignant questions punctuated with humour. The story begins with Kekeyi, shown as a seductive nurse with a plunging neckline, hinting at the control she enjoyed over her husband Dasrath,[13] warning Ram in contemporary American lingo, 'Don't let the door hit your ass on the way out.' Nina uses everyday language in the film; thus the environment and times of the maker find a reflection in the creation. The tale is modern and American, funny and sad because she is all of those things, describing both the film and her own character as 'a strange hybrid'.[14]

The use of colours and the body is one of the highlights of a complex film which sends out complex messages. Ram is blue, as he is described as dark-complexioned in all Indian texts. Blue also stands for maleness, meaning that Ram's complexion and physique emphasise his gender. Sita is depicted in a pink that underscores her femininity, with a thin waist and a buxom, voluptuous hour-glass figure, devised largely from circles by the animator. She lives happily with Ram in the wilderness, singing romantic songs like a hackneyed Bollywood heroine; their romance in a lush green garden indicates her desirability and sexuality, underscoring the fact that she is a normal young woman with normal human desires. Apparently both Sita and Ram deserve and complete each other as the male and the female. The colour green suggests Nature blooming and blossoming and also fertility, recalling Sita's original role as an earth goddess. The flora and fauna in fluorescent colours and absolute synchronisation lend the scene a fairy-tale element, underscoring the fantastical element in it. The Indian part of the story is a riot of colours. It is not only the visual text but also the written one that draws on many resources as music, colours, songs, landscape and performative references, recalling the poet Prakashram in his *Ramavtarcharit*,[15] which creates a reciprocal relationship between literature and film. Ram's masculinity, his carnal male body, is an object of desire and fulfilment. Yet, in the epic, he was not man enough for his woman; hence his perfectly censured body evokes irony and serves as an instrument of satire.

The use of nature as a reflection of Sita's moods also suggests the concept of eco-feminism; Sita's depiction in nature, painted in bright and bold colours, draws equally on the Indian myth that woman is nature personified or that she symbolises nature with all its colours and contours. An ancient Indian hymn says that the male principle is the activating force of the cosmos, illustrated forcefully by Lord Indra causing lightening to strike, bringing forth rains to make the earth fertile as in the *Rig Veda*. The sun is depicted as a bull whose virility is transmitted through rays of light that bring forth life on the Earth; the moon god's virility is the semen that seeps through vegetation and enlivens all things; the sky is seen as a father shedding its seeds or rain to bring forth vegetation resulting in life on Earth that pulses with *rasa*.[16] These ideas, which have been a staple of Indian mythology, show the comparisons continually drawn between nature and humans. The film employs the myths of the *Ksheersagar*,[17] or the churning of the great milky ocean, and also that of the *Ardhanarishwar*,[18] which says that Shiva and Shakti are both each other's counterpart, who together constitute a complete being, emphasising that no man or woman can be called complete in isolation. It also suggests that cosmic plurality is but a mirage and that there exists within all creatures a singular divine spirit. The film *Sita Sings* thus makes the Sita myth omnipresent, and free of all spatial and temporal barriers.

The tongue-in-cheek irreverence in the conversation of the puppets while discussing the *Ramayana* also helps us to understand the story better, with gods dancing to techno funk music, a fusion of the ancient with the modern which sets the tone for the rest of the film. The three puppets compare Ravan with Mogambo (the archetypal Bollywood villain from Shekhar Kapur's *Mr. India* (1987)), which hints at the intertextuality of the *Ramayana* and America's homage to Indian films. They mention *dashavatars* incorporating the incarnation theory of Lord Vishnu taking human form for a definite purpose and the welfare of mankind.[19] Sita's words, 'Ravan I don't burn you with my own gaze and power because Lord Ram has not ordered me to do so', depict a woman who knows her capabilities but is conditioned to believe in male superiority, internalising patriarchy as a part of her social, psychological and cultural construct. The puppets wonder why Sita did not return with Hanuman on his back, which interrogates and rethinks the epic from the perspective of the puppets, saying 'get on the monkey's back, go home and chill, hundreds could have been saved'. The puppets synergise humorous sarcasm with substantial food for thought, switching from comic songs to serious questions such as 'Why should Sita love someone who doesn't treat her right?'. They discuss various possibilities and piece together a mythological story which highlights the variations and the richness of the cultural traditions of this tale and difference in their cultural space as they grew up in different parts of the country listening to various forms of the *Ramayana*.

The contribution of the songs and dances in representing the sexuality of the heroine is noteworthy. When Ram picks up Sita in his arms it enhances the suggestive but subtle physicality of love, but only hinting at whatever happens outside the view, which appeals to Indian cultural logic. All this fusion is made plausible by the creator depicting a new form of Sita with the use of Rajput-style paintings, songs and the visual impact that the film creates. The clever use of songs as frames of the story is part of the narrative technique. Sung by the early twentieth-century American singer Annette Hanshaw, they tell about Sita's feelings and carry the tale forward. When Sita falls in love she sings, 'I would lean on his shoulder/Would never grow older.' After her rejection she sings 'You are mean to me', while on their reconciliation she sings, 'If you want a rainbow you must have the rain.' During her second exile she sings 'Moaning low, am I blue', and when longing hopelessly she sings 'Lover, come back to me'. Last of all, in the state of self-discovery and self-love after rejecting Ram and while disappearing into the earth she sings 'I have a feeling I am falling'. The songs bring out her pain and humiliation as an effective and eloquent tool which simultaneously mirrors and updates Sita's original words. They free the epic from its limited cultural context and by framing the tale around a familiar and relatable problem create a form of the epic with global appeal. This universalisation of female experiences liberates the Sita story, allowing it to transcend cultural, geographical, spatial and historical barriers, suggesting

Figure 12.2 The songs of *Sita Sings the Blues* frame the epic around a familiar and relatable problem with global appeal.

that the Sita theme is universal and that its universality is external to itself but inherent in human experience. Pattanaik extends this to argue that mythology represents the subjective truth of people and that divine tales in Indian myth are not bound by history or geography, time or space.[20] They exist everywhere. All songs end with a twinkling 'That's all', suggesting the narration of a story in the song and the completion of an episode. The film includes fusion numbers from *Chill Aum*,[21] alongside songs from an album of original music by Michelson, Tchaikovsky's *Romeo and Juliet*, and the ironic 'Rama's Great'.

In another episode from *Sita Sings the Blues*, Sita is shown singing 'What wouldn't I do for that man?', oblivious to her impending fate while she is alone in the hut and Ravan watches and waits for an opportune moment to abduct her. A serious situation here is depicted as a parody, denying it the decorum and gravity it deserved. On the other hand it brings out her innocence in an ordinary situation as an unsuspecting victim of fate and impending turn of events. When Sita longs for Ram she sings 'Daddy won't you come home', which has a subverted hint of Sylvia Plath's poem 'Daddy', suggesting the oppressive male, which also universalises the themes of the song by contextualising the suffering of Sita within broader global themes of fatherhood and patriarchy, linking Sita's struggle for autonomy with what Harold Bloom, referring to Plath, terms 'the eternal sameness of patriarchy and of women's singular relationship to it'.[22] While a fierce battle is fought between Ram and Ravan she sings 'Who's knocking at my door?'. A river of blood flows past Sita, which suggests the futility of the battle and the loss of lives associated with it, an issue also echoed in the graphic novel *Sita's Ramayana* by Moyna Chitrakar, a Patua scroll painter from Bengal.

After Dave leaves Nina there is a fire dance shown in the film; here fire is understood to be a metaphorical expression of Nina's repressed emotions, appearing as something of a revolt, a catharsis of pent-up emotions to give visual expression to the fire within her heart. This spectacular sequence enhances the effect of the conflict within, which both consumes and creates something new. Though it may not have been Paley's intention to challenge the Indian myth, by juxtaposing the ancient with the modern she has done so through *Sita Sings*, contributing in the process to a better and more sensitive understanding of a woman's agony by updating the past and relating the modern to an age-old issue. It can be called both a reworking of an Indian myth (adapted to contemporary life and issues) and an international translation of the Sita myth for women across the world. It is, hence, an important suggestion for redesigning a society and culture, creating a new text with global appeal. The film can be seen as an outcome of the meeting of two cultures, Indian and American, each seeming exotic to the other. Both co-mingle and exist side by side with a variety of possible interactions in the future. Paley has also been applauded for her creativity in mixing, matching and fusing together different works and styles, rendering and re-rendering the tale making it enchanting, keeping it alive and contemporising it by making the Sita story a dynamic plot in place of a fixed one. The way of life depicted in the film has been localised, with the backdrop of San Francisco, USA and, later, Trivandrum, India, reinventing Sita as a newly repositioned global *avatar*. Its cultural impact was such that the film inspired a Bangkok fashion line designed by Raj Singhakul in April 2009 called 'Sita Sings the Blues'.

At the same time, however, the film is not without its shortcomings. Paley has been criticised by some for using the *Ramayana* tale as a vehicle for her personal story, releasing it under a free licence; these critics deem it a form of cultural imperialism because Nina is neither Indian nor Indian-American; she is a white American of Jewish descent. It is also conjectured that such an attempt may be motivated by monetary gain. The film's popularity opened up merchandising possibilities, and shirts, accessories, Sita pins and pendants, books, charms, water bottles, bags and Sita dolls can all be ordered from the website, things whose saleability suggests to some that the holy religious tale of oriental India has been commodified by capitalist America. Whether this is true, or indeed whether it represents the use or the abuse of the *Ramayana*, is a question which remains unanswered.

Likewise, at the level of gender politics, resistance to patriarchy by Sita is expressed as suicide, the ultimate self-denial. Unlike in *Laying Janaki to Rest*, which adopts a discursive approach, the absence of a second voice in *Sita Sings the Blues* risks making it opinionated and one-sided, lacking in objective balance. Ram is the second most prominent character, but his voice has been totally silenced. Both films highlight Ram's eventual treatment of Sita, which, though extremely troubling, is only a minor part of the epic, but in both films it has been emphasised for thematic reasons as if it were the focal point of the *Ramayana*, which makes them somewhat feminist retellings. This may cloud the judgment of those who have no awareness about the *Ramayana*. Furthermore, the global appeal of the epic is somewhat diminished by the intertextual references which pervade both *Sita Sings the Blues* and *Laying Janaki to Rest*, which suggest that knowledge of the original tale is a prerequisite for both films. On the other hand, however, they fit very well with the Indian tradition of alternative *Ramayanas* and may engage people with Indian mythology, making the *Ramayana* an engaging device of story-telling and shared experiences.

CONCLUSIONS

Thus, despite these films being about individual experience, their titles, dialogues, symbolism and references collectively evoke tradition and myth and have resonances far beyond the individual, taking in the collective cultural memory of Sita. The myth functions as a medium for bringing about self-realisation for all the women depicted and dealt with. Both films are anguished critiques of romantic love and are a creative outpouring of their women directors, transgressed and violated in their broken marriages; both, like Valmiki, appear in their own tale, projecting ordinary women on an extraordinary journey rationally. Anxious to avoid being consumed by failed relationships, they metamorphosed into self-assured women, in the process questioning all social constructs. Both films are open-ended, operating within the *Ramayana* tale but transcending the epic and its context. The protagonists shift from one set of cultural habits to another, and by the end of it all a stereotyped Sita becomes a prototypal one.

In both the films, the ancient and the modern Sitas combat not only tradition but also their dependence on and attachment to their husband. The original Sita myth underpins the films, and *Sita Sings* can be seen as beginning of a new, more international culture which, though made up of composite elements from the past, also addresses future generations which are hybrid in more ways than one: they represent fusions of cultures, languages, food, clothing and so on. The lines of demarcation have either melted or become invisible. The last scene justifies the rejection of the Sita within Nina, the Sita with whom she associates domesticity, sacrifice and love. In a way it can be seen as self-assertion: Nina comes out of a bad marriage, is comfortable handling herself and her new identity, and has exorcised her ailing marriage –

however painful the process may have been. In her final gesture of picking up the *Ramayana* and reading it as a bedside book, Nina moves out of the frame of the story and returns from the outside, as a reader in search of recovery and self-healing. The employment and use of digital media also challenge the presentation or acting out of mythology. The myth is an attempt at a cross-cultural translation of the Sita myth and its collective memory, and stands as a testament to the creative potential of social imagination; the possibility thus exists that in future such attempts may result in redefining and re-inventing culture. The character of Sita seems to be potent enough to trigger off such a process. As Patrick Colm Hogan suggests, 'Prototypical narrative structures show remarkable cross cultural consistency. Prototypes also must vary with context and time.'[23]

While every film tells a story, *Sita Sings the Blues* tells two. The Indian Sita myth has gone global, with innovative attempts that should give Sita an international identity, if she does not have one already. The embellished Sita image of the Indian imaginations, calendars, movies and mythological tales is now perpetuated not only at home but also in the world outside, protecting Sita from the danger of fading out from collective memories. The very title of the film evokes myth as well as modernity. The world's curiosity, interest and appreciation of such a creative attempt focusing on the most memorable Indian human figure will result in more such attempts, each more imaginative and original than the last, and which fuse tradition and modernity, reverence and belief, adapting them all for modern times. Now that she has broken free from the form or the genre (epic) she was found in, and has adopted a new, artistically adventurous and culturally omnivorous, global avatar, the possibilities are endless. Every interpretation is valuable as the *Ramayana* belongs to everyone.

The classical myths are thus linked, by their reinterpretation in modern media, to contemporary issues. The interaction of myths and social issues can hence take any direction and form. But the only way writers can attempt to make a difference is by writing; the only way a filmmaker can do so is by making a film. Alternative views enrich the *Ramayana* and avoid its scholarly isolation; a rethinking of it is hence a reflection of an understanding of an ancient myth in modernity, in cross-disciplinary sociological and literary contexts. The future holds promise of many such creative experiments. Thus, both films challenge viewers' understanding of epic films, by taking epic source material and reworking it in ways which are relevant to the everyday lives of women and which, as Burgoyne argues, result in a negotiated form of epic with significance for both national identity and the wider, global realities of women's lives.

NOTES

1. Swami Vivekananda, 'On Lectures from Colombo to Almora: The Sages of India'. http://www.ramakrishnavivekananda.info/vivekananda/volume_3/lectures_from_colombo_to_almora/the_sages_of_india.htm, last accessed 10 October 2012.
2. The stories of Ram. *Kath* is a word found in Sanskrit and Hindi which means 'to speak'. *Katha* means an oral tale.
3. For more on the variations of the *Ramayana*, see Paula Richman, *Questioning Ramayanas: A South Asian Tradition* (Berkeley and Los Angeles: University of California Press, 2001).
4. Ibid., p. 2.
5. Robert Burgoyne, 'Introduction', in Robert Burgoyne (ed.), *The Epic Film in World Culture* (New York: Routledge, 2011), pp. 1–16 (p. 3).
6. Robert Burgoyne, 'Generational Memory and Affect in *Letters from Iwo Jima*', in Robert A. Rosenstone and Constantin Parvulescu (eds), *A Companion to the Historical Film* (Hoboken, NJ: Wiley, 2012), pp. 349–64.
7. Savitri is a female character in Indian mythology who brought her dead husband, Satyavan, back to life.
8. *Sahaj* is a Hindi word meaning 'spontaneous, effortless and natural'.
9. Lalitha Lenin, 'In the Shadow of Sita', *Namukku Prarthikkam (Let us Pray)* (Thiruvananthapuram: DC Books, 2000), pp. 39–41; reprinted in Paula Richman (ed.), *Ramayana Stories in Modern South India: An Anthology* (Bloomington, IN: Indiana University Press, 2008), pp. 108–10.
10. *Sutradhar* was the chief narrator of the tale in old Indian dramas appearing in the beginning of the play and also whenever the narrative had to be carried forward verbally.
11. Old American films used the word 'intermission' to indicate an interval.
12. *Sudarshan* is the name of the circular weapon lord Vishnu holds on the tip of his finger which if released beheads its target. Literally the word means 'good to look at'.
13. In the *Ramayana*, Kekeyi was one of the wives of King Dasrath.
14. Nina Paley and Malashri Lal, 'Sita Sings The Blues', in Malashri Lal and Namita Gokhale (eds), *In Search of Sita* (New Delhi: Penguin Books, 2009), pp. 124–30 (p. 127).
15. *Ramavatarcharit* is a version of the *Ramayana* written by the nineteenth-century Kashmiri poet Prakashram Kulgami in the Kashmiri language. It is the only published Kashmiri text out of the seven *Ramayanas* written in Kashmiri.
16. Devdutt Pattanaik, *The Goddess in India: The Five Faces of the Eternal Feminine* (Rochester, VT: Inner Traditions International, 2000), p. 11.
17. *Ksheersagar* was the ocean of milk in the Indian myth which was churned by the Gods and Demons, as a result of which all things that are beneficial to man and make his life beautiful and bountiful emerged. Pattanaik, *The Goddess in India*, p. 20.
18. Half man and half woman is the *Ardhanarishwar* form.
19. *Dashavatar* refers to the theory of the ten incarnations of Lord Vishnu. *Dash* means 'ten' and *Avatar* means 'descent'.
20. Devdutt Pattanaik, in his address 'Mythology in Indian Films', *FTII*, Pune, 22 March 2009.
21. *Chill Aum* is a CD of music by Masaladosa, a group of five musicians known across the world from Jamaica to Rajasthan and from London to Calcutta. Their music is characterised by songs of energy and fusion, sitar songs, and Indian ragas, with Jamaican grooves and drum & bass, blending Indian and Western music.

22. Harold Bloom, *Sylvia Plath* (New York: Infobase, 2007), p. 49.
23. Patrick Colm Hogan, *Understanding Indian Movies: Culture Cognition and Cinematic Imagination* (Austin, TX: University of Texas Press, 2008), p. 15.

Notes on the Contributors

Saër Maty Bâ gained his PhD from Exeter University in 2006. He has lectured in film studies and in visual culture at the universities of East London, St Andrews, Portsmouth and Bangor, and at other UK universities. He is co-editor of special issues of journals such as *Crossings: Journal of Migration and Culture* (3:2, 2012), and of the book *De-Westernizing Film Studies* (2012). He is associate editor of *The Encyclopedia of Global Human Migration* (2013). His research focuses on race, 'documentary' voices, African/black diasporas, and francophone films/cinemas. His publications cover a range of themes including 'emergent method', ethnographic film, black aesthetics, body studies, labour and migration.

Deborah Bridge has been a Lecturer in English at Mount Royal University in Calgary, Alberta, Canada since 1986, where she currently teaches courses in critical reading and writing, and introductory literature. Most recently, she contributed to the volume *The World-Wide Influence of Harry Potter*. Although her educational background is in contemporary Arthurian literature, her research and interests are wide-ranging and eclectic, and include Harry Potter as an unprecedented cultural phenomenon.

Robert Burgoyne is Professor of Film and chair of the Department of Film Studies at the University of St Andrews, UK. His books include *The Epic Film in World Culture* (2010), *Film Nation: Hollywood Looks at U.S. History* (1st edition 1997, 2nd edition 2010), *The Hollywood Historical Film* (2008), and *New Vocabularies in Film Semiotics: Structuralism, Poststructuralism, and Beyond* (1992, republished 1993, 1994, 1995, 1999).

Aarttee Kaul Dhar is a *Ramayana* scholar, editor, writer, translator and corporate trainer of English and Communication Skills in New Delhi, India. She has postgraduate degrees in both English and Management, has worked at *The*

Times of India, and has taught at the the National School of Banking and in a number of high-ranking university colleges. The author of *The Banishment of Seeta, Language Can Be Fun, Creative English* and *Ramayana: Comics, Graphic Novels and Films*, she also edited a report on early childhood education for the National Council for Educational Research and Training. Her research is in the field of the *Ramayana* and its retellings in all genres.

Andrew B. R. Elliott is a Senior Lecturer in Media and Cultural Studies at the University of Lincoln, UK, where he teaches on a range of courses in film, television and cultural studies. He is the author of *Remaking the Middle Ages*, his research focusing on the representation of history in film, television and popular culture. He has published on a range of topics from accuracy and authenticity to Vikings and violence, and is the co-editor with Matthew Wilhelm Kapell of *Playing with the Past: Digital Games and the Simulation of History* (2013), a collection on the representation of history through video games.

Sheldon Hall is a Senior Lecturer in Stage and Screen Studies at Sheffield Hallam University, UK. He is the author of *Zulu: With Some Guts Behind It: The Making of the Epic Movie* (2005), co-author (with Steve Neale) of *Epics, Spectacles, and Blockbusters: A Hollywood History* (2010) and co-editor (with John Belton and Steve Neale) of *Widescreen Worldwide* (2010). He has contributed articles on various aspects of American and British cinema to numerous books and periodicals, and is currently working on a monograph about the screening of cinema films on UK television, entitled *Armchair Cinema: Feature Films on British Television*.

Kevin J. Harty, Professor in and chair of the Department of English at La Salle University in Philadelphia, is the dean of medieval cinema studies. He is either author or editor of: *The Vikings on Film: Essays on Depictions of the Nordic Middle Ages* (2011); *Strategies for Business and Technical Writing* (7th edn, 2011); *Cinema Arthuriana, Twenty Essays* (2001/2011); *The Reel Middle Ages: American, Western and Eastern, Middle Eastern and Asian Films About Medieval Europe* (1999/2006); *King Arthur on Film: New Essays on Arthurian Cinema* (1999); *The Chester Mystery Cycle, A Casebook* (1993); *Cinema Arthuriana: Essays on Arthurian Film* (1991); and (with John Keenan) *Writing for Business and Industry: Process and Product* (1987). His most recent publications are essays on the Disney Robin Hood films and the First World War Joan of Arc films, and essays are forthcoming on Malory and Cornwall and on George Macfarren's 1860 opera *Robin Hood*.

Mark Jancovich is Professor of Film and Television Studies at the University of East Anglia, UK. His books include *The Cultural Politics of the New Criticism* (1993), *Approaches to Popular Film* (1995), *Defining Cult Movies: The Cultural*

Politics of Oppositional Tastes (2003), *Quality Popular Television: Cult TV, the Industry and Fans* (2003), and *Film Histories: An Introduction and Reader* (2007), co-edited with Paul Grainge and Sharon Monteith.

Jeffrey Richards is Professor of Cultural History at the University of Lancaster, UK, and a leading expert on the depiction of the past in film, as well as on Victorian popular culture. He is the author of over a dozen books, his publications including *Hollywood's Ancient Worlds* (2008), *The Ancient World on the Victorian and Edwardian Stage* (2009), *Films and British National Identity* (1997), *Swordsmen of the Screen: From Douglas Fairbanks to Michael York* (1977) and *Visions of Yesterday* (1973).

Robert Stow is a graduate of Newcastle University, UK, where he read Classical Studies and graduated with Honours. He later completed his MA in International Film: History, Theory and Practice. His research focuses on audience perceptions of historical accuracy and authenticity in film, with particular focus on the 'Sword and Sandal' Roman epics, and on the contrasts and comparisons between these perceptions, and those of academics and the film's directors.

Paul B. Sturtevant is currently an Experienced Research Fellow on the EU collaborative project 'Power and Institutions in Medieval Islam in Christendom', where he is collaborating with Centro de Ciencias Humanas y Sociales and Lopez-Li Films to create a Media School for Historians in Madrid. His previous research has focused on the degree to which cinematic depictions of the medieval world influence the contemporary public's understanding of the Middle Ages. He received a PhD from the University of Leeds in 2010, and has subsequently done post-doctoral work at the Leeds Humanities Research Institute, the University of Cambridge, and the Smithsonian Institution in Washington, DC.

Index

3D (film technology), 59, 69, 70, 130
9/11 (September 11th attacks), 25, 120
55 Days at Peking (1963 film), 24
300 (2006 film), 2, 11, 58, 66–8, 69, 70, 118, 130, 133, 139, 170, 171, 179, 182
300 Spartans, The (1962 film), 67
1492 (1992 film), 60

Academy Awards, 57; *see also* Oscar
accuracy
   historical accuracy, 74–9, 83, 89, 90, 122
   inaccuracy, 74, 75, 83, 85, 88, 89, 122
   see also authenticity
Achilles, 58, 62, 99, 131
Adventures of Quentin Durward, The (1955 film), 19
Adventures of Robin Hood, The (1938 film), 22, 121
Agricola, Gnaeus Julius (Roman general), 47, 48, 49, 75
Akomfrah, John, 182
Alexander (2004 film), 1, 4, 6, 11, 12, 15n, 58, 63–5, 66, 69, 70, 95, 96, 97–102, 106
Alexander the Great (1956 film), 58
Alexander the Great (historical person), 6, 49, 64, 98
Amazing Grace (2006 film), 170, 175–8, 182
anamorphic lens *see* widescreen
Anand, Madhureeta, 202, 204–5
Arianne (character in *Centurion*), 48, 49, 83
Aristotle, 100, 105, 192
Arn (series of films 2007–10), 116–17, 118, 125, 126, 127n
   Arn: The Kingdom at Road's End (2008 film), 110, 127n

Arn: The Knight Templar (2007 film), 3, 11, 110, 127n
Arn: The Knight Templar (2010 TV miniseries), 127n
Attila (1954 film) aka *Attila the Hun, Attila, Flagello di Dio*, 37, 38, 40–2
Attila the Hun, 37–42, 54n
Aurelius, Marcus, 21, 22, 23–4, 43–5, 47, 87, 90
authenticity, 8, 20, 74, 76, 78, 86, 90, 133, 135, 141
   plausibility, 12, 139–40
   verisimilitude, 12, 131, 137, 139, 140, 141
Avatar (2009 film), 59, 69

Babylon, 7, 54, 98, 99, 100, 135
Badiou, Alain, 182, 184n
Baldwin IV, King (character in *Kingdom of Heaven*), 26–8, 116
Balian (character in *Kingdom of Heaven*), 25–8, 29, 32, 33, 34, 65, 114–16
Ballistae (Roman missile weapon), 82,
Baron-Cohen, Simon, 113
Barthes, Roland, 102
Batchelor, David, 96–7, 98, 99, 100, 103
Ben-Hur (1959 film), 6, 8, 57, 97, 98, 133, 135
Benioff, David, 62
Beowulf (2007 film), 110
Birth of a Nation, The (1915 film), 148, 172, 182, 183
Black Hawk Down (2001 film), 23
Blanchett, Cate, 33
blockbuster film, 5, 9, 136, 140, 147, 148, 149, 156, 162, 190
   association with spectacle, 5, 136, 147, 162
   first uses, 147–64

Bloom, Claire, 58
Bloom, Harold, 210
Bloom, Orlando, 27, 65
Bombardier (1943 film), 150, 153
Booker, Christopher, 193, 194, 199n
Braveheart (1995 film), 20, 22, 112, 118, 120, 126
Bronston, Samuel, 8, 15n, 23, 24
Brooks, Xan, 58, 59
Burgoyne, Robert, 4, 5, 12, 20, 111, 115, 133, 139, 189, 194, 197, 203, 213
Burton, Richard, 58, 60
Bush, George W., 25, 62, 64; *see also* Iraq, War on Terror
Butler, David, 28

Camelot (1967 film), 63, 119
Camelot (2011 TV series), 119
Cameron, James, 61, 140
camp, 61–3, 64, 66, 68
Campbell, Joseph, 194
Centurion (2010 film), 3, 11, 12, 47–9, 75, 78, 82–5, 88, 89
CGI (Computer Generated Imagery), 6, 9, 12, 46, 58, 59, 61–5, 67–9, 70, 129, 130–41, 192
   byte crowds, 59
   crowd-building software, 9, 59, 130, 131, 136, 138, 192
   DVFx (Digital Visual Effects), 137, 141
   special effects, 59, 61, 137–40, 141
   visual effects, 129, 131, 132, 133, 135, 138, 140
Chicago Sun-Times, 150
Chitrakar, Moyna, 211
chivalry, 19, 25, 27, 29, 31, 32
Christianity, 11, 20, 23, 25–9, 30, 31, 37, 38–40, 65, 112, 126, 175–7
Christie, Julie, 59
Chronicles of Narnia, The, 112, 191
Cicero, 36
CinemaScope, 28, 130, 134; *see also* widescreen
Clash of the Titans (1981 film), 130
Clash of the Titans (2010 film), 2, 57, 58, 59, 68–9, 70, 130, 139
Cleopatra (1917 film), 7
Cleopatra (1934 film), 20
Cleopatra (1963 film), 1, 8–9, 10, 24
Cold War, 4, 11, 37, 40, 41, 42, 53, 65; *see also* Communism, McCarthyism, Red Scare
Coleman, Kathleen, 76, 78, 79
Coliseum *see* Colosseum
Colosseum, 13, 47, 61, 96, 133, 136, 137, 141

Commodus, 21–4, 34, 43–6, 80–1, 87, 90
Communism, 38, 40, 42, 43, 54n; *see also* Cold War, McCarthyism
Connery, Sean, 32
Conqueror, The (1956 film), 63
Costner, Kevin, 32–3, 121
Crawford, Joan, 64, 66
Crowe, Russell, 21, 32, 33, 60, 65
Crusades, 25–7, 30, 31, 32
Crusades, The (1935 film), 20, 30, 31, 126
Currie, Finlay, 44
cycle (of films), 22, 24, 57, 58, 66, 67, 69, 70, 129, 130
   epic films as cycles, 3, 5–7, 8, 9, 58, 129, 130, 141
Cyrino, Monica, 4, 5, 6, 8, 11, 81, 129, 134

David and Bathsheba (1951 film), 157, 160, 161, 162
De Mille, Cecil B., 6, 20, 30, 31, 57, 98, 126, 130, 133, 138, 148, 161
Deleuze, Gilles, 105–6, 108n, 186n
Doyle, Christopher, 105
Dyer, Richard, 171, 173, 177

Eagle, The (2011 film), 11, 49–53
Eagle of the Ninth, The (1954 novel), 50
Ebert, Roger, 59, 60, 61, 63, 65, 66, 67, 68, 69
Eco, Umberto, 119
Eisenhower, Dwight D., 42, 43
El Cid (1961 film), 24, 112, 118, 126
Elizabeth (1998), 21
Elley, Derek, 8, 105
empathy, 102, 112, 113–14, 193, 196; *see also* sympathy
Entertainment Weekly, 83
Etain (character in *Centurion*), 47, 48, 49, 86
Excalibur (1981 film), 119

Fairbanks, Douglas, 32, 121
Fall of the Roman Empire, The (1964 film), 1, 6, 8, 21–2, 23, 25, 27, 42–5, 58, 76, 82, 86, 90, 135, 192
Flynn, Errol, 32, 121
Foster, Gwendolyn Audrey, 172, 173
Founding Fathers, American, 36, 55n
framing (Erving Goffman theory), 85–6
Francisci, Pietro, 3, 37, 38, 40–2, 54n
Franzoni, David, 10, 22,
French, Philip, 61, 63

gay, 62, 67 *see* homosexuality
genre, 3, 4–7, 9, 12, 50, 60, 90, 95, 97, 114, 117, 130, 137, 147, 169, 189

epic as genre, 1, 2–4, 5, 21, 60, 75, 76, 95, 102, 108, 110–11, 112, 114, 117, 194, 213
genre studies, 2, 11, 108
sub-genre, 110, 112
Germania, 45, 87
Gérôme, Jean-Léon, 22
Gibbon, Edward, 23, 37, 42, 53
Gladiator (2000 film), 1, 2, 3, 4–6, 9, 10, 11, 12, 19, 21–3, 26, 31, 33–4, 45–7, 57–8, 59–61, 65, 69, 70, 74, 75, 76–82, 83, 84, 85, 87, 88, 90, 96, 118, 121, 125, 130, 133, 135, 136, 137, 138, 140, 141
Glissant, Édouard, 167, 177
Goffman, Erving, 85
Gone with the Wind (1939 film), 148, 149, 160
Gracchus (character in *Gladiator*), 22, 34
Greatest Show on Earth, The (1952 film), 161, 162
Greatest Story Ever Told, The (1965 film), 1, 8–9
Greeks, Greece, ancient Greece, 7, 63, 66, 101–2, 131, 135, 139
Greene, Richard, 32, 121
Guardian, The (British newspaper), 58, 63, 64, 65, 67

Hanshaw, Annette, 209
harem, 99–100
Harris, Richard, 59
Harrison, Rex, 28
Harry Potter 188–97
books, 191
character, 191, 195–6
film franchise, 2, 13, 188, 189, 190, 194, 195, 197
. . . *and the Chamber of Secrets* (2002 film), 192
. . . *and the Deathly Hallows: Part II* (2011 film), 192
. . . *and the Goblet of Fire* (2005 film), 192, 194
. . . *and the Philosopher's Stone* (2001 film), 189, 192, 193
. . . *and the Prisoner of Azkaban* (2004 film), 194
Harryhausen, Ray, 69
Harty, Kevin J., 58, 12, 126
Harvey, Laurence, 28
Heidegger, Martin, 181, 182
Hero (2003 film), 3, 12, 95, 96, 97, 103–7
Heston, Charlton, 58, 112, 174
Hitler, Adolf, 38, 87; *see also* Nazi

Hobbit, The (2012 film), 110
Hollywood, 3, 6, 7, 9, 10, 12, 13, 19, 22, 28, 29, 58, 60, 63, 91, 112, 127n, 133, 134, 135, 136, 137, 147, 149, 153, 154, 156, 161, 162, 164, 171, 173, 180
homosexuality, 67, 96, 173; *see also* camp, gay
House of Flying Daggers (2004 film), 97, 103
House Un-American Activities Committee, 154; *see also* McCarthyism, Red Scare
Huntington, Samuel P., 37

I, Claudius (abandoned 1937 film), 20
I, Claudius (1976–7 BBC series), 3
Iliad, The, 131, 189
In the Shadow of Sita (2000 poem), 205
Indiana Jones (film series), 111
Inglourious Basterds (2009 film), 87–8
Intolerance (1916 film), 100, 135
Iraq, 11, 25, 47, 48, 49, 58, 63, 65, 66; *see also* George W. Bush, War on Terror
Islam, 25, 26
Christianity and Islam opposition, 25, 29
see also Muslim
Ivanhoe (book by Walter Scott), 121, 123, 128n
Ivanhoe (1952 film), 19
IX Legion, The *see* Ninth Legion, The

Jackson, Peter, 2, 110
Jarl, Birger, 117
Jerusalem, 25–6, 27, 31, 34, 115, 116, 138
siege of, 116
JFK *see* Kennedy, John F.
Joan of Arc, 20
Joan the Woman (1916 film), 20
Jolie, Angelina, 64
Juba (character in *Gladiator*), 22, 82, 141
Julius Caesar, 6, 47

Kekeyi (Indian mythological figure), 207, 214n
Kennedy, John F., 24, 42, 43, 44, 55n
King Arthur (2004 film), 11, 58, 61, 63, 66, 69, 70, 88, 89, 110, 119–21, 122, 126, 128n, 189
Kingdom of Heaven (2005 film), 1, 4, 11, 12, 20, 25, 29, 31, 33, 34, 58, 61, 65–6, 67, 69, 70, 110, 114–16, 117, 121, 125, 126, 138
King, Geoff, 130, 132, 134, 135, 137, 138
King John, 33–4, 122
King of Kings, The (1927 film), 20
King of Kings (1961 film), 24
King Richard I, 28, 29–30, 122, 123

King Richard and the Crusaders (1954 film), 19, 28, 31
Kracauer, Siegfried, 10
Kristeva, Julia, 100

Ladyhawke (1985 film), 119
Lamont, Peter, 85
lancea (Roman javelin), 83
Laxmi (Indian goddess), 206, 207
Laying Janaki to Rest (2007 documentary), 202, 204–6, 211, 212
Legend (1985 film), 60
LeRoy, Mervyn, 79, 148, 153
Lewis, C. S. *see Chronicles of Narnia*
Lionheart *see* King Richard I
Livius, 22, 24, 27, 43–4, 46
Lollobrigida, Gina, 63
Lord of the Rings, The (film trilogy, 2001–3), 2, 110, 112, 117–9, 189, 191
Loren, Sophia, 112
Lost Legion, The, 50; *see also* Ninth Legion
Lucilla (character in *The Fall of the Roman Empire* and *Gladiator*), 21, 22, 24, 43, 44, 45

Mabinogion, The, 189
McCarthyism, 37, 41; *see also* Cold War, Red Scare
McClean, Shilo, 133, 137, 141
Macdonald, Kevin, 11, 49, 53
Maciste (character in peplum film), 3
Magna Carta, 33, 122, 124
Mahabharata (Indian epic poem), 202
Maid Marion *see* Marion
Mann, Anthony, 1, 8, 22, 23, 24, 42–3, 44–5, 46, 58, 76, 82, 86–7, 112, 192
March, Fredric, 58
Marcus Aurelius *see* Aurelius, Marcus
Marion, Maid Marion, 123, 124
  Maid Marian (character in 2010 *Robin Hood*), 33
  Robin and Marian (1976 film), 32
Marshal, William (character in 2010 *Robin Hood*), 122, 124
Marshall, Neil, 3, 47, 75, 83, 85, 90
Massoud, Ghassan, 29
Mature, Victor, 58
Maximus, Maximus Decimus Meridius (character in *Gladiator*), 21, 22–3, 33, 34, 45–6, 82, 96, 112
Mayo, Virginia, 28
Men in Black 3 (2012 film), 170, 180, 182, 183
Merlin (BBC TV series 2008–12), 119

MiB3 see Men in Black 3
Middle East, 58, 116
  war in Middle East, 11, 62, 138
  see also George W. Bush, War on Terror
Miller, Frank, 58, 67, 72n
Monahan, William, 25–6
Mount Olympus, 61, 68
Muslim, 25, 31, 32, 33, 115, 116
  Muslims and Christians, 25–6, 27, 29, 31, 65, 116, 126
  see also Crusades, Islam

Nama, Adilifu, 174, 175
narrator, narration, 86, 88, 105, 106
national identity, 12, 13, 36, 44, 96, 97, 105, 108, 127n, 139, 195, 201, 203, 213
nationalism, 52, 122, 123, 126, 127n, 131, 138, 195
Nazi, National Socialism, 40, 41, 60, 87, 121, 126, 150
Neale, Steve, 2, 5, 134, 136, 147
Neeson, Liam, 27, 65, 68
Neill, Alex, 113–14, 127n
New York Times, The, 30, 59, 62, 63, 68, 69
Ninth Legion, The, 47–52, 55n, 75, 88
Norman, 19, 32, 121, 122, 123
  Norman yoke, 121, 128n
  Normandy landings, 33
Nottingham, 124
  Sheriff of Nottingham, 122, 123
nuxia pian (Chinese female warriors), 96, 106, 107

Observer, The (British Newspaper), 61
Odoacer, 37
Olympias (character in *Alexander*), 64, 100, 101
Olympus, Mount *see* Mount Olympus
Once Upon a time in China (film series), 60
opacity, 167–8, 169, 170, 171, 172, 173, 175–6, 177, 179, 180, 181, 183
Oscar, 21; *see also* Academy Awards
O'Toole, Peter, 59, 62, 178
Outlander (2008 film), 110

Palance, Jack, 37, 40, 185n
Paley, Nina, 202, 206, 211
Paul, Joanna, 4, 100
Pella (caves), 98–100, 101
peplum (Italian films produced in the 1950s and 60s), 3
Persia, 39, 44, 66–7, 68, 139, 171, 179
Petersen, Wolfgang, 1, 2, 5, 6, 13, 58, 59, 62, 130, 131, 136, 189

INDEX 223

Phantom Menace, The (1999 film), 61; *see also Star Wars*
Philip of Macedonia (father of Alexander the Great), 99–101
Phoenix, Joaquin, 80, 81
Picts, 47, 48, 49, 85, 89
pilum (Roman javelin), 83
Pitt, Brad, 58, 62
Planet of the Apes (1968 film), 170, 173, 174–5, 182
Pope Leo, 37, 38, 41, 54n
Potter, Harry *see* Harry Potter
Prakashram (Indian poet), 208
presentist (historians), 10–11, 20
Prieto, Rodrigo, 98, 100, 102
Prometheus, 99
Proximo (character in *Gladiator*), 22, 61, 79; *see also* Reed, Oliver
Psycho (1960 film), 64
Ptolemy, 99
Puritans, 44

Quinn, Anthony, 37
Quintus Dias (character in *Centurion*), 47, 48–9, 88
Quo Vadis? (1925 film), 6, 134
Quo Vadis (1951 film), 6, 78, 79, 148, 158, 160, 161, 162

race, 40, 95, 167, 168, 170–1, 174, 175, 177, 178, 180, 181, 182, 183, 184n, 201
racism, 168, 174, 175, 177, 178, 184n
Raiders of the Lost Ark (1981 film), 59; *see also* Indiana Jones
Raise the Red Lantern (1991 film), 103
Ram (character in *Ramayana*), 201, 202, 204, 205, 207–8, 209, 210, 212; *see also* Sita
Ramayana (Indian epic), 13, 201–4, 206, 207, 209, 211, 212, 213
rape, 49, 121, 124, 171
Reagan, Ronald, 44
Red Cliff (2008 film), 97
Red Scare, 37, 41, 53; *see also* Cold War
Reed, Oliver, 59, 60; *see also* Proximo
Richard I *see* King Richard I
Richards, Jeffrey, 4, 5, 10, 12, 15n, 40, 42, 58, 126, 148
Riefenstahl, Leni, 23, 60, 65, 109n; *see also* Nazi
Rig-Veda (Indian collection of hymns), 202
Robe, The (1953 film), 60, 148
Robin and Marian (1976 film), 32
Robin Hood (character), 20, 32, 33, 34, 119, 121, 122, 123

Robin Hood (2010 film), 11, 12, 20, 32, 34, 110, 121, 122–5, 131
Robin Hood: Prince of Thieves (1991 film), 32, 125
Robin of Sherwood (1980s TV series), 32
Rocky (film series), 60
Rogues of Sherwood Forest (1950 film), 33
Rome
    ancient Rome, 1, 4, 7, 10, 21, 22, 36, 38, 41, 45, 50, 63, 78, 79, 88, 90, 135, 139
    as city, 8, 23, 37, 38, 39, 40, 41, 43, 61, 78, 79, 81, 97, 138
    as synecdoche to suggest empire, 22, 23, 34, 36, 37, 39, 40, 42, 43–7, 48, 49–53, 75, 82, 86, 88, 138, 141
    fall of Rome, 12, 23, 36, 37, 42, 44, 47, 53, 86
pax romana, 23, 43
Roman Empire, 20, 22, 24, 36, 38, 39, 44, 47, 53, 78, 79, 83, 87, 133, 139
Romans, 36, 40, 48, 49, 79, 115, 139
Rowling, J. K., 190, 191
Runciman, Sir Steven, 26–7
Russell, James, 5, 9, 130, 133, 135

Saladin, 25–9, 30, 31, 115, 116
Samson and Delilah (1949 film), 106, 148, 157, 160, 161
Sanders, George, 28
Santas, Constantine, 4, 7, 9, 110–11, 125, 139, 189, 192
Savitri (Indian mythological figure), 202, 204, 214n
Saxons, 19, 32, 33, 119, 120, 121, 123
'Scope *see* CinemaScope; *see also* widescreen
Scotland, 19, 28, 38, 49, 75, 83, 112
Scott, Ridley, 1, 12, 13, 19, 20, 21–3, 25–6, 27, 29, 31, 32, 33, 45, 47, 59, 60, 61, 65, 82, 87, 90, 110, 114, 121, 122, 125, 135, 140
Scott, Walter, 19, 26, 28, 29, 30, 31, 121, 123
Senate (Roman), 23, 24, 43, 47, 50, 51, 52
September 11th attacks *see* 9/11
Sign of the Cross, The (1932 film), 20
Sign of the Pagan (1954 film), 37, 38–40
Sin City (2005 film), 58, 67
Sirk, Douglas, 37, 38–40, 41, 54n
Sita (Indian mythological figure and character in *Ramayana*), 201–3, 204, 205–12, 213
Sita Sings the Blues (2008 film), 202, 206–12, 213
Smith, Gary Allen, 111
Sobchack, Vivian, 10, 102, 104, 129, 192

Solomon, Jon, 4
Solomon and Sheba (1959 film), 63
Sorlin, Pierre, 10, 74, 75
Spartacus (character), 112
Spartacus (1960 film), 6, 11, 22, 57, 60, 98, 112, 135, 192
spectacle, 1, 8, 12, 20, 37, 53, 59–61, 62, 66, 70, 97, 101, 108, 129, 131, 133–6, 138–40, 141, 148, 156, 158, 162, 192, 199n
Stallone, Sylvester, 60
Star Wars (film franchise), 61, 65
   Episode I: The Phantom Menace (1999 film), 61
Sternberg, Josef von, 20
Stone, Oliver, 6, 15n, 59, 63–5, 95, 97–100, 102, 106
Sutcliff, Rosemary, 50
sword and sandal, 5, 58, 67, 76, 130
sympathy, 112, 113–14, 193; *see also* empathy

Tacitus, 75
Talisman, The (novel by Sir Walter Scott), 19, 26, 28, 29, 30
Tarantino, Quentin, 87–8
Tea Party (US political movement), 37, 52–3
Templar Knights, 3, 26, 30, 116
Ten Commandments, The (1956 film), 6, 57, 98, 133, 138, 148
Thucydides, 76, 79
Time (magazine), 30, 61, 63, 64
Time Out (magazine), 63, 64, 67
Titanic (1997 film), 9, 61, 140, 199n
Todd, Richard, 32
Tolkien, J. R. R., 126n, 188, 189, 191
Triumph of the Will (1935 film), 23, 60
Troy (2004 film), 1, 2–4, 5, 6, 11, 58, 61, 63, 64, 69, 130, 131, 133, 136, 138, 189, 199n
Tyerman, Christopher, 26, 27

U571, 81, 84, 91n
USA Today (American newspaper), 64

Valmiki (ancient Indian poet), 201, 202, 206, 212
Variety (trade journal), 59, 62, 63, 65, 67, 69, 147–8, 150, 151, 152–3, 154, 155–7, 160, 161, 163, 164n
Vénus noire (2010 film), 170, 173–5, 182
Verstehen (concept), 113, 127n
Vietnam (war), 24, 32, 42–3
Vikings, The (1958 film), 22
Village Voice, The (American weekly newspaper), 6, 59, 63, 64, 65, 67
Voldemort, Lord (character in *Harry Potter* series), 192, 193, 196

Wallace, Lew, 6
Wallace, William, 20, 120
War on Terror, 11, 25, 31, 66; *see also* George W. Bush, Iraq, Middle East
Ward, Allen, 79
whiteness, 98, 167, 168–9, 170–2, 173–5, 177, 178, 179, 180, 181, 182, 183, 184n; *see also* race
widescreen, 129–30, 134, 163; *see also* CinemaScope
Wilcoxon, Henry, 31
Wild Bunch, The (1969 film), 22
Willow (1988 film), 119
Winkler, Martin, 4–5, 8, 11, 15n, 74, 76, 78
Wyke, Maria, 4, 5

Xerxes (Persian king), 66, 68, 71

Yimou, Zhang, 95, 97, 103, 106

Zeus, 68
Zulu (1964 film), 170, 178, 179, 182
Zulu Dawn (1979 film) 170, 178, 179, 182